AF580131

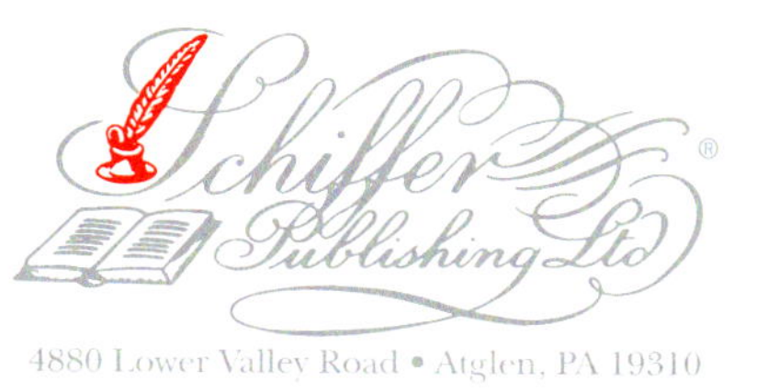

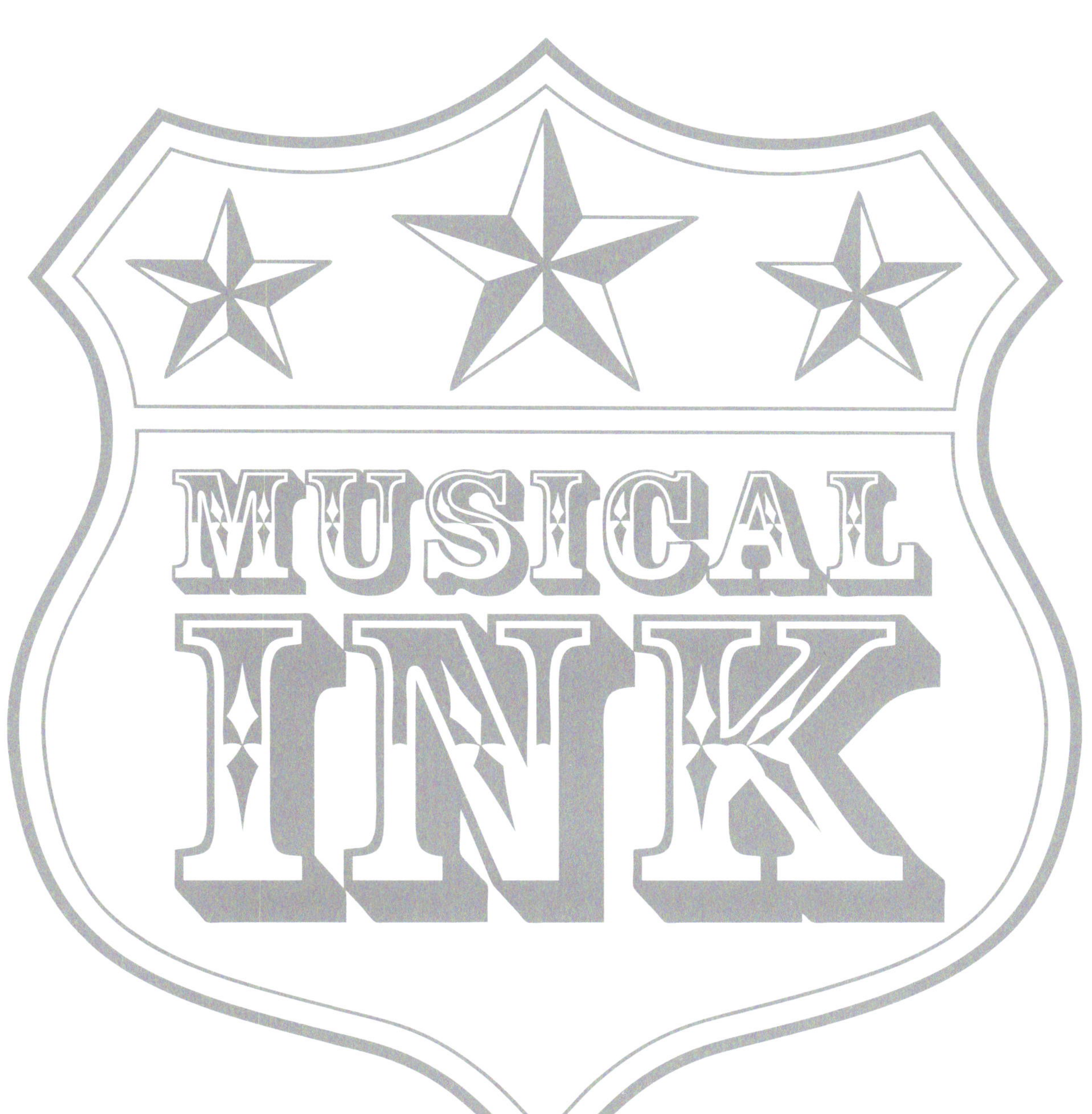

JON BLACKER

Other Schiffer Books on Related Subjects:

War Paint: Tattoo Culture & the Armed Services,
978-0-7643-4086-4, $34.99

The Tattoo Project: Body, Art, Image,
978-0-7643-4245-5, $45.00

TattooIsMe,
978-0-7643-4298-1, $39.99

Library of Congress Control Number: 2013932497

Designed by Justin Watkinson
Type set in Boomshanker/Minion Pro/Zurich BT

ISBN: 978-0-7643-4443-5
Printed in China

Published by Schiffer Publishing, Ltd.
4880 Lower Valley Road
Atglen, PA 19310
Phone: (610) 593-1777; Fax: (610) 593-2002
E-mail: Info@schifferbooks.com

For our complete selection of fine books on this and related subjects, please visit our website at www.schifferbooks.com. You may also write for a free catalog.

This book may be purchased from the publisher. Please try your bookstore first.

We are always looking for people to write books on new and related subjects. If you have an idea for a book, please contact us at proposals@schifferbooks.com

Schiffer Publishing's titles are available at special discounts for bulk purchases for sales promotions or premiums. Special editions, including personalized covers, corporate imprints, and excerpts can be created in large quantities for special needs. For more information, contact the publisher.

In Europe, Schiffer books are distributed by
Bushwood Books
6 Marksbury Ave.
Kew Gardens
Surrey TW9 4JF England
Phone: 44 (0) 20 8392 8585; Fax: 44 (0) 20 8392 9876
E-mail: info@bushwoodbooks.co.uk
Website: www.bushwoodbooks.co.uk

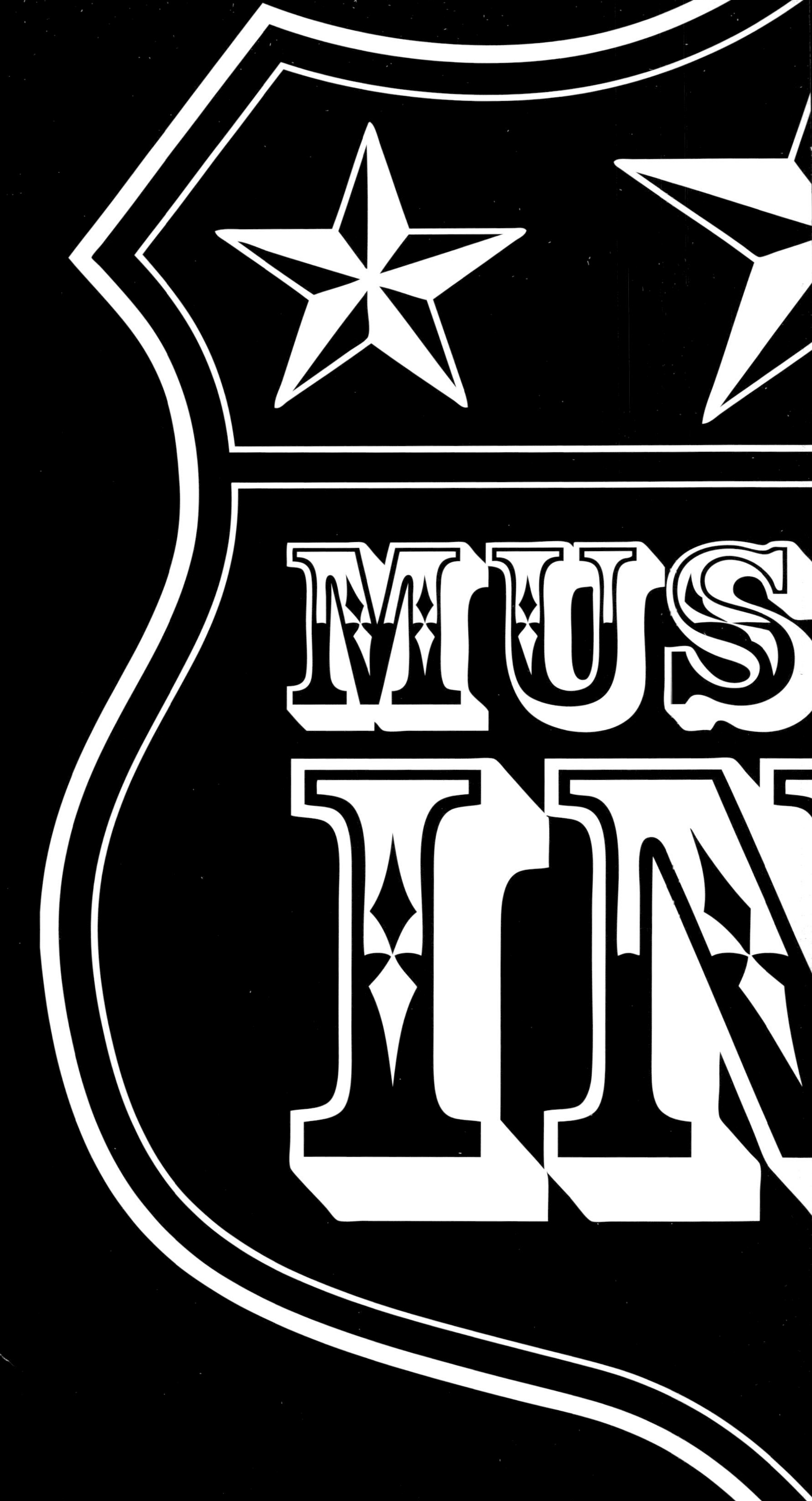

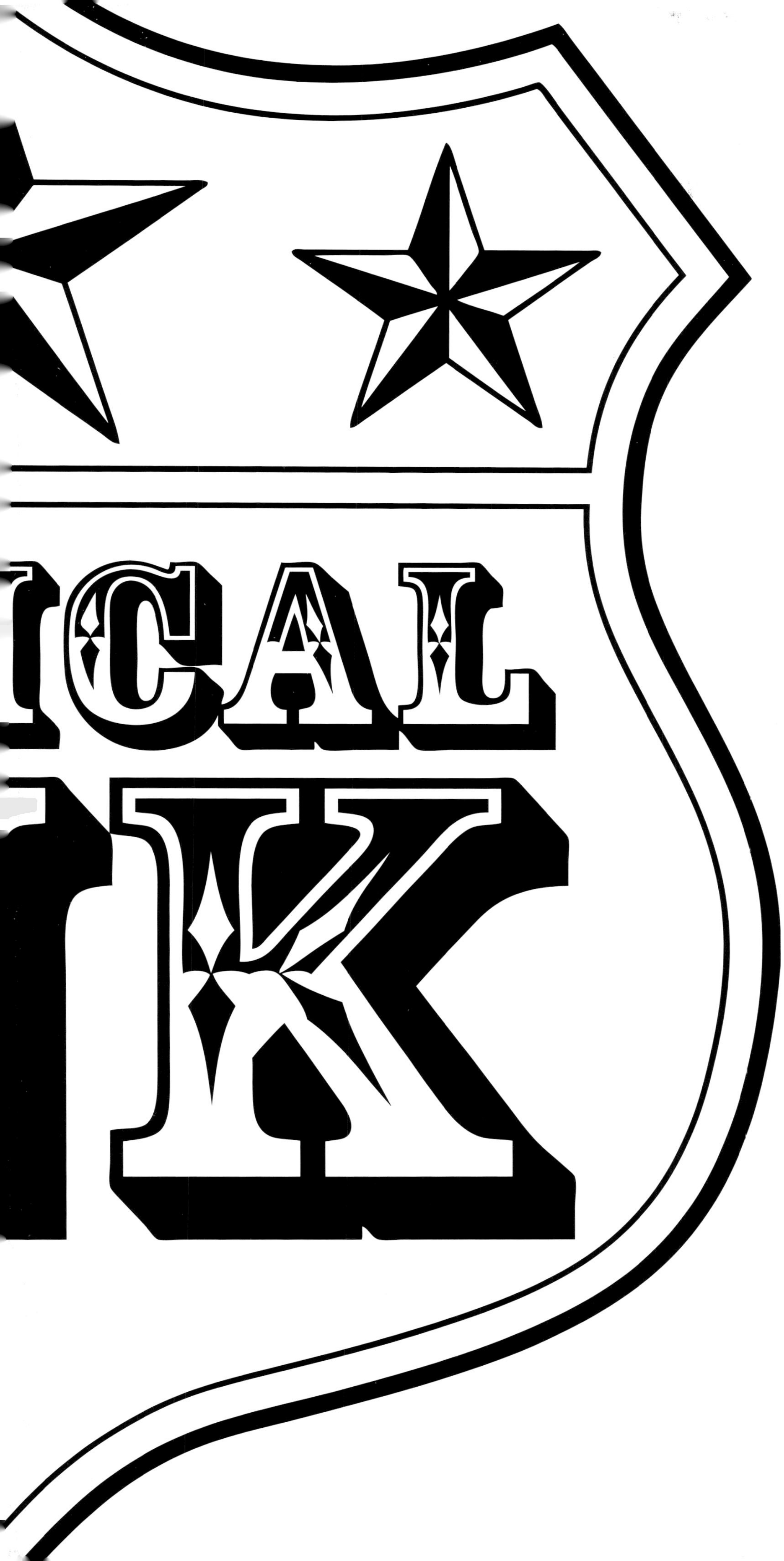

CONTENTS

ACKNOWLEDGMENTS

I've been tremendously fortunate to have made some close and lasting friendships, and worked with some true professionals during the course of creating this book.

Of course without the participation of the musicians, this book wouldn't exist. Without exception, they were simply amazing to work with; giving me a few minutes of their time back stage that they didn't really have in the middle of a long tour, or inviting me into their homes to make their portrait, they were gracious, accommodating, and open to my sometimes odd posing requests.

To all of the band managers, tour managers, assistants, publicists, and PR people—largely unsung heroes who have assisted me along the road of putting this collection together—you have my humble and profound thanks.

A number of people have gone above and beyond to help me put this project together and they deserve special recognition: Kristen Mulderig, Andrew Stuart, and Larissa Swan in Los Angeles. These individuals have not only gone far out of their way to align me with a number of artists who appear in these pages, but have become close friends.

Rose Slanic and Dean Pogue in Toronto. I first met Rose and Dean on set while I was making a portrait back stage at Toronto's Air Canada Centre. Within days, they were calling me asking if they could put me in touch with a laundry list of artists. Thank you both for your support and friendship.

And of course my family and friends, who have believed in me and this project from the beginning…I wouldn't be writing this without your support.

INTRODUCTION

They're cool. They're creepy. They're funny. They hurt. They bleed. When they're old they fade and get a little blurry, a little fuzzy. Just like us. They commemorate a turning point in our lives. Or they don't. They're dark and brooding. They're bright and colorful. They're tiny, private, and hidden. They're big, bold, and in (or on) your face. THEY'RE TATTOOS.

With the prevalence of tattoo-influenced styles in fashion and reality series on prime time television, mainstream society has embraced tattoos as true art. In 2008, more than 43 million people in the United States had at least one tattoo. And in 2008 alone, CD sales and album downloads were more than 420 million units.

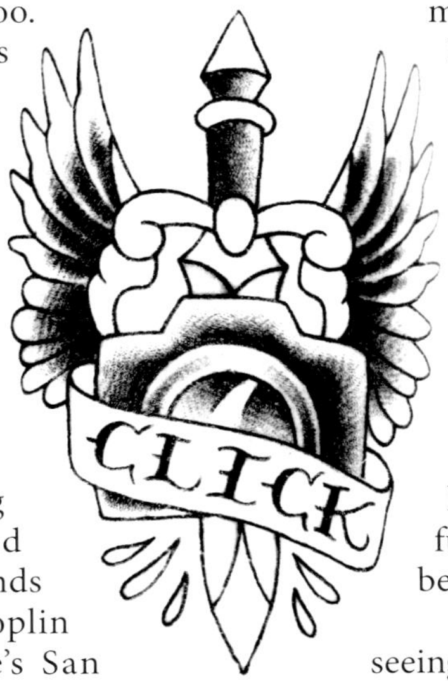

For more than 40 years, music and tattoos have been indelibly linked together. Borne into the rock 'n' roll rebellion of the 1960s, musicians have long expressed a different side of their creativity by permanently painting themselves with ink and needles at the talented hands of tattoo artists. Janice Joplin walking into Lyle Tuttle's San Francisco tattoo shop to be adorned with an ink bracelet and a heart on her breast marked a turning point for music and tattoos.

From the brightly lit studios in Las Vegas hotel lobbies pumping out bass tones so low you can feel them thumping in your chest to the gritty old-school parlors off the beaten track piping classic rock into an atmosphere of history so thick you can reach out and grab a handful, they have three things in common: ink, needles, and music.

It had long been thought that in modern times (versus 4,000 years ago when tattoos were first worn by the ancient Egyptians as protection) tattoos were the sole domain of sailors, bikers, and gang members. Rock 'n' roll, the anti-establishment of the music world may have kicked things off, but now tattooed musicians of all genres from country to opera to heavy metal proudly show off their inked artwork. There are as many different resasons for wearing tattoos as there are people who wear them. Everyone has a story and every one has a story; it can have a deeply moving, heartfelt meaning, a really funny tale, or simply be just because.

CLICK

The first tattoo I can recall seeing on a musician was a small rose on the arm of KISS front man Paul Stanley shortly after they released their *Destroyer* album in 1976. Curiously enough, that tattoo was also done a couple of years earlier by Lyle Tuttle. KISS was the "Hottest Band in the World," larger than life, and that one tattoo added to the mystery of the masked members of the group.

All these years later, that single rose may seem tame when compared against arms fully covered in inked dragons and demons and flowers and waves, yet it is just as much a part of the culture of ink and music as it was when it was drawn onto Paul Stanley's arm. Just as in this collection of portraits and stories you will find artists with more tattoos than you could have imagined, you will find artists with small tattoos you would never have otherwise known they had. Some appear to have a life of their own; winding around their owner's body like a snake (okay, some of them actually *are* snakes) while others are only visible because the curators of these living art galleries have chosen to let us see them.

I made a point of telling every artist in this collection that the tattoo which was going to be the spotlight of their story was to be entirely of their choosing; I did not want to influence them in any way—these are their tattoos, their stories, their words. I wanted them to have the opportunity to tell their story their way. Some of them chose the tattoo everyone knows, others chose the tattoo that no one has seen before. All of the artists I worked with on this project openly shared not only the meanings to the tattoo they chose to spotlight, but also told the story behind it. From Tyler Connolly's falling down a flight of stairs after getting a tattoo to Chad Smith's hernia operation that delayed him from getting one, they laid it all out for *Musical Ink*...and for you.

I hope you enjoy viewing the images and reading their stories as much as I enjoyed shooting their portraits and hearing their tales.

JB: I understand that you have been tattooing for a long time and you've tattooed a lot of musicians. I also understand that you see a direct correlation between music and tattoos. Can you talk about that a little bit?

KVD: I've always said that music and tattoos…I think music and art directly influence each other. I think they're one in the same thing in a lot of ways. In the end I think it's all a form of self expression. As a tattooer, I've been tattooing a long time and I've tattooed everything from portraits of people's favorite musicians to band logos to lyrics and I think music speaks volumes in people's lives; I know it has in mine and it only makes sense that people would want to transfer it into tattoos.

JB: Do you see a difference from musical genre to musical genre as to what types of tattoos artists get on themselves?

KVD: I think if you're a musician, obviously music is a big part of your life and when you're getting tattooed for the most part it tends to be a very monumental thing or something that means a lot to the person wearing the tattoo, so I think it would make sense that it would be very music related.

JB: I ask that question specifically because this *Musical Ink* project is covering as many musical genres as possible from guys like Kerry King of Slayer all the way to Andrea Gruber who is a soprano who has performed with the Metropolitan Opera in New York and has a line of an aria on the small of her back. I wouldn't imagine that being an opera singer she's going to want to have full sleeves.

KVD: You never know…

JB: You never know, but that would be out of character with that genre.

KVD: Sure. I think people would be surprised to see who has tattoos and who doesn't. I think for a long time people had the misconception that it was something that scumbags get. Tattoos can get pretty pricey sometimes; I've tattooed everyone from physicians to aerial logistics engineers and rock stars and everything in between.

JB: Do you find that having been in relationships with musicians sort of draws musicians to you to tattoo them?

KVD: I don't know. I would never flatter myself into thinking that I'm awesome or I'm the best. I try my best at what I do and people tend to get tattooed by me because I believe they like what I do. There's a million tattooers out there and it all depends on what style you like. I've always been very open about my passion for music in general so I don't know if that's necessarily why musicians want to get tattooed by me or not.

JB: Over the past 15 years or so there's been a trend of musicians getting more ink. My first recollection of a musician with a tattoo is Lyle Tuttle's rose on Paul Stanley in 1974. Do you think that trend is going to continue?

KVD: When you think about people in the limelight with tattoos, you're probably going to see more musicians with tattoos because their lifestyle caters to that, whereas actors and actresses can't get as heavily tattooed because it interferes with their ability to get certain jobs. Members of Mötley Crüe were some of the first people in the spotlight that were openly getting a lot of tattoos. They were one of the first out there that was heavily tattooed and a lot of people emulated that style. I think Mötley Crüe incorporated everything from punk rock to glam to biker style. Bikers in the '70s were the next big movement that had tattoos in the "style" and before that, sailors were the ones that were sporting the most amount of tattoos. Nowadays it's everybody; it's crazy. We have 18-year-olds coming in here on their birthday wanting to start with sleeves, so that's kind of cool. For me as an artist and a big fan of music, I really get excited when clients come in and want to get tattoos of some of my own favorite bands, even some of the more obscure ones. To me I know how it feels to be inspired by music. Music has probably been the most influential thing, even more than my parents, in my life. I have a lot of band- or music-related tattoos; I have four different Beethoven tattoos. I've been playing classical music since I was six and I love Beethoven. I always say that without Beethoven you wouldn't have Slayer; he was the original punk rocker.

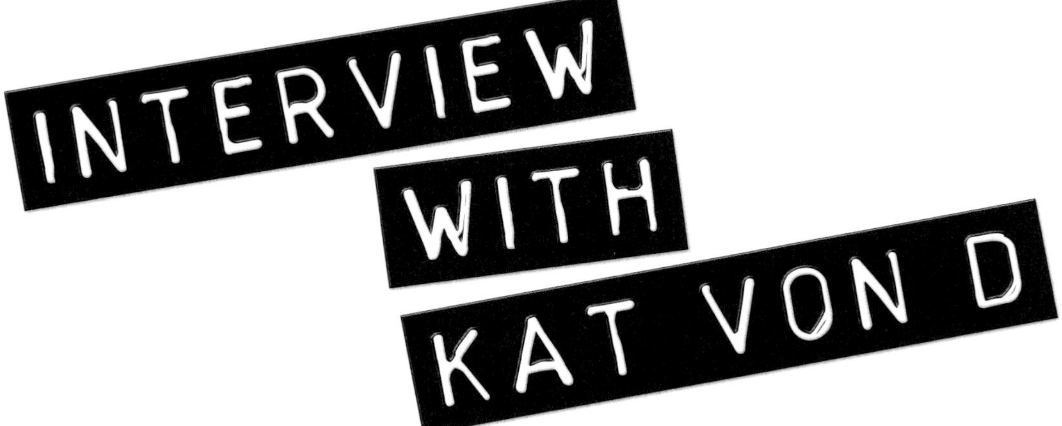

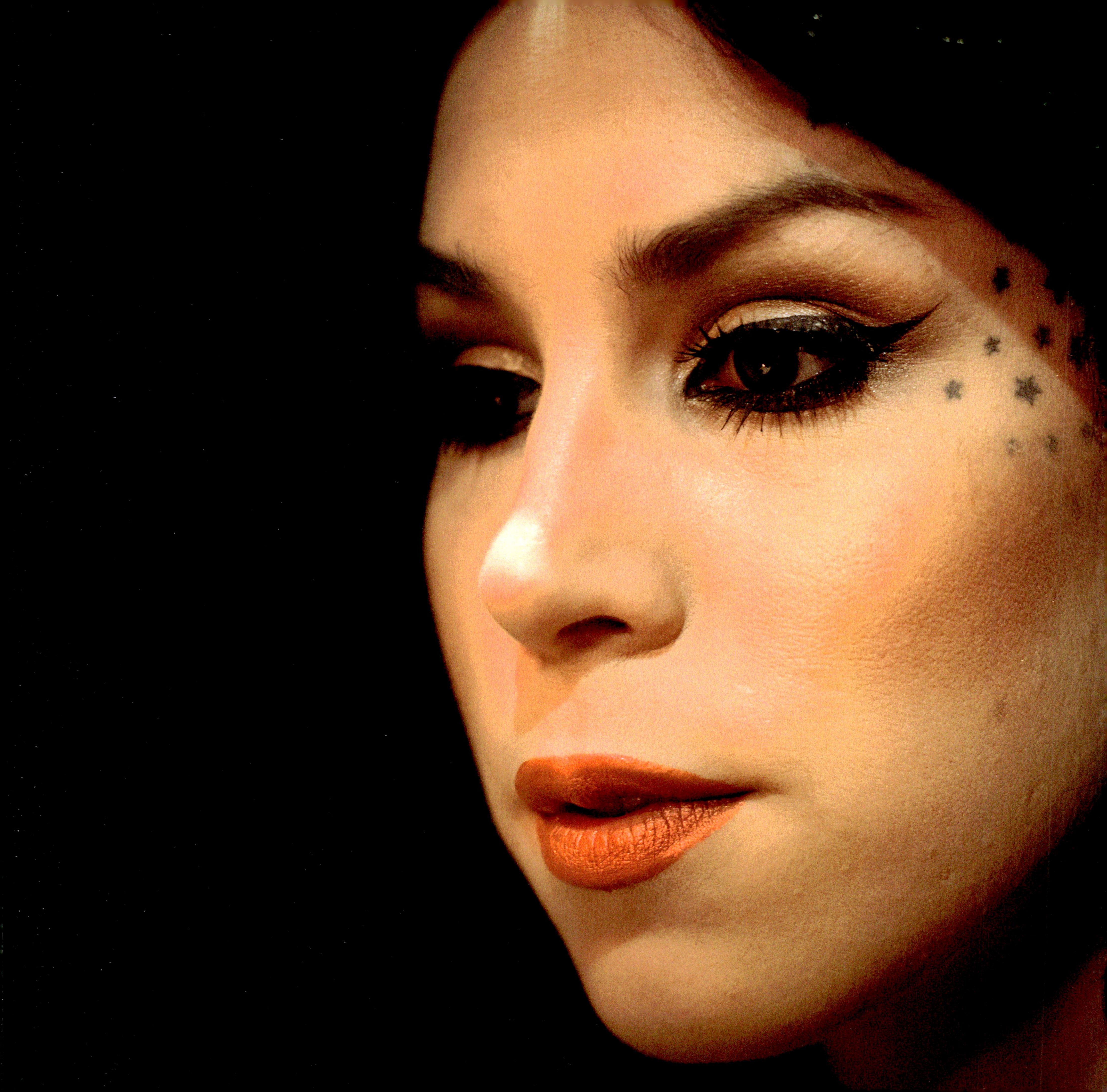

JB: Do you see the trend continuing of both the prominence of tattoos and the correlation between tattoos and music?

KVD: I think that nowadays the correlation between tattoos and music is at its strongest and it can only go higher from here. Now that people are a lot more open to getting tattooed, you're probably going to see a lot more band-related tattoos. I know I've done a lot of them.

JB: And you've tattooed a lot of musicians.

KVD: I've been lucky enough to tattoo some of my favorite musicians of all time. I don't get star struck at all, it's more like, "Oh, cool. I never could have imagined that a member of the Misfits would want to get tattooed by me." That was one of my first tattoos I ever did when I was 14 years old, so it's interesting to see that circle complete.

JB: I think there's a mutual respect there, artist to artist.

KVD: I think there's always been a mutual respect from musicians to tattooers. If you look at…I forget which tour it was that Axl Rose wore that Sunset Strip Tattoo t-shirt on stage, and every rocker kid went and bought that same shirt. Now it's a collectable if you have it. I think there's a certain relatability because tattooers are very much like a musician. We travel, whether it's to a convention or to tattoo friends out of the country. Wherever we go, we take our equipment with us. I've seen tattooers go on mini-tattoo tours, and it's very much like being on the road with a band. It's not as glamorous as people would think it is. The expectations, the more negative side of being successful at what you do, there's a lot of similarities that you can find in tattooing and in music.

JB: The glamour of life on the road is held by the people who don't do it?

KVD: Exactly. Exactly. But I guess it's good; keep the dream alive.

To hear Scott Ian's reasons for the portrait, for him as a younger kid being influenced by musicians, [Angus Young] was one of his biggest influences. Anthrax and AC/DC, you don't necessarily see that much of a similarity, it's rock and roll, but to see where all of that begins is so cool, somebody celebrating that and saying, "This is my hero." He's so many musician's hero and it's kind of neat.

JB: Everybody has seen the Paul Booth piece on the back of Kerry King's head, but he's got a molar on his throat for Dimebag Darrell and not many people know about it because it's always covered up. That's the story he decided to share for this book.

KVD: Of course! That's the stuff that the fans want to see. I think fans are going to be excited to see their reasoning behind it; that is a window into their soul. Tattooing is such an intimate thing, so it's being able to see what their influences are that's so cool.

I'm just glad that you wanted me to be a part of this. I always feel really weird because I'm not a musician but I do a lot of interviews for MTV or whatever and they always kind of peg me as kind of a commodity, so I always get excited when people respect what I do.

Jon Blacker (JB)
Kat Von D (KVD)

PORTRAITS

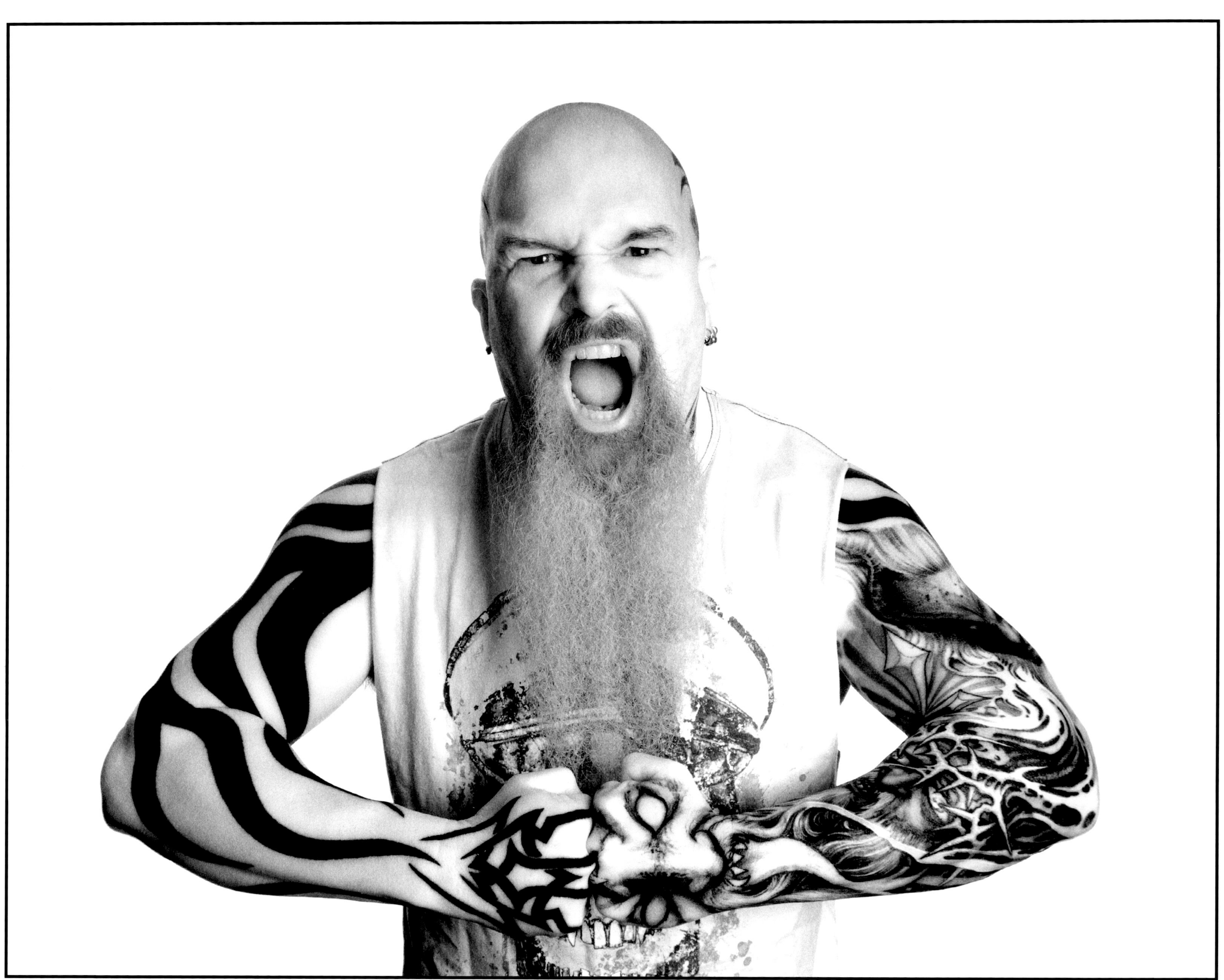

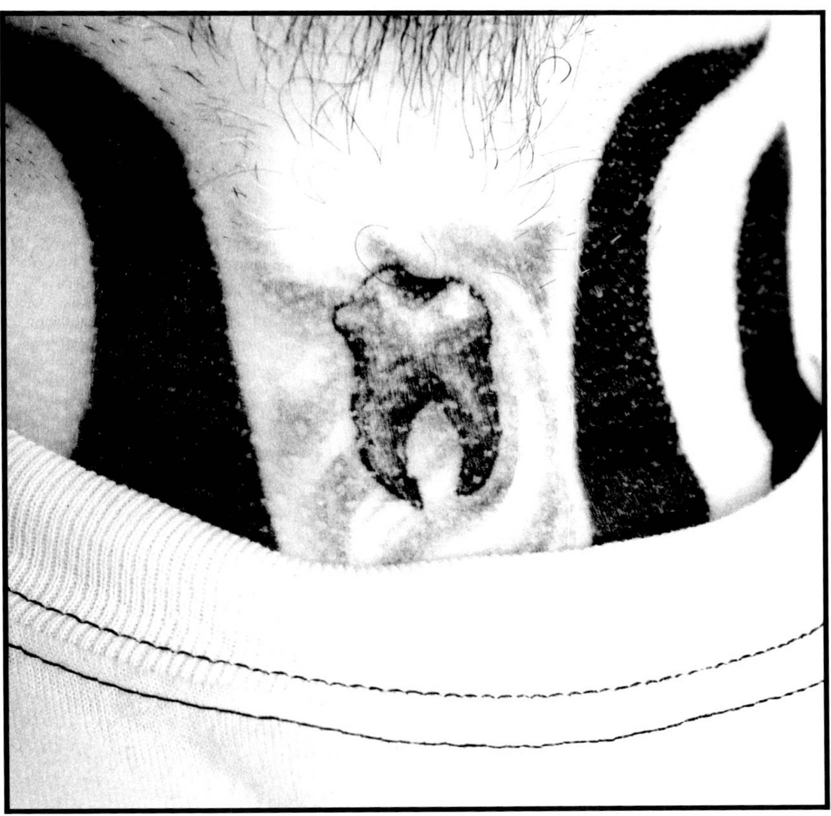

The tattoo on my throat I got on the second anniversary of Dimebag Darrell's death. It's a black tooth, which is Dimebag's drink. A buddy of mine, tattoo artist Jeremiah Barba, was coming over to my house to tattoo my wife and to do something on me and I said, "Dude, it's December 8th. I gotta get a fuckin' Black Tooth for Dime." I put it on my throat, not because I wanted to hide it but because it's a cool spot and it definitely came out cool. Now I have a little piece of Dime with me all the time...

–Kerry King

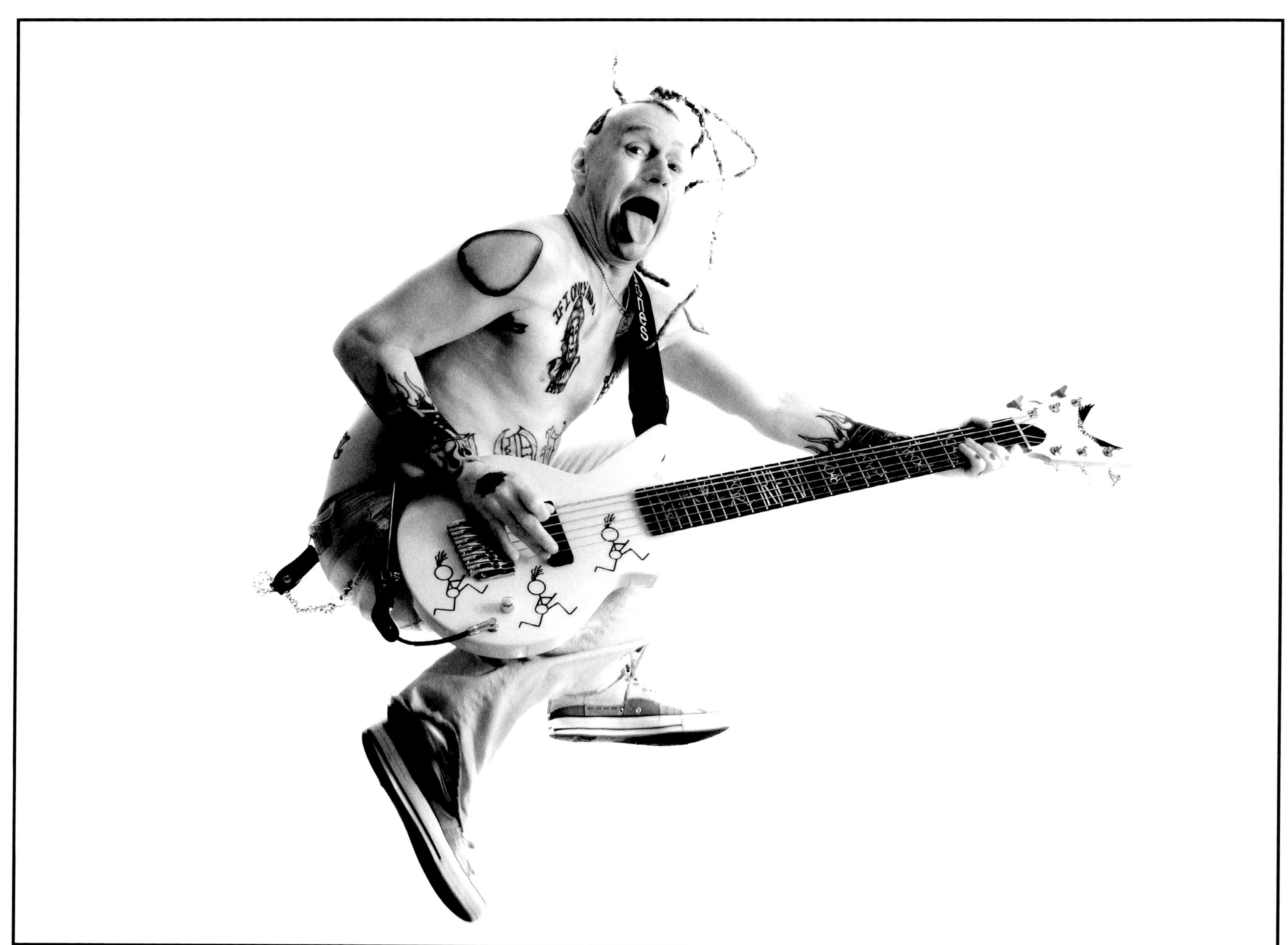

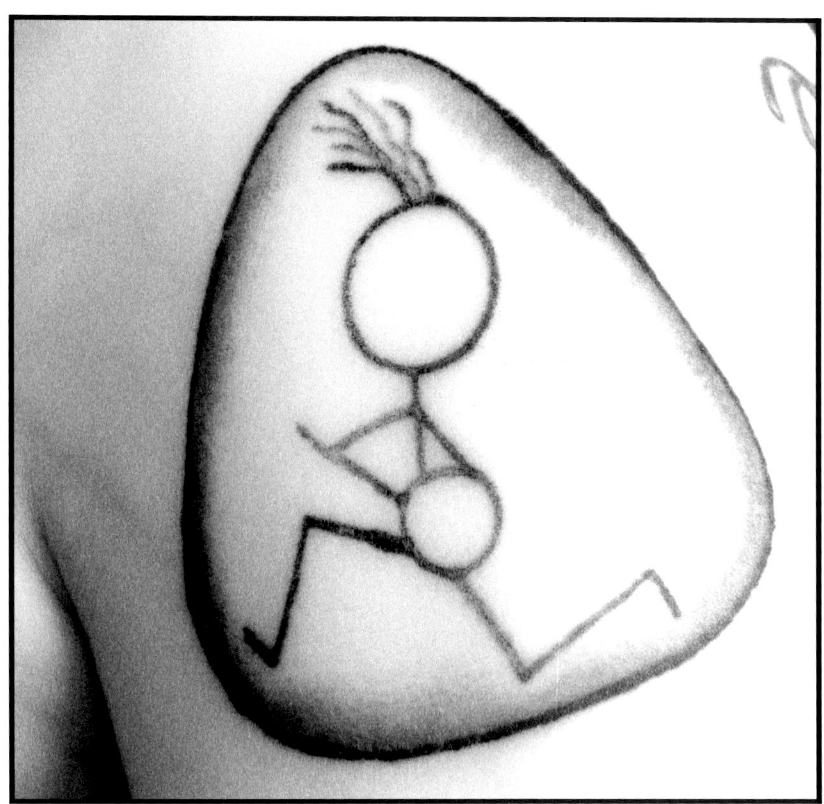

For most of my career, every time I sign an autograph I draw a little stick figure of myself, which is the center of this tattoo. A few years ago while on tour in Germany, I was with a friend who was getting a tattoo. While talking with the artist, I informed him about the fact that tattoos were illegal in Oklahoma, so actually I had broken the law getting all the tats that I have on my body. After hearing that, he laughed and offered to do a tat for me so I could say I had a legal one. I said, "How about a self portrait?" He looked at me and said, "How can we do this today?" I showed him my stick REV man, he laughed, and we decided to put one on each shoulder. After I got back home I realized two things: the Oklahoma law changed, making tattoos legal now and getting the tat in Germany at the guy's house was basically the same as getting all my others since it wasn't a shop. So I went in and had my buddy D.J. put a guitar pick outline around both of them, so now they're legal. The best part is that the picks I use on stage have the same stick figure on them, so it's like I always have two extra picks.

–Rev Jones

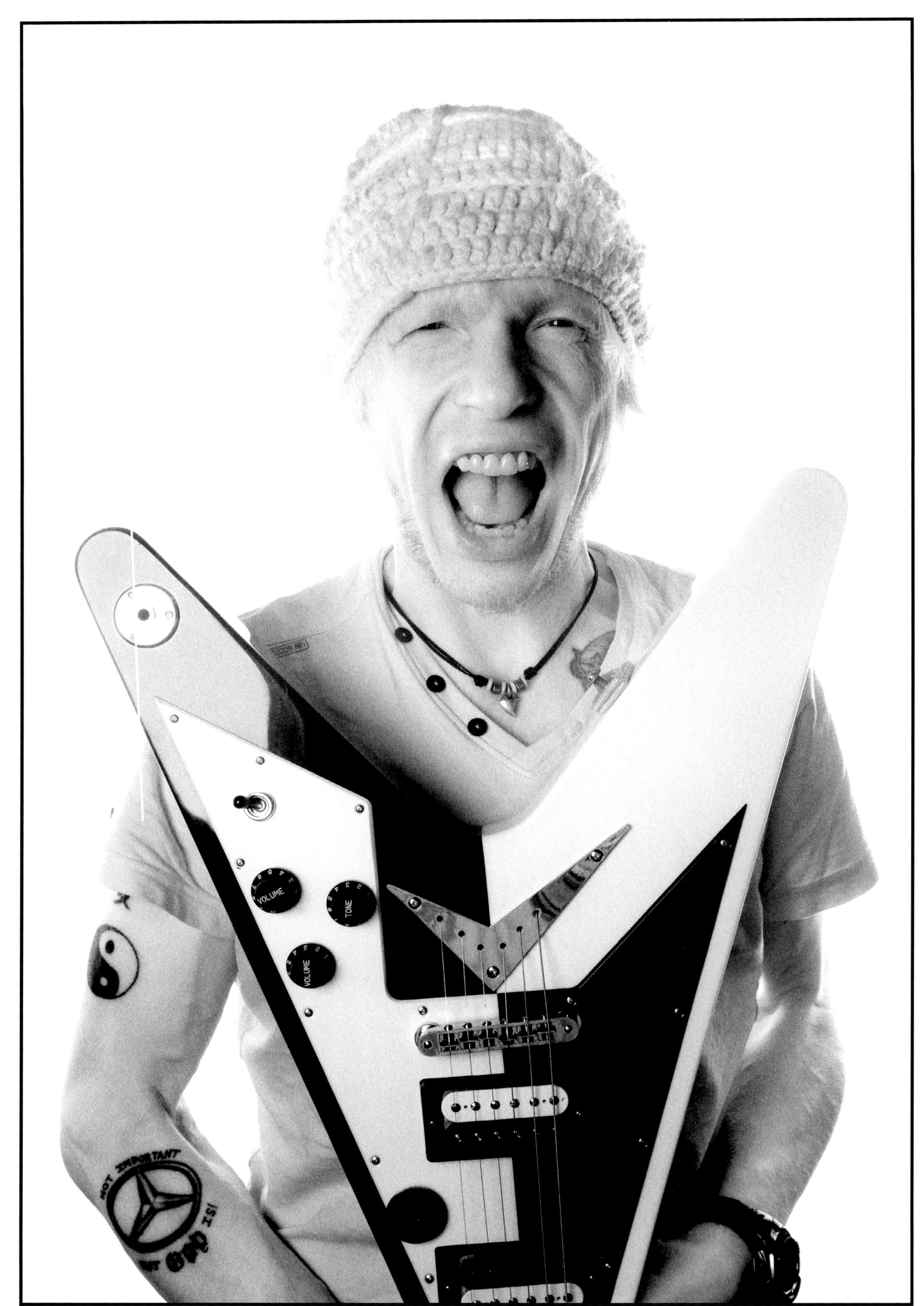
VOLUME
TONE
VOLUME

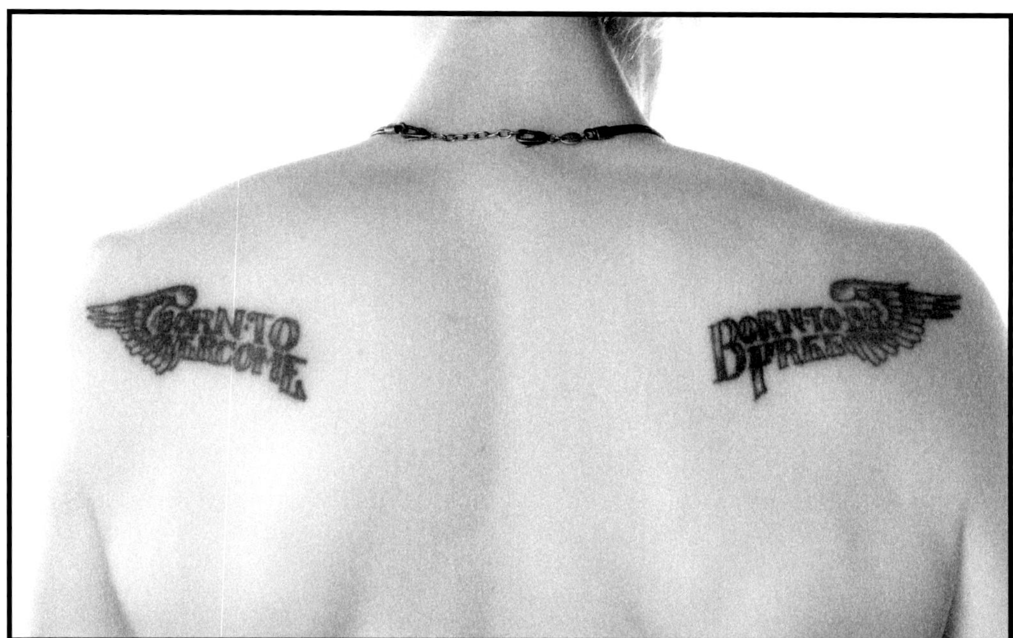

The story behind these two tattoos, "Born To Overcome" and "Born To Be Free" is basically the story of my life.

–Michael Schenker

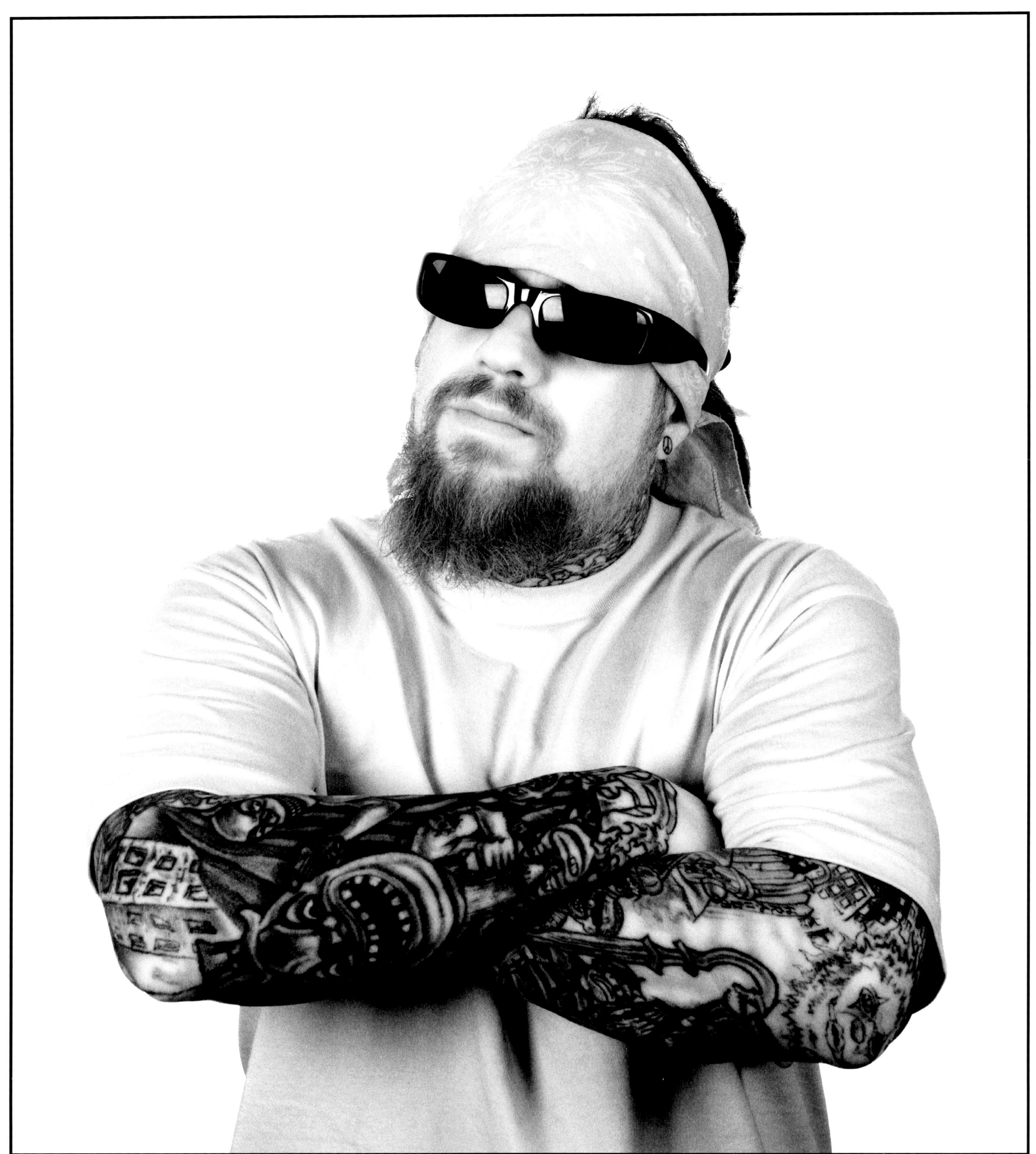

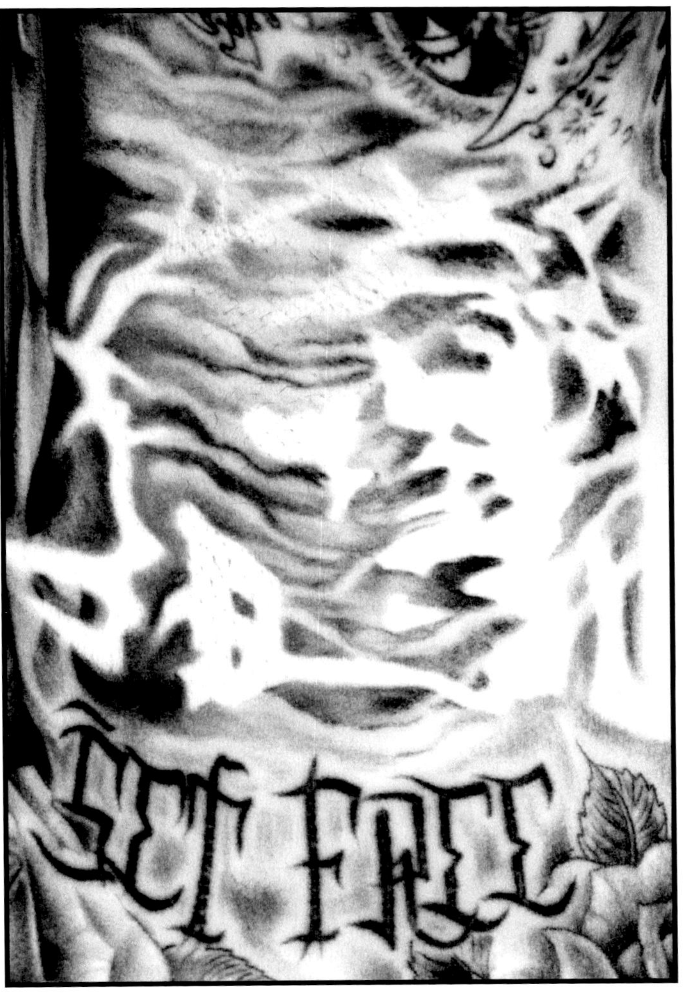

I got this tattoo in my armpit through a dude named Mario Barth. He's a famous artist and he distributes tattoo ink from all over the world. He flew me and a friend of mine out to New Jersey to tattoo me. I didn't really know what I wanted because I'm pretty covered up, but of course, my armpits weren't done yet. I wanted to do something different, and being a Christian, I wanted to get Jesus on me. He's like, "Why don't we do it in your armpit?" And he showed me this shot. "Let's just do it in white ink only..." and I'm like, "Oh, that'd be crazy," that might look cool. So he did it and after it was done and healed up, I'm noticing...man, it looks like deodorant, like it sucks. It just looked like deodorant on my armpit, you know, and I was like how can I fix it. I didn't know what to do, so I ended up throwing some black cloud stuff behind it when we were in Germany touring. I was in so much pain doing my armpit. I could barely take it, squirming around. It was rough man. That's why people don't have their armpits tattooed, but we got it done. It's finished and that one probably has the best story.

–Fieldy Arvizu

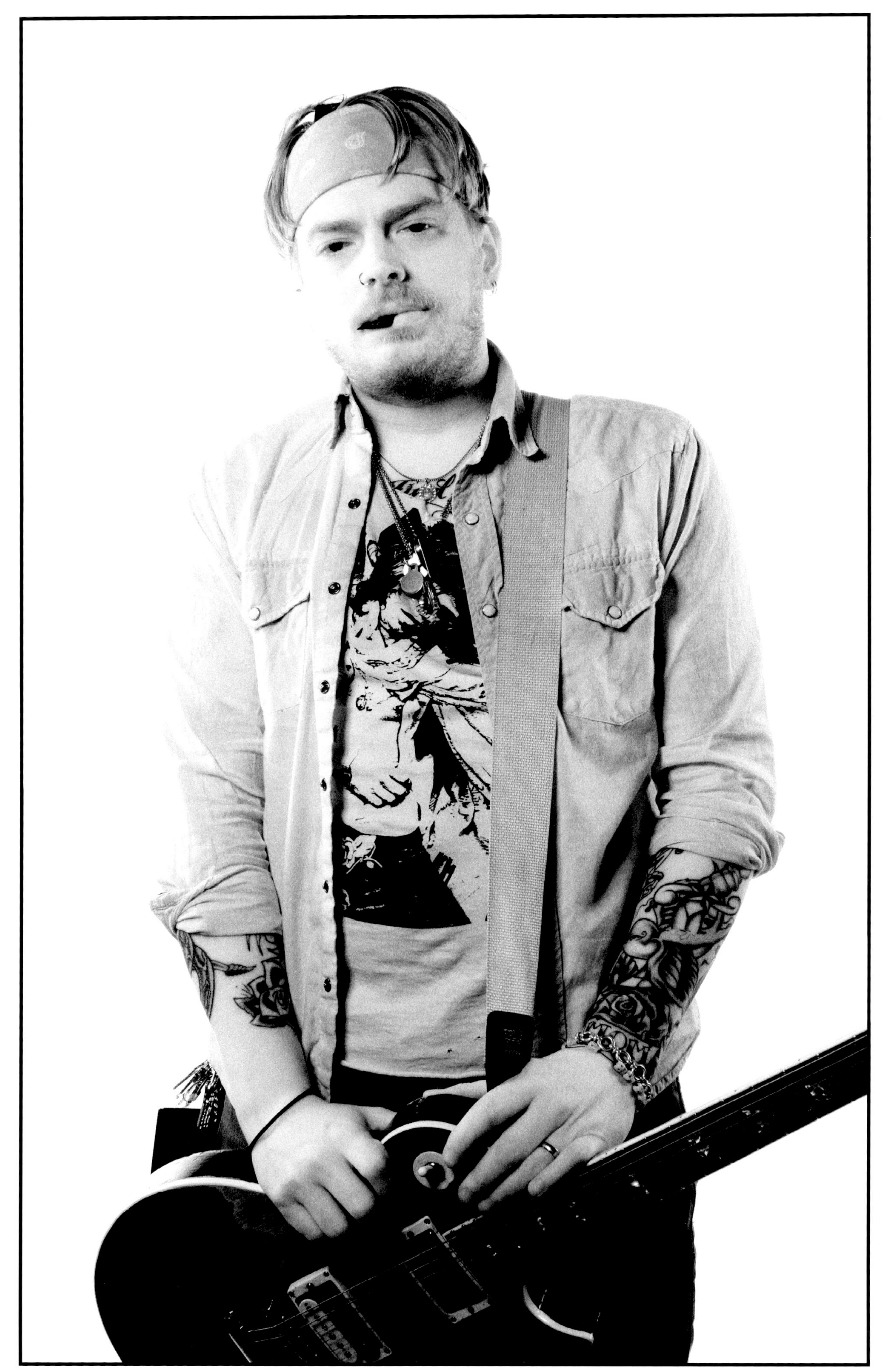

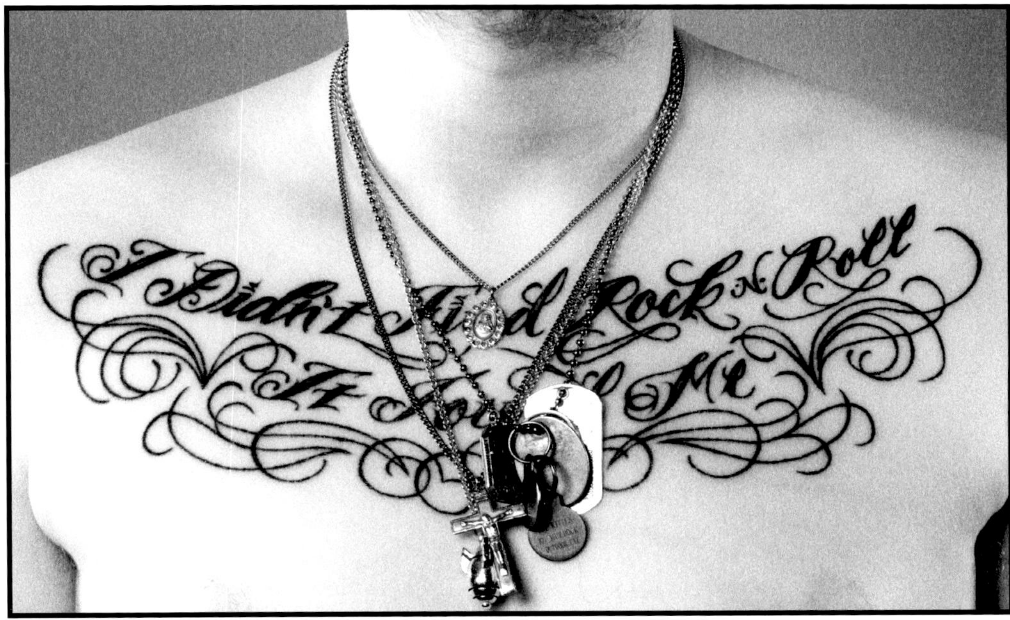

The tattoo I choose is one on my chest: it says, "I didn't find rock and roll, it found me," and there's a lot of reasons why it's important. When my aunt saw it, she said to me, "You could have saved yourself a lot of time and just got 'DNA' written on your chest," and the idea is that I come from a very incredible family, all musicians, all into rock and roll, and it's something I almost felt like I didn't have a choice about. I was born to do this. I was born to be in a rock band and there's also something about sitting through that and the pain and getting your chest done. It really starts to feel like armor when you come out of that. You feel like you earned it. You feel like you're in a secret club almost with anyone else who has gone through that experience and, ah, I don't know—it's one that I think about a lot and if I could only have one to keep, it would be that one.

–James Lynch

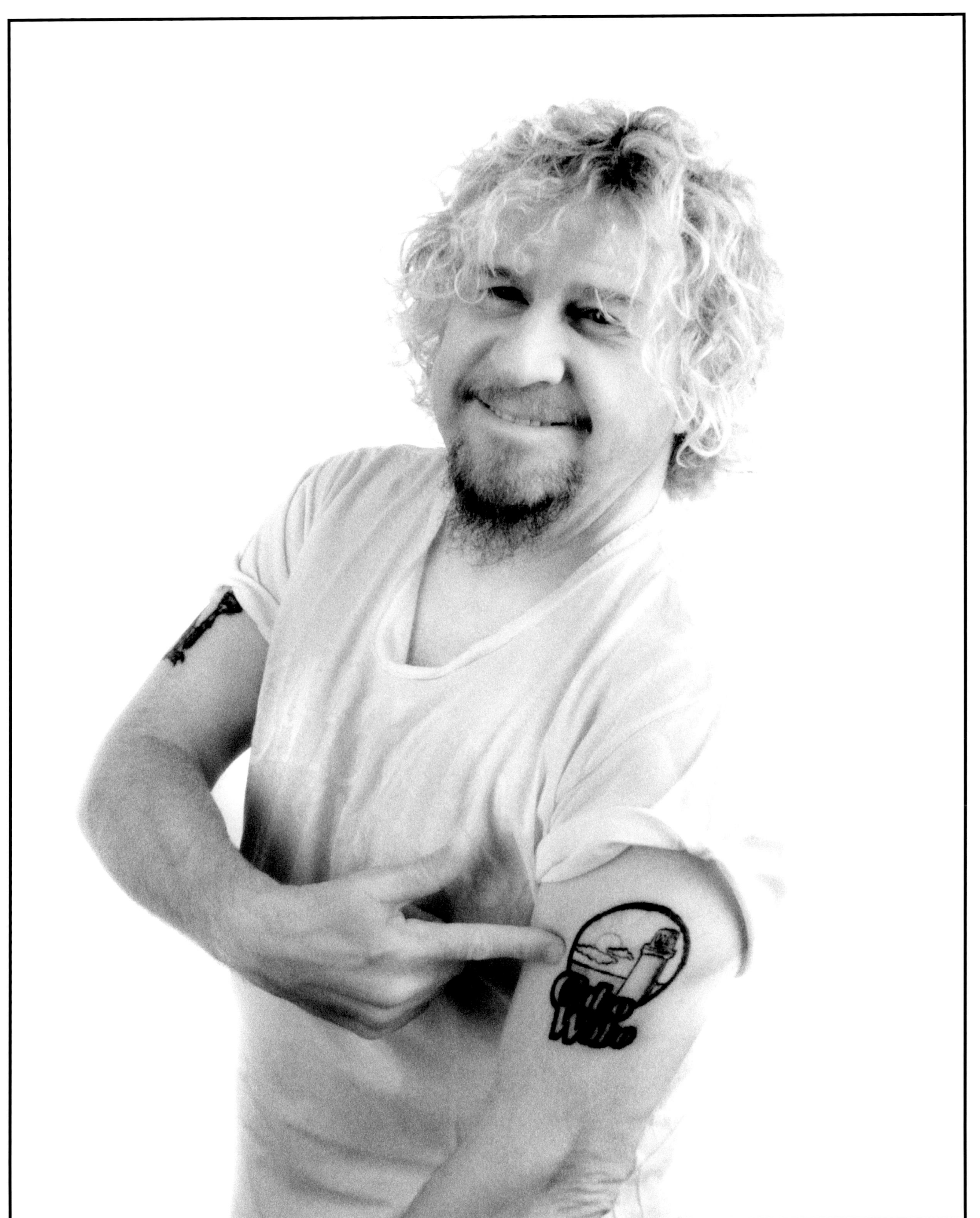

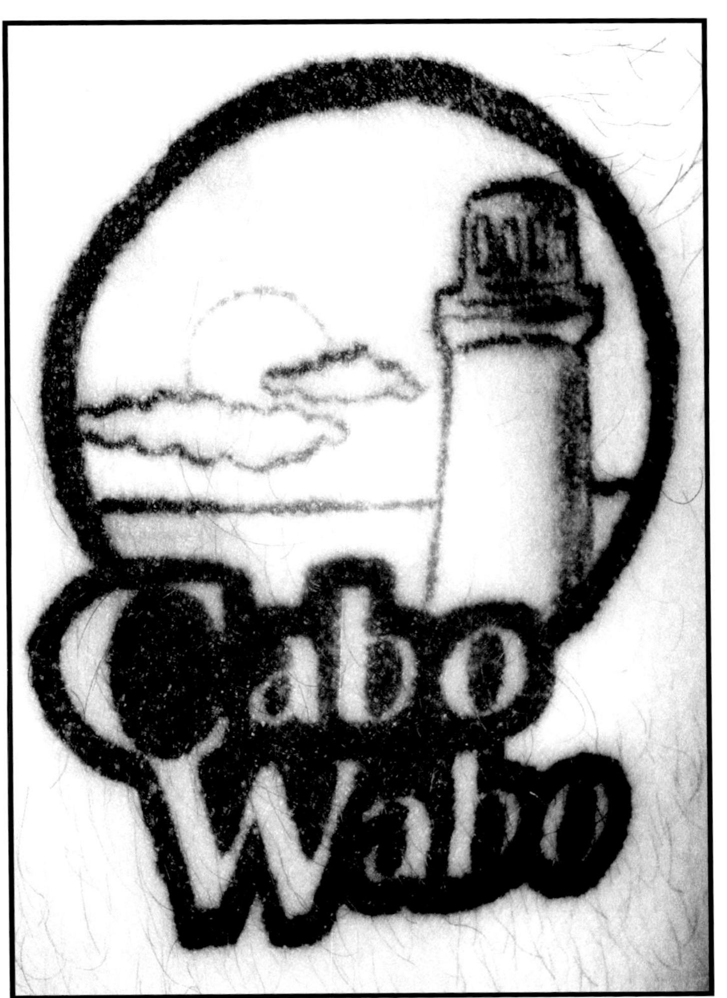

In 2004, when the Van Hagar reunion tour started, they put in the contract between me and the brothers that I wasn't allowed to wear Cabo Wabo t-shirts on stage. I thought, "how stupid." I thought it was just so childish and rather than say, "Take it out," you know, like "fuck you, I ain't doin' it," I just thought, I'm going to go and get a tattoo. So I went and got my tattoo and wore long sleeved shirts to rehearsals because it had a bandage on it. First gig, I popped out in a t-shirt rolled up and of course we had a 100-foot giant video screen, and being the lead singer I was on it a lot of the time. I can tell you straight up, the video guys were my friends and they would come and do close-ups on my tattoo and the whole place would cheer. That's all I can say. It's a true story!

–Sammy Hagar

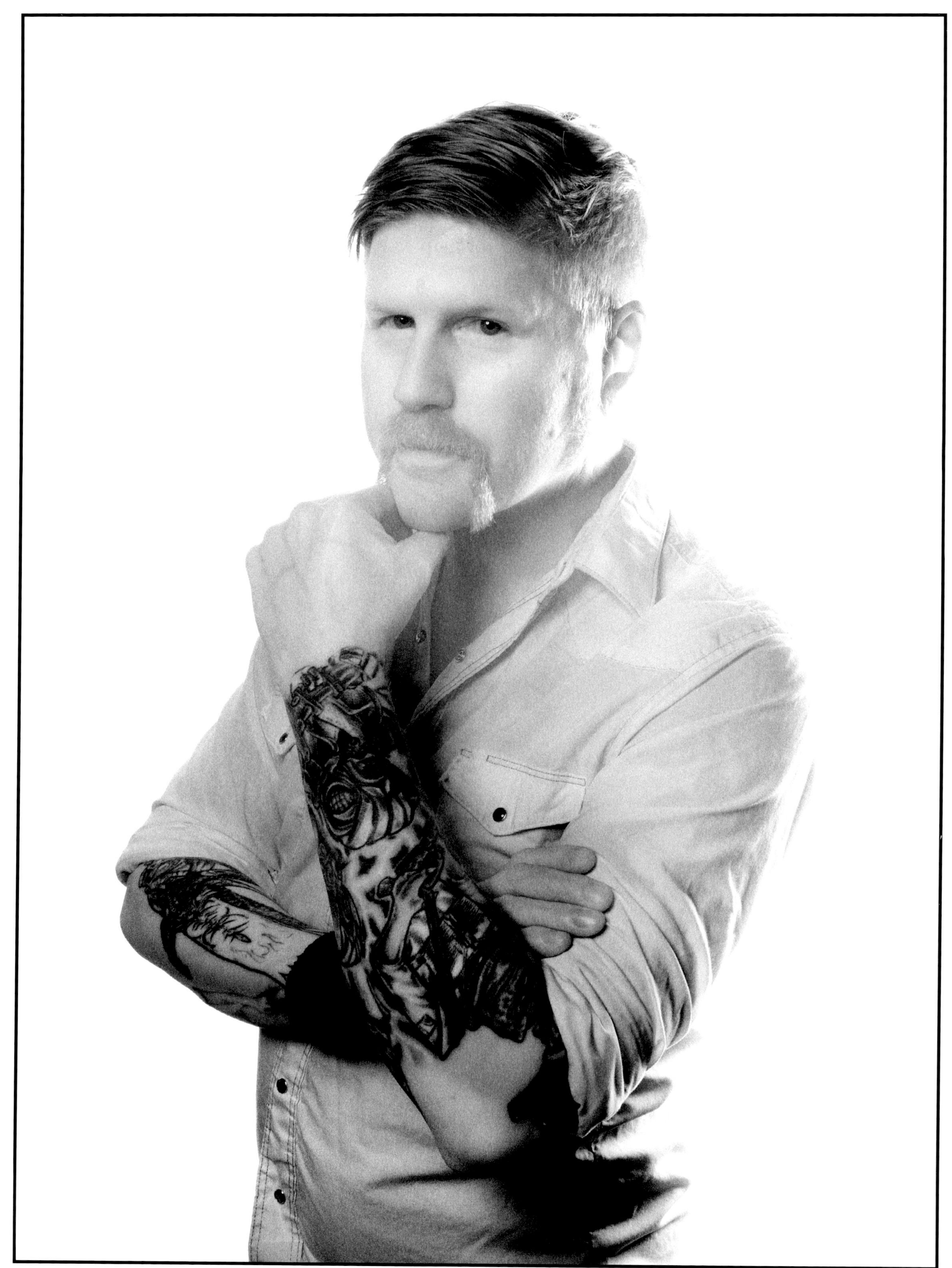

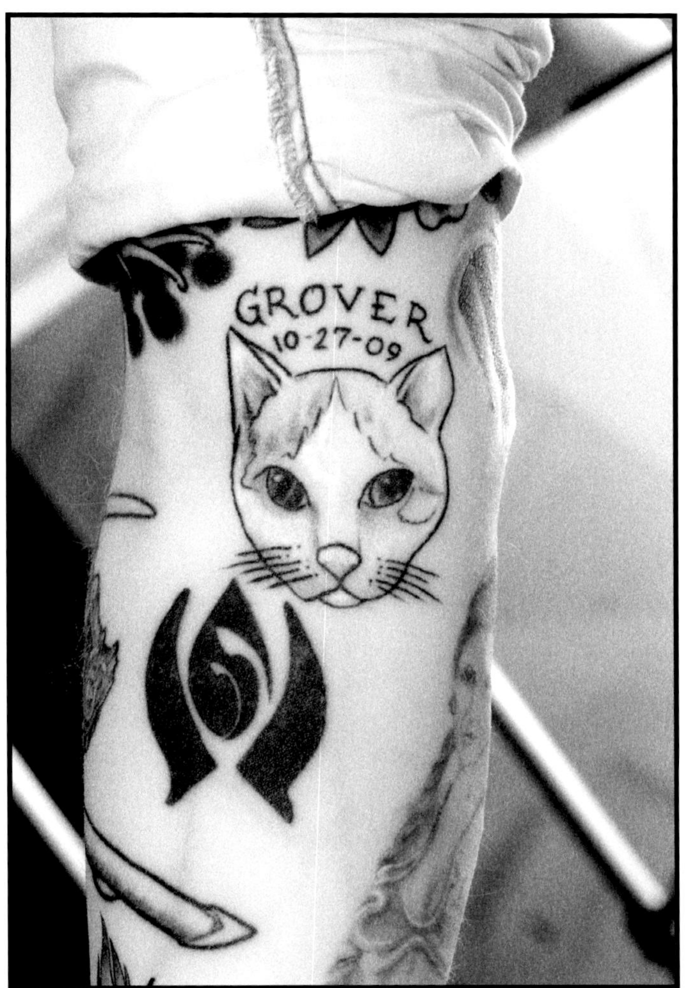

One of my favorite tattoos is a tattoo of my cat Grover, who passed away two years ago. I was on tour and my wife had to put my cat down. He was more my cat. I had him for about 19 years. He was pretty old and lived a really good life. I got to see him about a week before he died; he was getting really bad, really thin. I was playing at the House of Blues in Boston, Massachusetts, that night and there happened to be a tattoo artist there who was a friend of ours and I thought what a great way to immortalize my cat on my arm. So every time I look down, he's still with me by my side 'cus that's the kind of cat he was. A good friend and I miss him.

–Bill Kelliher

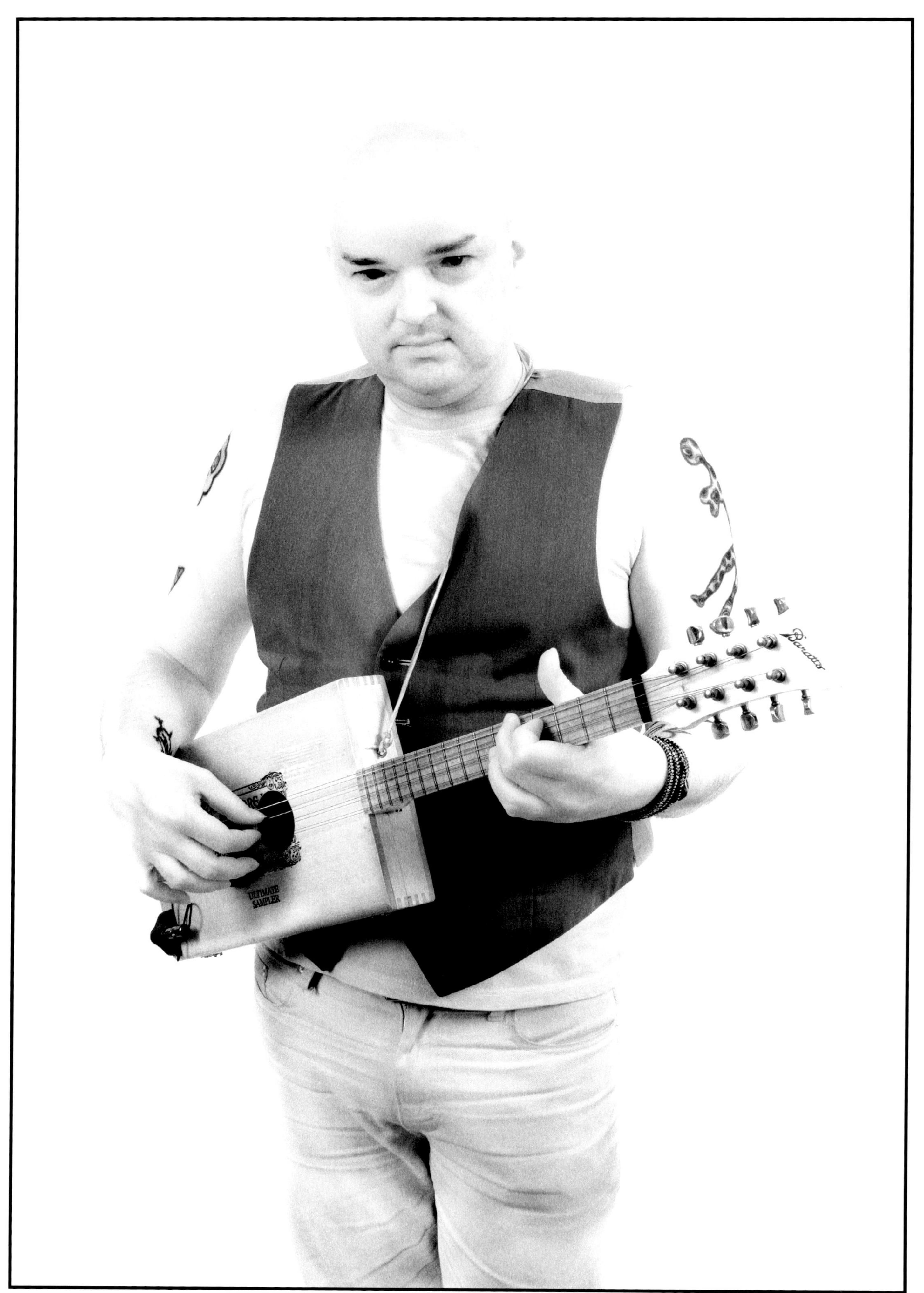
ULTIMATE
SAMPLER

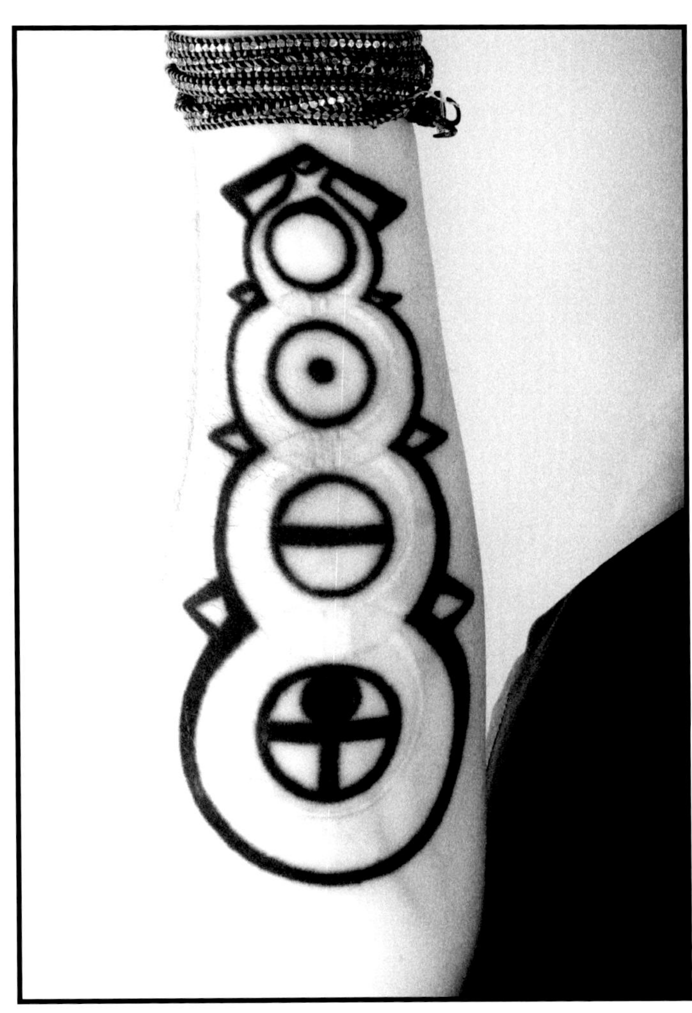

My very first tattoo was this one right here. There was a club that we used to play a lot with my band Eleven called Black & Blue on Sunset Boulevard and right next door was a shop called The Purple Panther. My friend Matt Denis ended up getting a tattoo by Kore Flatmo who was just starting out back then, and I really loved what he was doing, so I went over to Kore and we started out with just the line work and then did the color later. The tattoo itself, I designed and it's basically a snake biting its own tail, which represents infinity. The perfect circle without any content represents the absolute, the dot below that represents birth, the line across is duality, and the ankh for life, so basically the process of folding and unfolding from the source back into itself is represented. I remember getting into a zone because we would have quite long sessions and parts of it were quite painful and a couple of times I had an almost out-of-body experience, which helped with the significance of the tattoo; for years to come it marked a very important shift for me, evolving in my own abilities and my quests, my perceptions and full power really and started to be demarcated by my tattoos.

–Alain Johannes

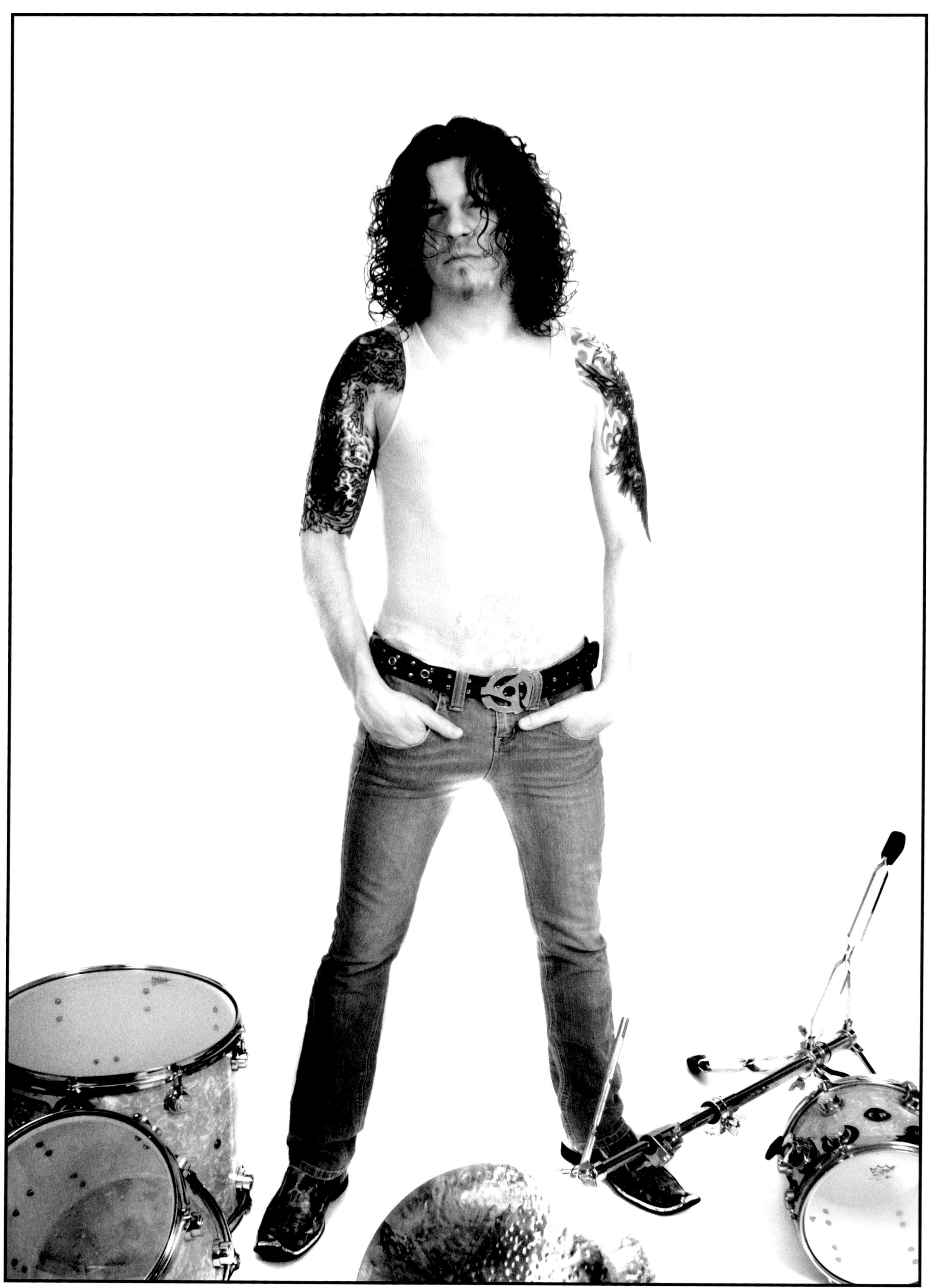

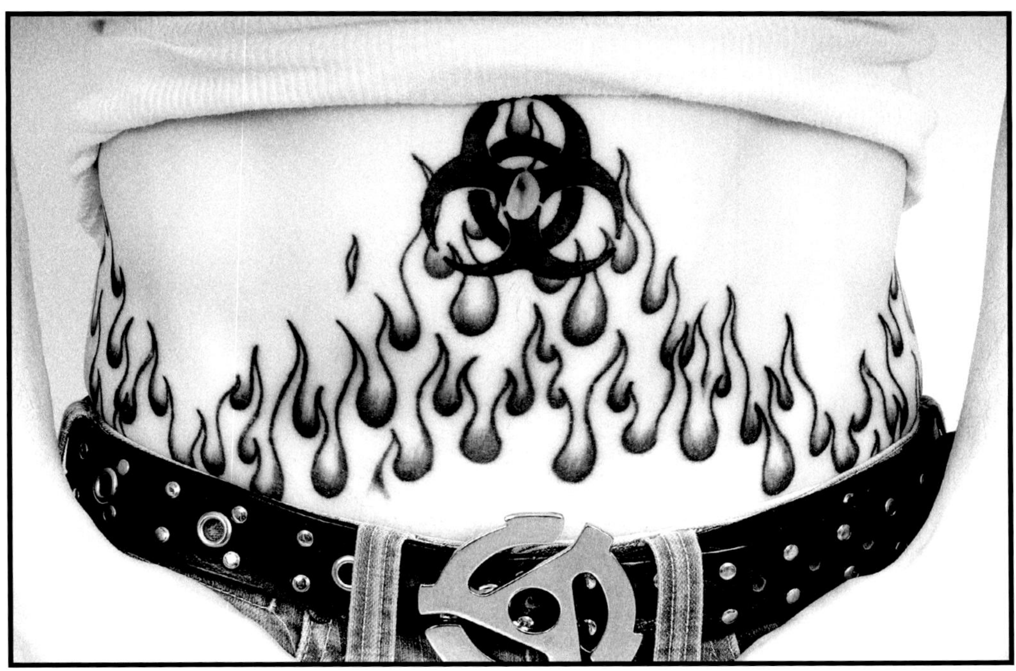

I wanted to look like I was on fire! I was hanging out with a good buddy of mine who does tattoos, and I had come up with this idea where I wanted to look like I was on fire. It starts around my hips and goes all the way around. At the back, I wanted it to look like the sun sets on my ass, like it rises and sets on my ass. Ha ha ha! We had a few beers and they put me on three chairs at the kitchen table and basically put me on a rotisserie and we went through the whole thing. It took about eight hours…and about 28 beer. It was almost a religious experience, it hurt so bad, but I stuck it out. Healing was a bit of a drag because you gotta wear pants!

–Darren James Smith

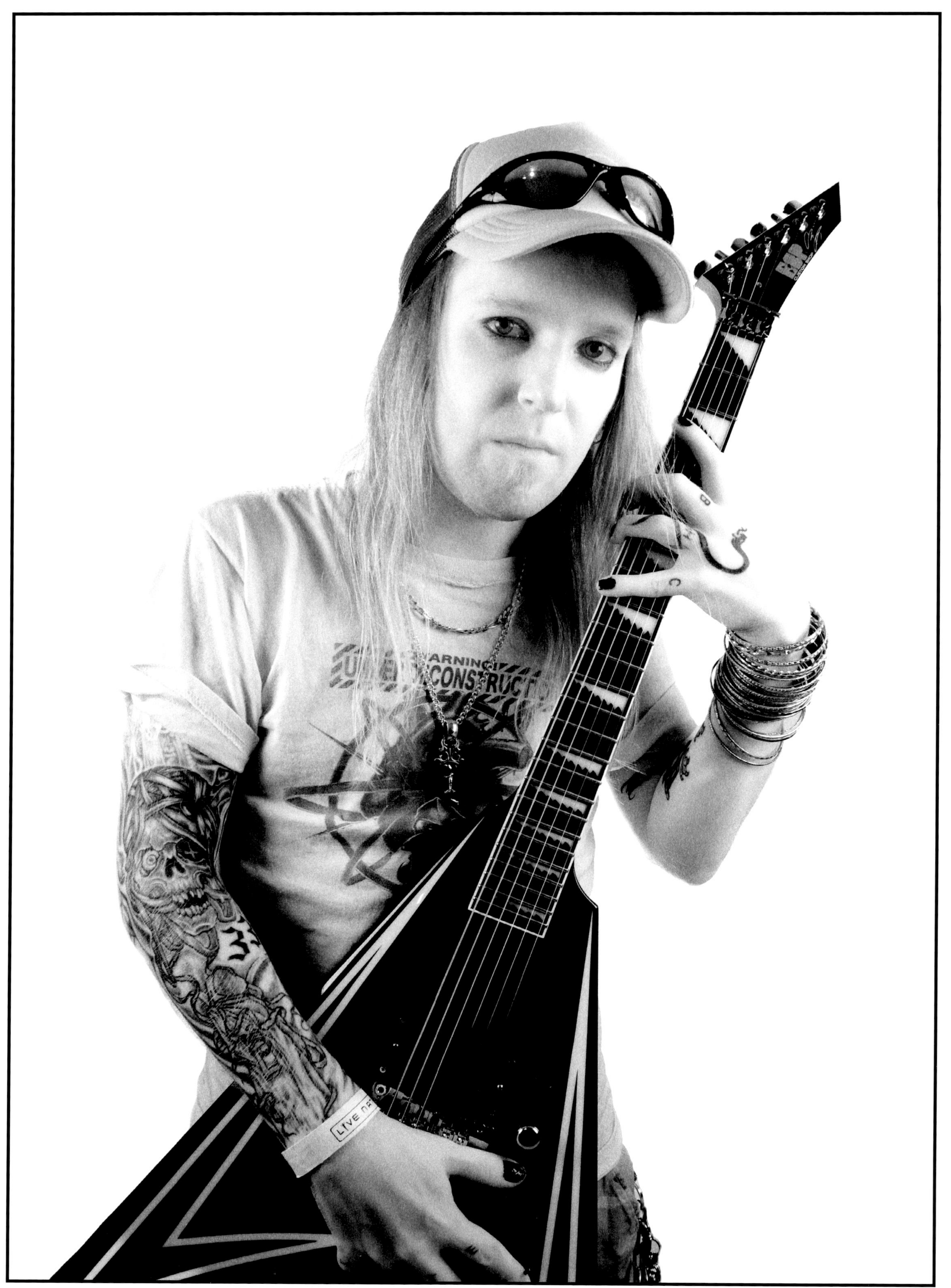

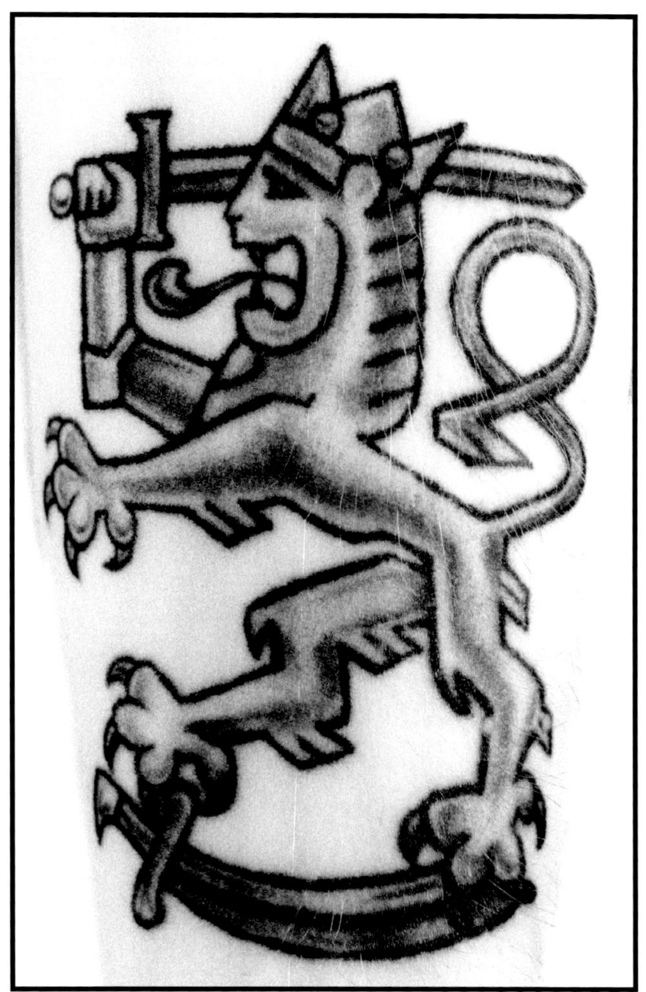

This tattoo here probably has the most... the biggest...meaning for me ever because it's like the emblem of family, and my grandparents used to actually fight; they were in a war against the Russians and for me this is like a sign of respect for my grandparents and just the fact that I was brought up and I'm proud of being Finnish.

–Alexi Laiho

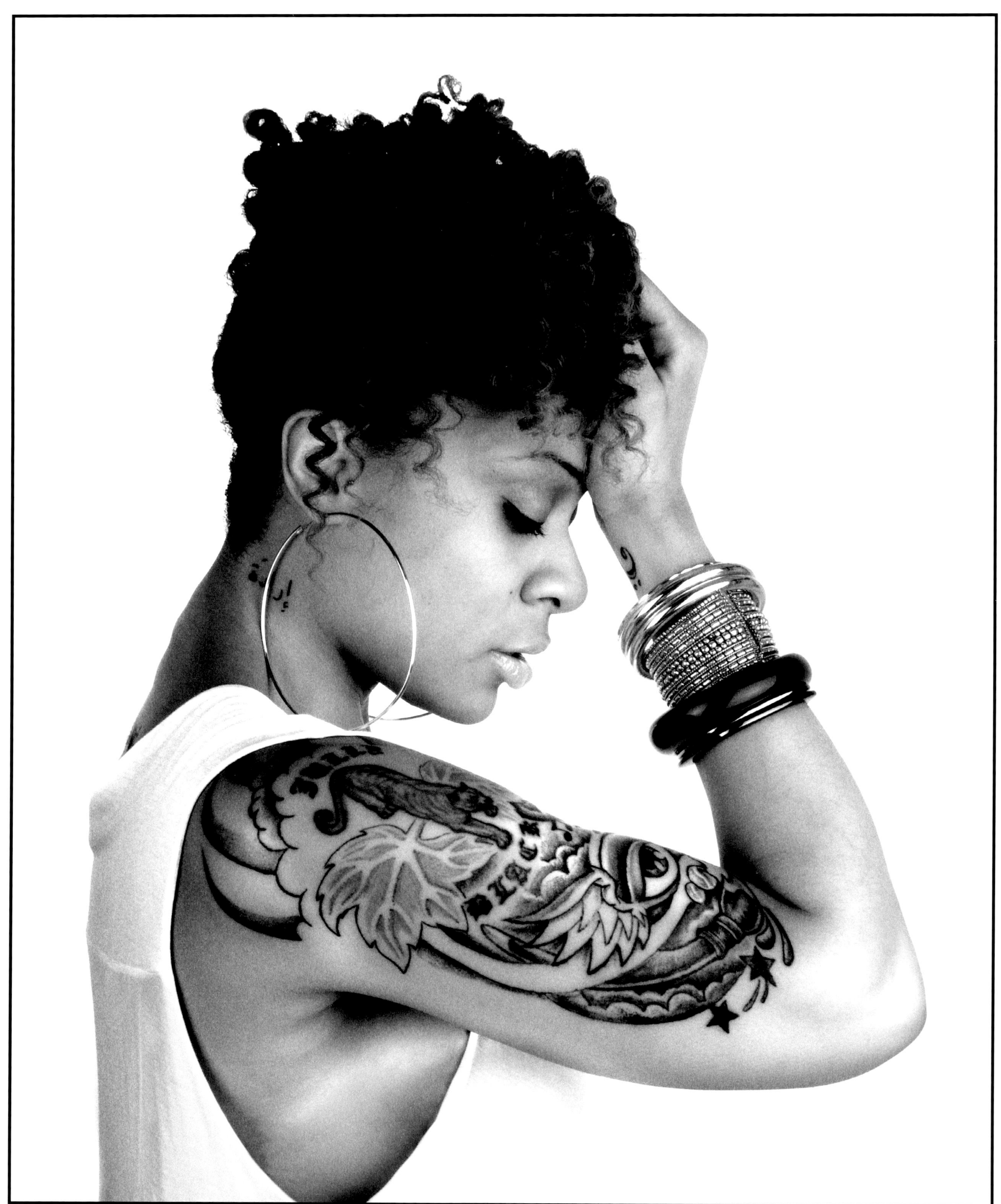

This tattoo has been a work in progress that began with the panther. 1996 was my first tattoo, the black panther and my name, Jully Black. I did some research and found that the panther was the one animal who's prey never hears it coming and I felt that when my music was finally heard around the world, that's the impact it was going to have. I wanted it to be when Jully Black arrives, no one will hear me coming. Fast forward to 2007, I added the wind bars, the clouds, and the maple leafs. I wanted to add some of who I am: I'm from Canada, so the panther is coming out of the leaves, which represent Canada. Then jump ahead now to 2008, when the rest of it happened. I went to Atlanta, Georgia, and met up with a tattoo artist named Miya Bailey. I told him I needed my tattoo to be in memoriam to commemorate the lives of my sister Sharon who passed away in 1990, my twin brother who passed away at birth, and one of my managers, Bonnie O'Donnell, who passed away in 2008. I let him know my sister was a painter, my brother was my twin, and Bonnie loved marbles. He took a Sharpie and just drew on my arm and drew my brother's eye with angel wings on it and his tear rolling down, my sister Sharon's paint brushes catching his tear and Bonnie's marbles flowing right into it and that completed the whole piece. He also knew I'm a musician, so he said let's add in some musical notes to it. And it was very important to me to have color on black skin and I've been to other tattooists who were very iffy about putting color on black skin, but Miya pulled it off. He got me some yellow and green and purple… and all that good stuff. It's not done; I'm going to be finishing up a half sleeve in the next few years, but it all has to mean something to me.

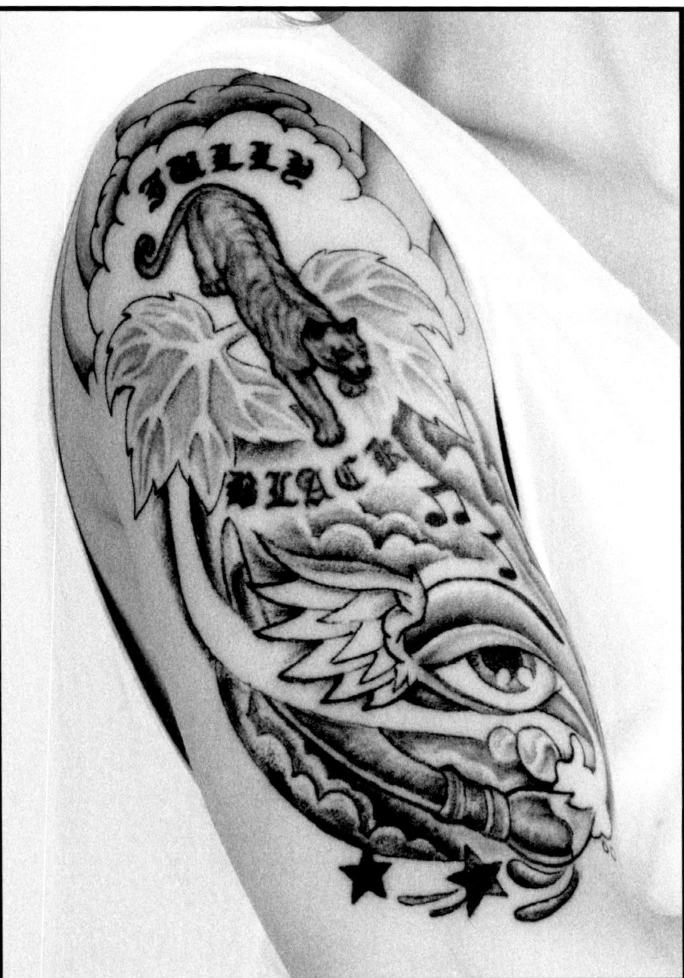

–Jully Black

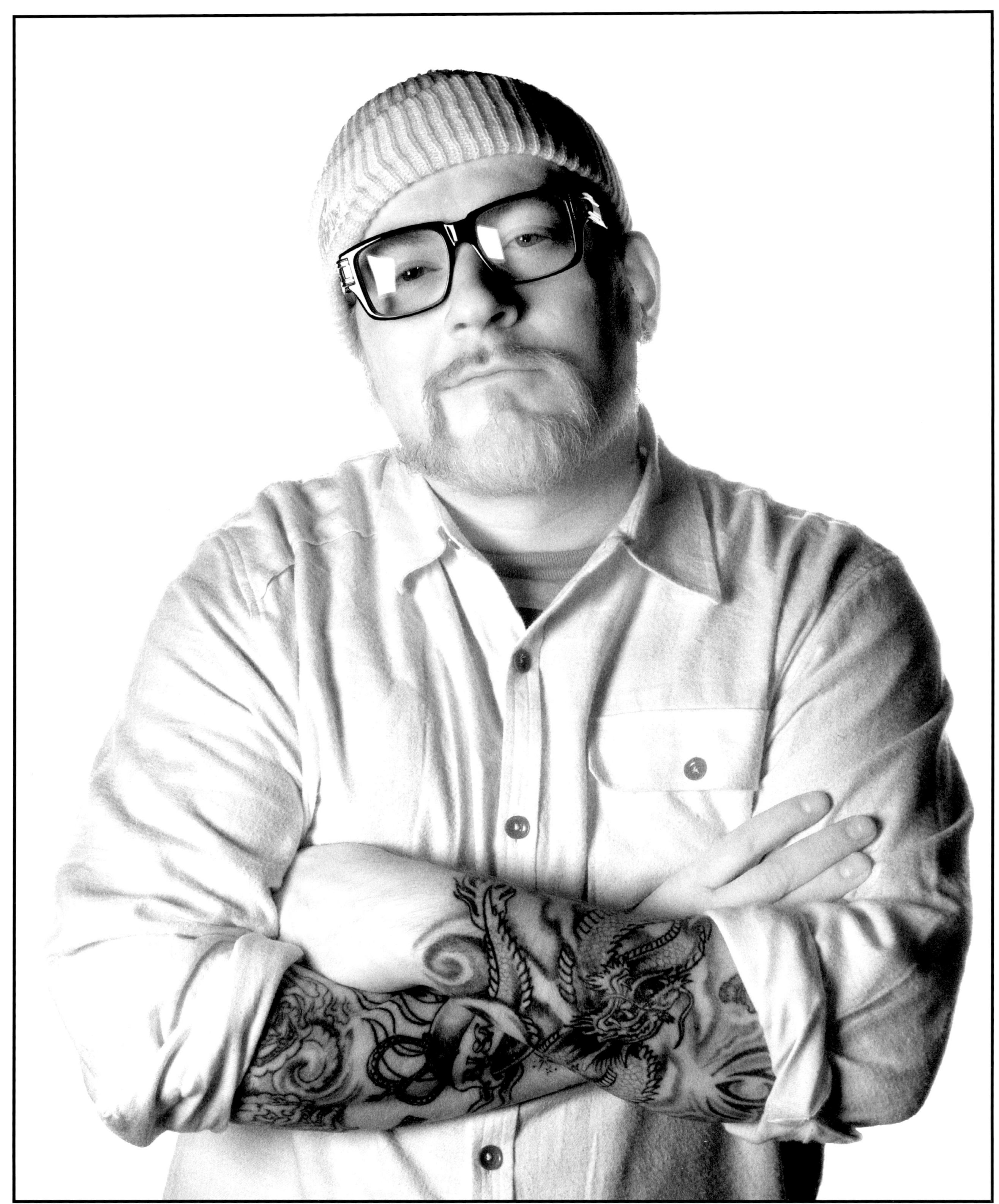

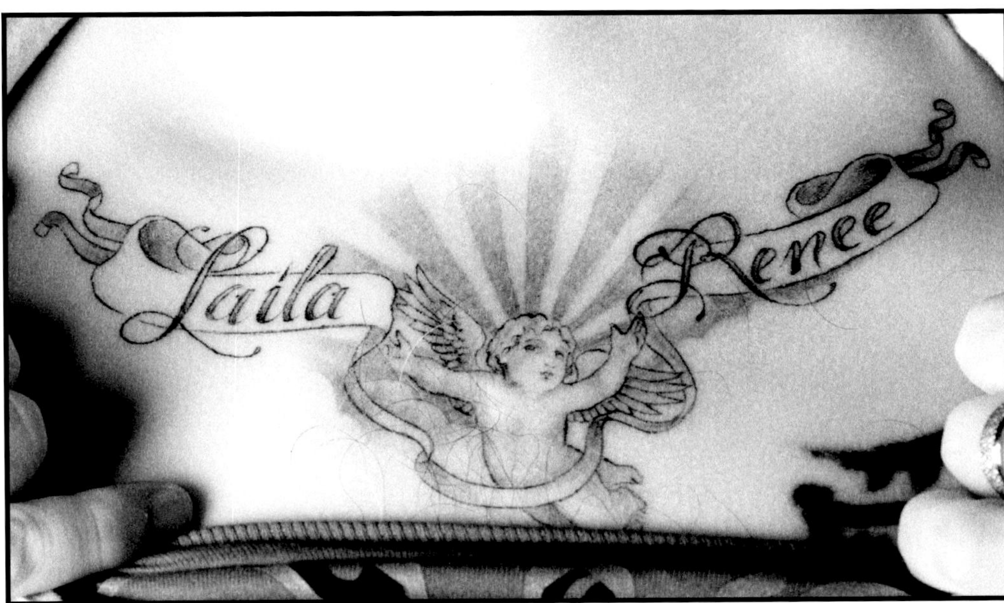

Once my daughter was born, I wanted to ink the occasion and knew there was only one cat I wanted to do it. The one and only Mark Mahoney at Shamrock Social Club in Hollywood. I had him work up a little angel to of course represent my little angel and surround it with a banner that has her name in it. Mark is one of the best to ever do it in the tattoo game and I love the results. It will definitely not be the last time he inks me.

–Erik "Everlast" Schrody

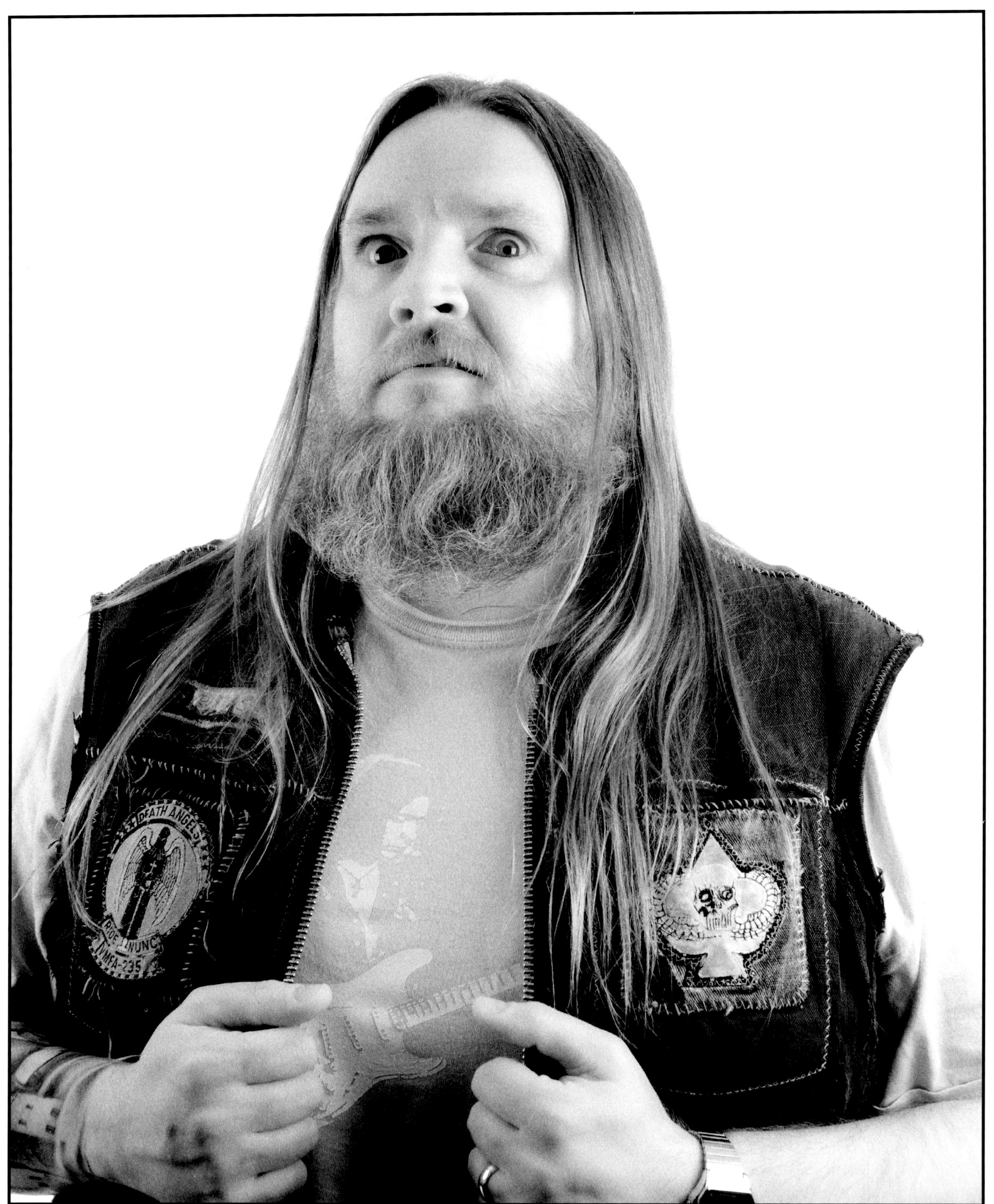
DEATH ANGELS
VMFA-235

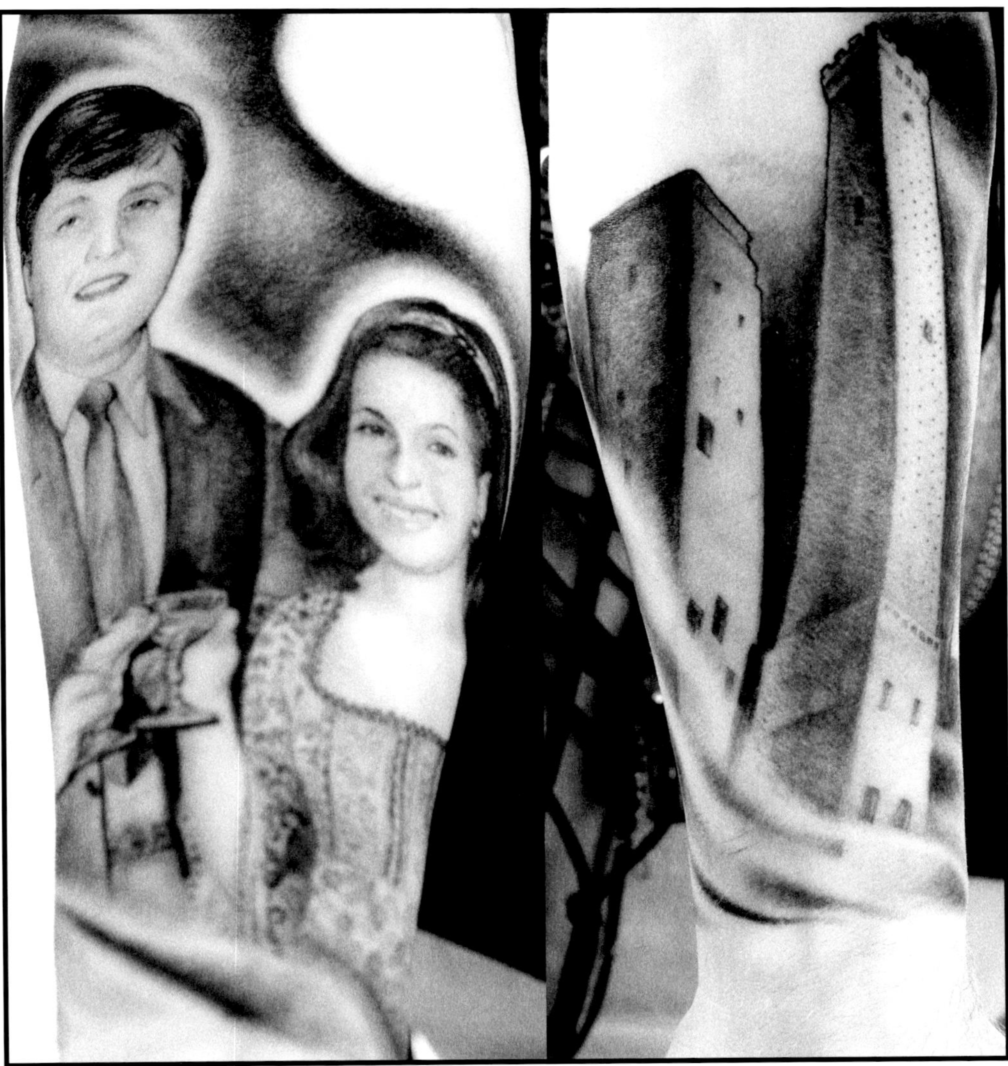

The reason I got the two tattoos on my right arm, obviously for my folks, who have moved on from this earth. That's the reason they are on my arm, but also on the back, the two towers that are in the town square in Bologna, Italy, are symbolic of where my parents started their life together. The two towers always remind me of the two of them, so I figured it was a good justification. I could be wrong.

–James Rota

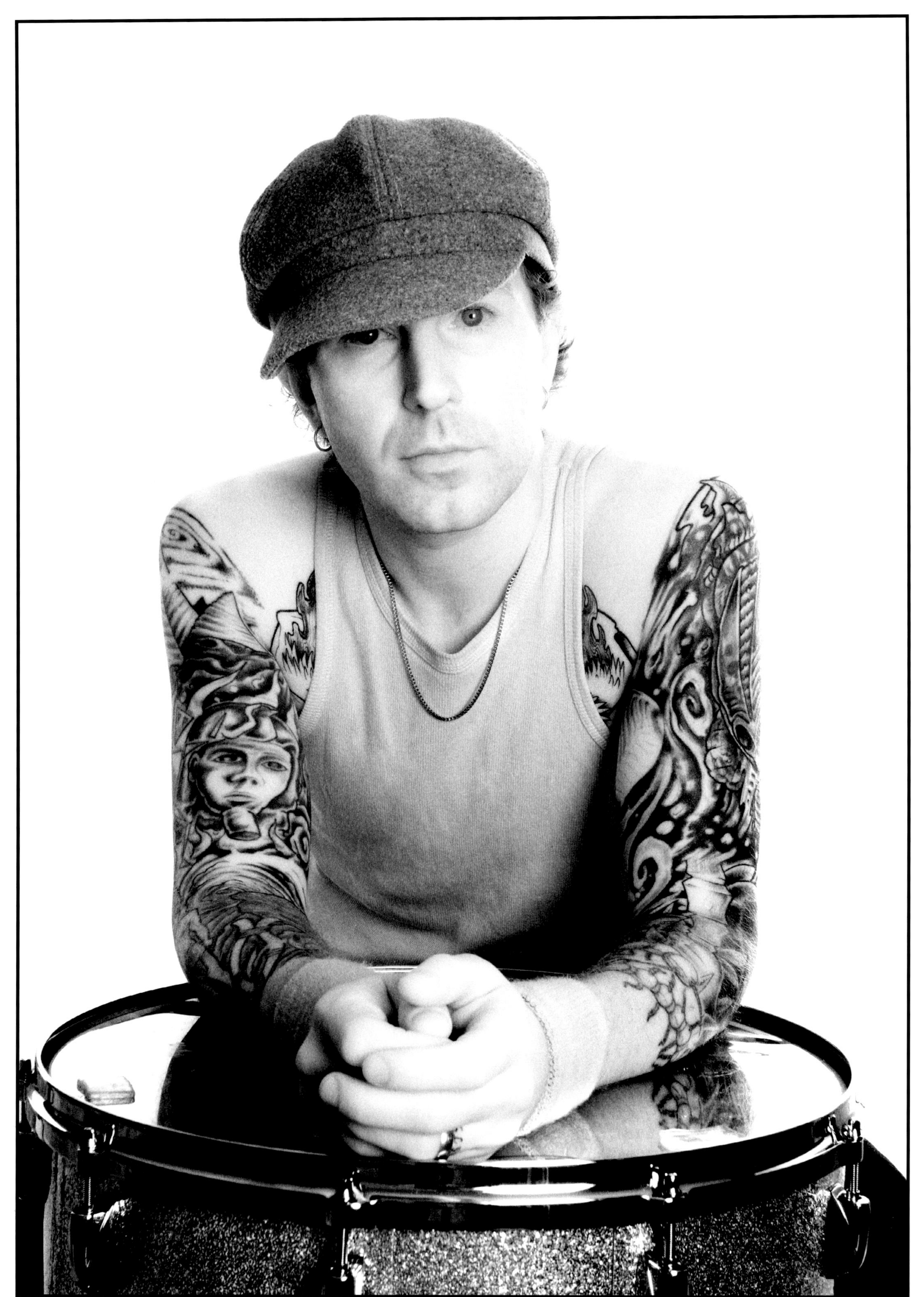

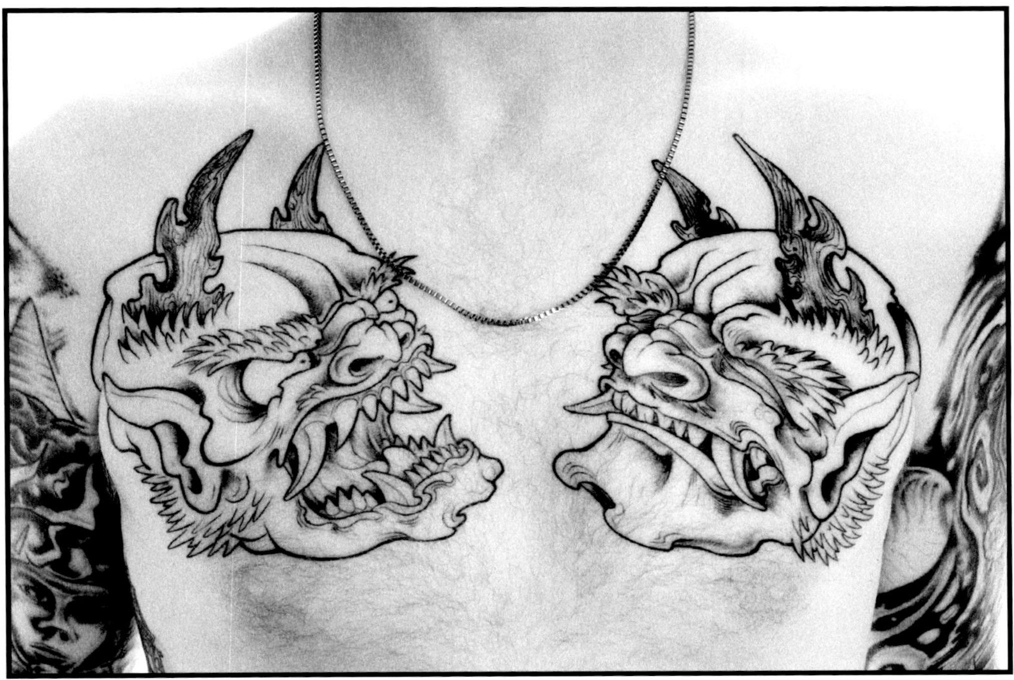

I just got these Japanese demons on my chest about a year and a half ago. I quit drinking and that was a pretty big life change for me. I drank pretty heavily for a long time and it was time for a change. Because it was such a big deal and such a big change, I thought a tattoo, something to symbolize it. I got these Japanese demons on my chest, one kind of screaming and the other sleeping, showing that there is always going to be a demon screaming in your ear, enticing you, and then the demon sleeping, but it's always there. It's like the good and the evil, showing that there is always the devil waiting and the other side, calmly sleeping but that can always be woken up.

–Rich Beddoe

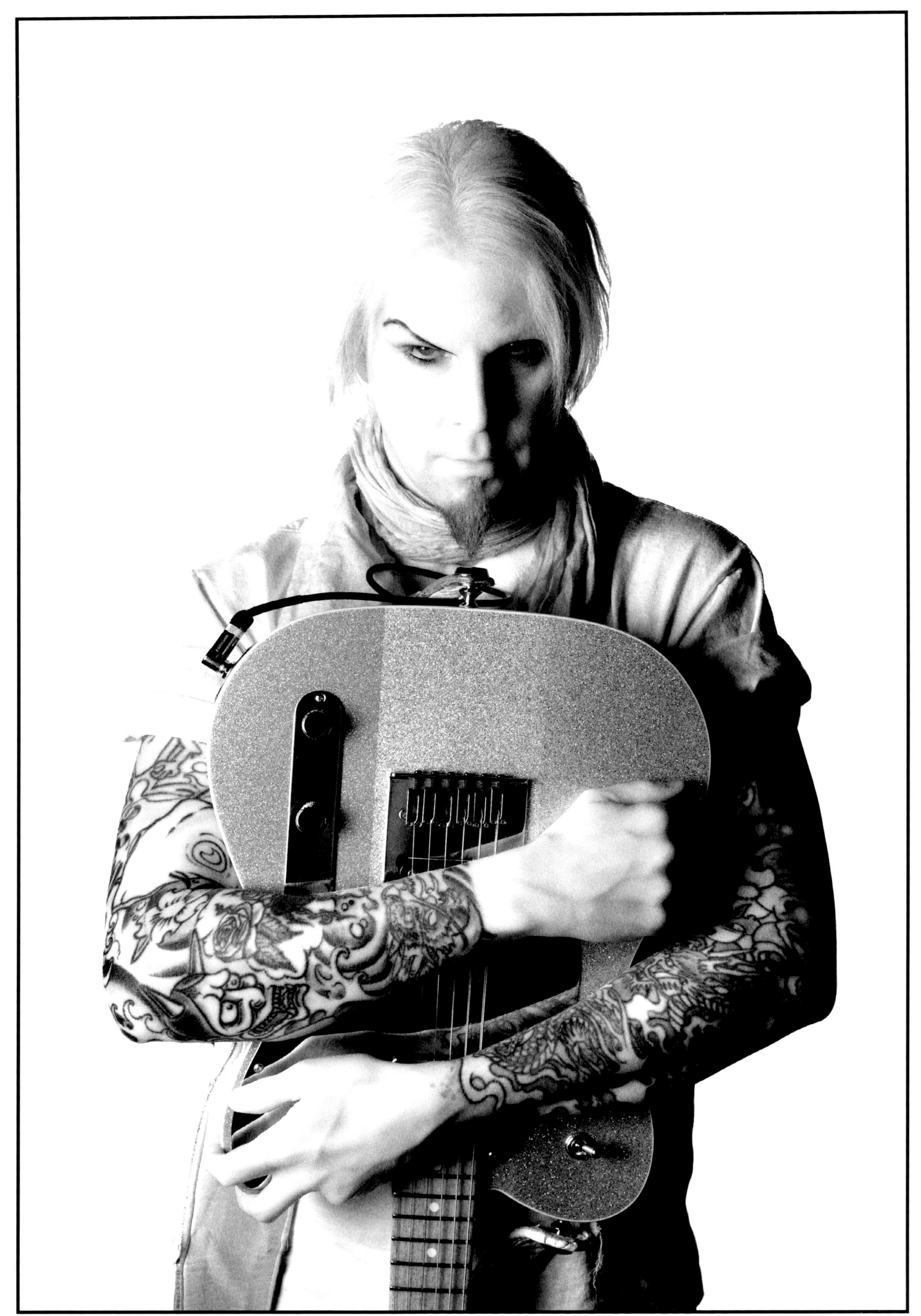

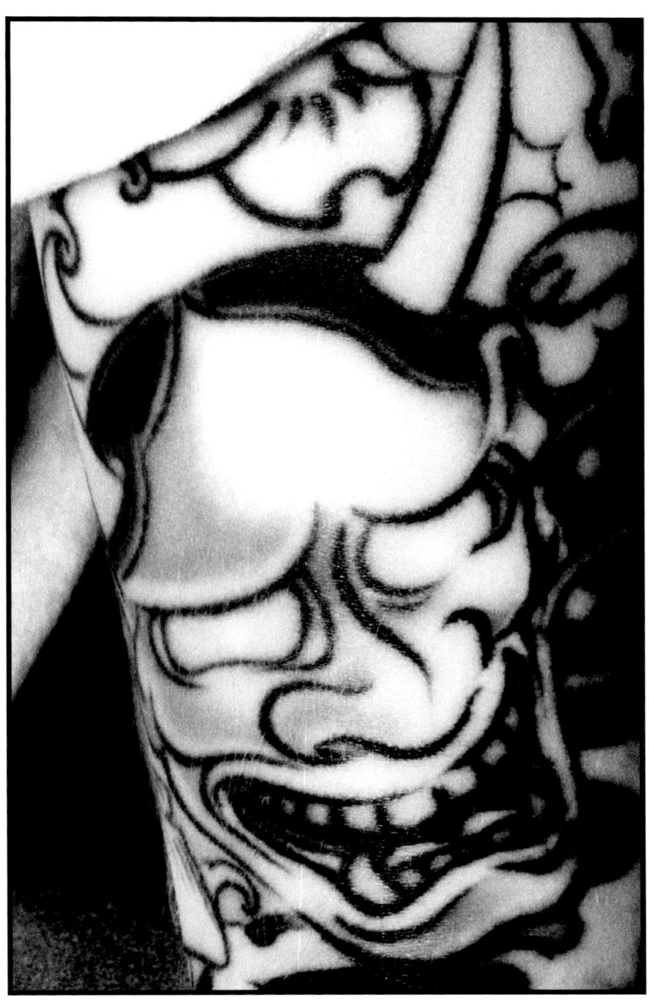

The reason I started getting tattoos: I was brought up in a kind of strict, well-off family and I was so determined to become a musician that I never wanted to give it up. I got my chest and both arms tattooed completely because tattoos last forever of course and that was my thing; I didn't want to give up until I made it. Because the tattoos will be on me forever and I never wanted to stop trying to make it forever and ever and ever. It's just what I wanted to do; I just wanted to be a successful guitar player my whole life and having these tattoos on me was going to be a life-long commitment with my career and my tattoos. I have a lot of Japanese-style tattoos because I love the work ethic, the discipline, and I love the art of it; it's just beautiful, beautiful art.

–John 5

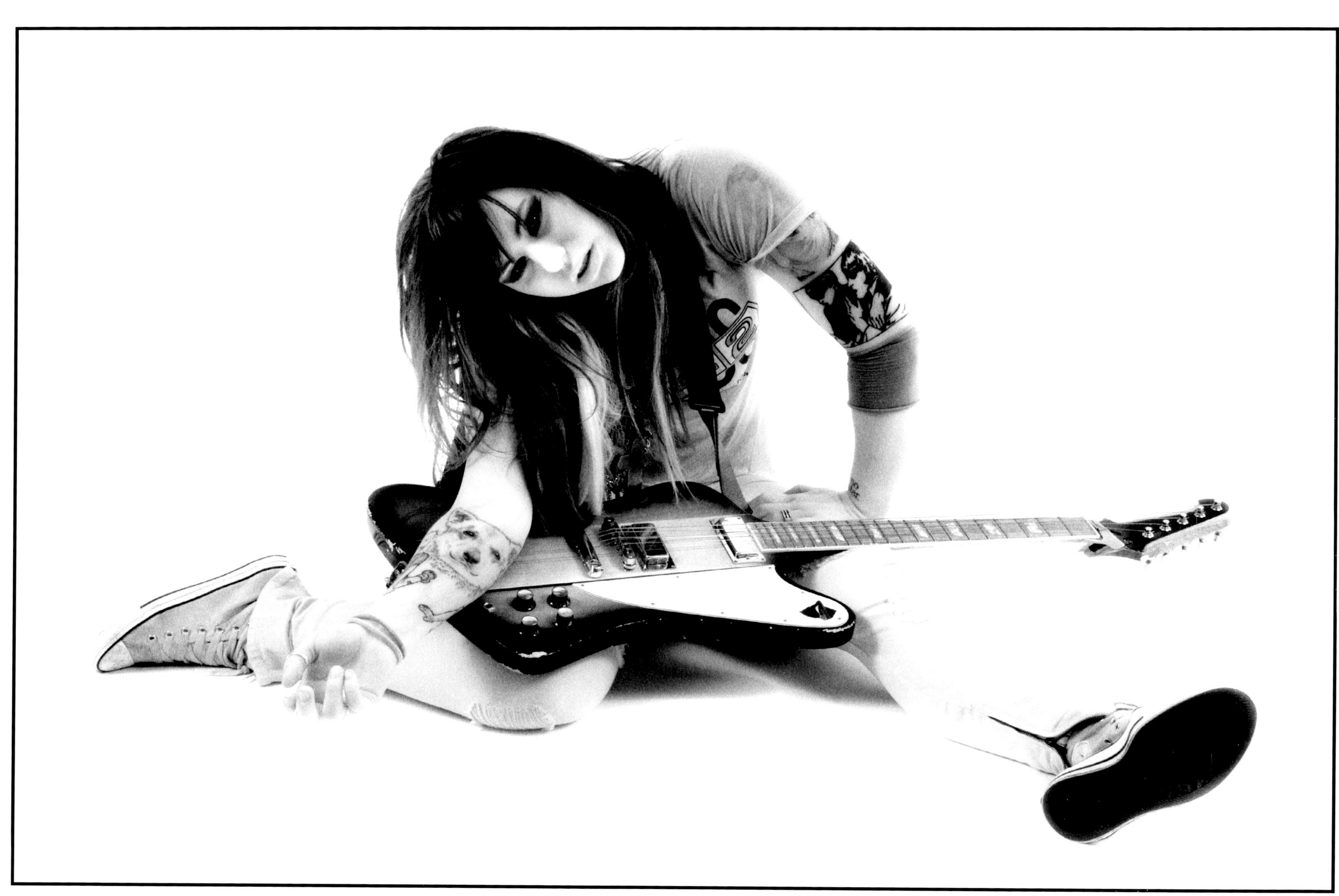

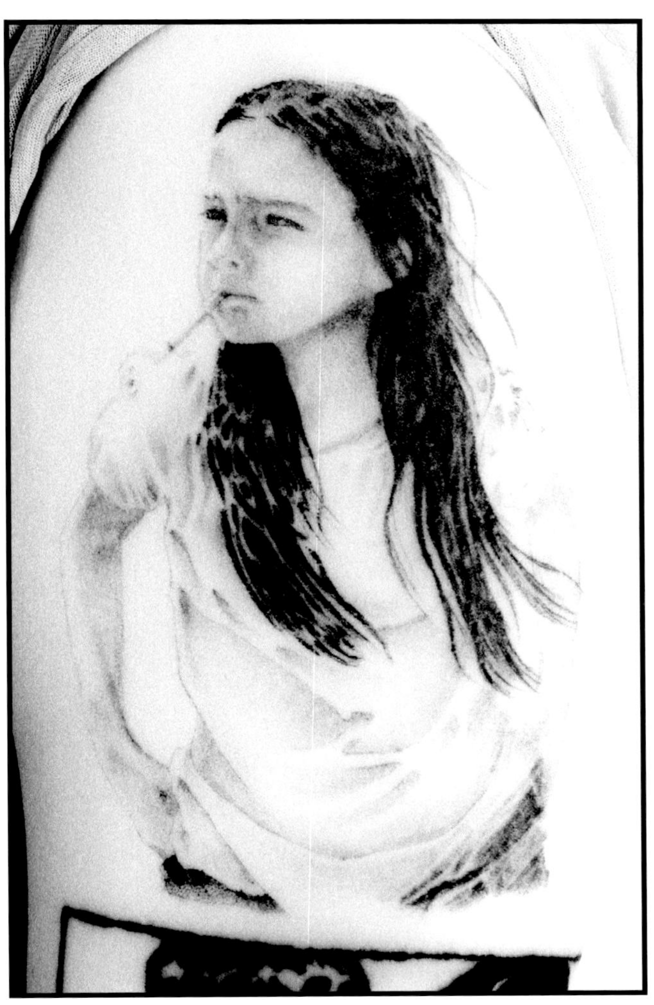

All of my tattoos are album covers besides my R.I.P. puppy. I started by trying to tell the story of my life with album covers; I have to like the record, I have to love it. I have to love the art, too, and it has to tell a story, so there's three things that have to happen. I have *Houdini*, and that's two kids discovering this two-headed puppy dog. It's curiosity, and I mean I left home at a young age, and that's the next one I want to talk about, which is the *Green Mind* cover from the Dinosaur Junior record. It's this 10-year-old native girl smoking a cigarette in a junkyard picking up her pants in the morning and she's naive but thinks she's all tough and she can handle the world, but at the same time that image of a child smoking a cigarette is what probably got to me the most. My pal Kelly who's done all of my good tattoos and this one really kind of resembles me when I was 16 and I left home, coming back later with my tail between my legs; that naiveté and thinking your really strong at the same time is what I like the most.

–Care Failure

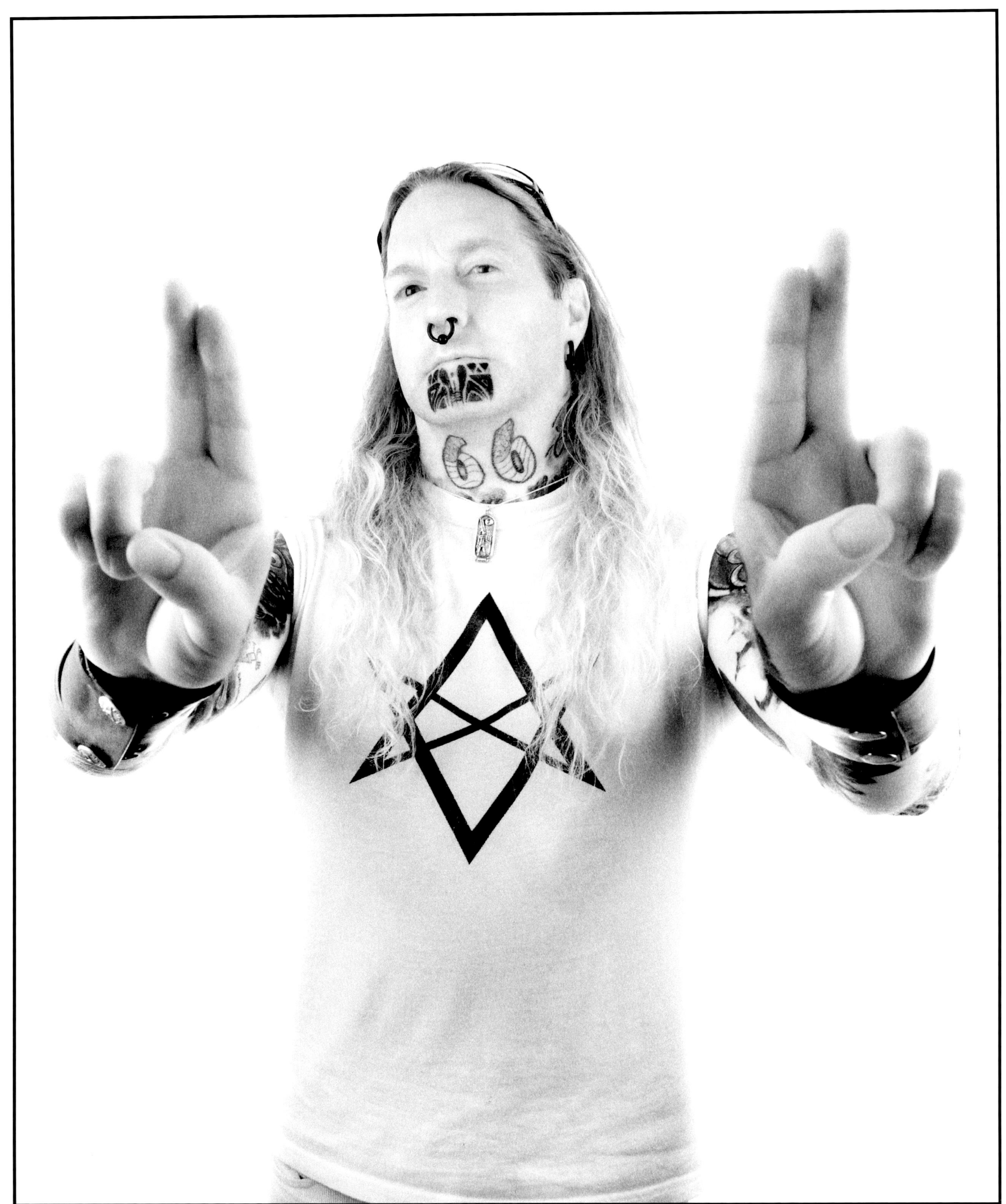

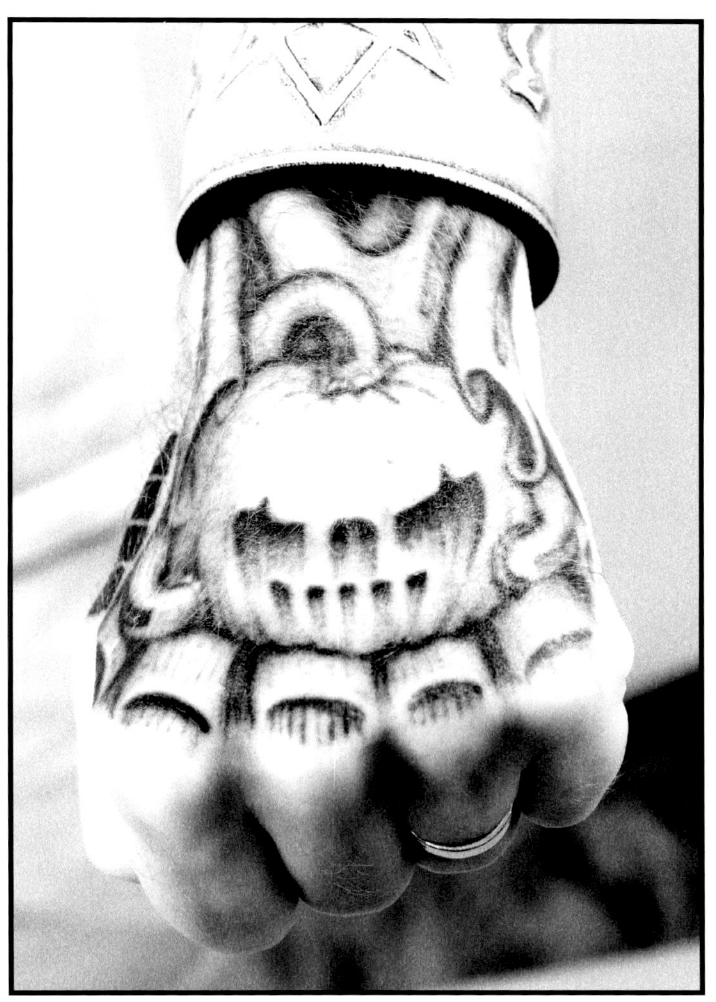

I got this tattoo by Paul Booth in 1998 at Oz Fest. We were backstage and Paul was tattooing, so he said "Who wants to go?" and I sat down. It's a mechanical pumpkin and I love it. It's one of my favorite works. I mean obviously Booth is an amazing artist and legend. The same day, he also tattooed Lynn Strait of Snot, same kind of mechanical skulls on his hands. So rest in peace Lynn. I got tattooed the same day together by Paul. This will always be special to me because of it.

–Dez FaFara

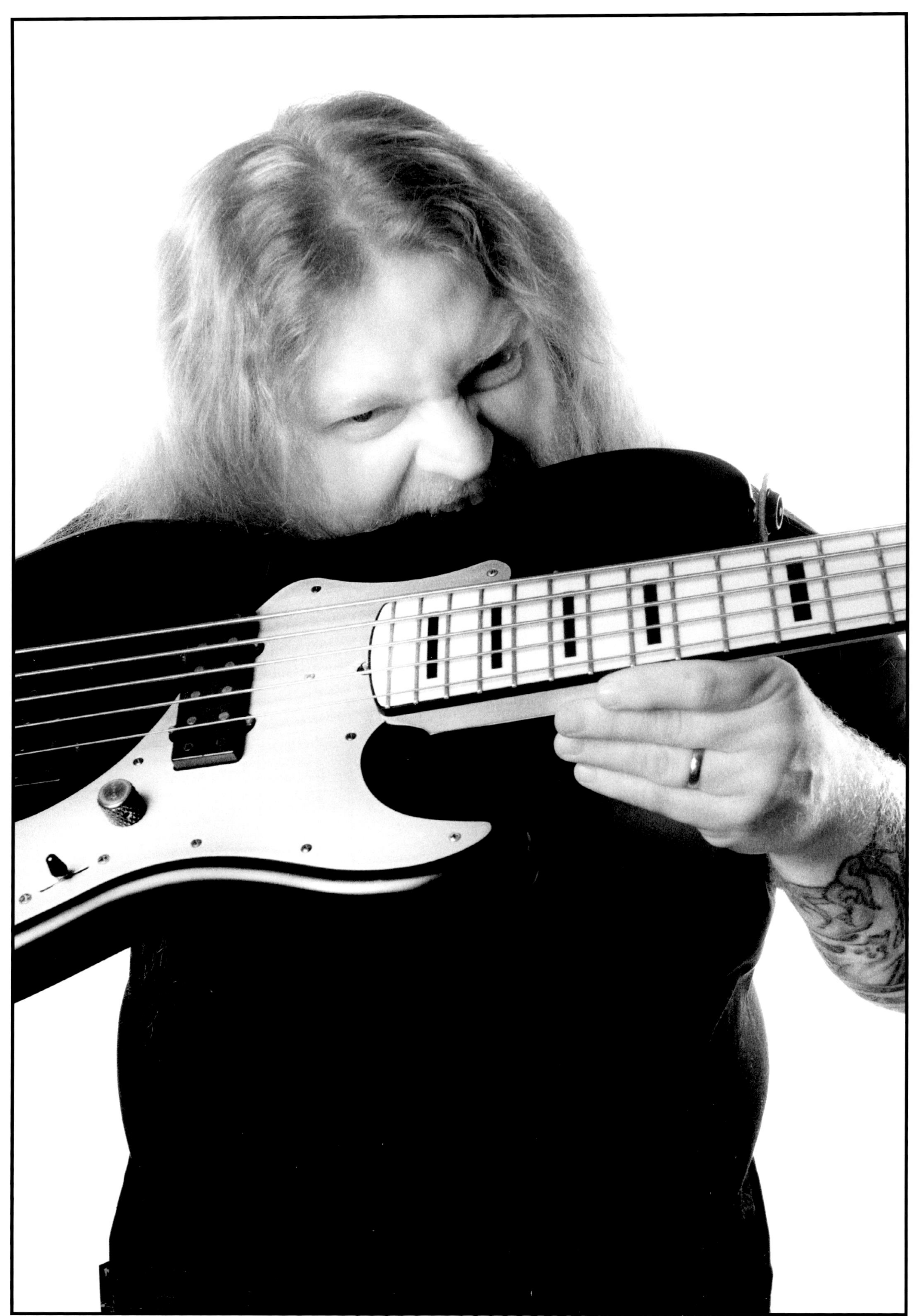

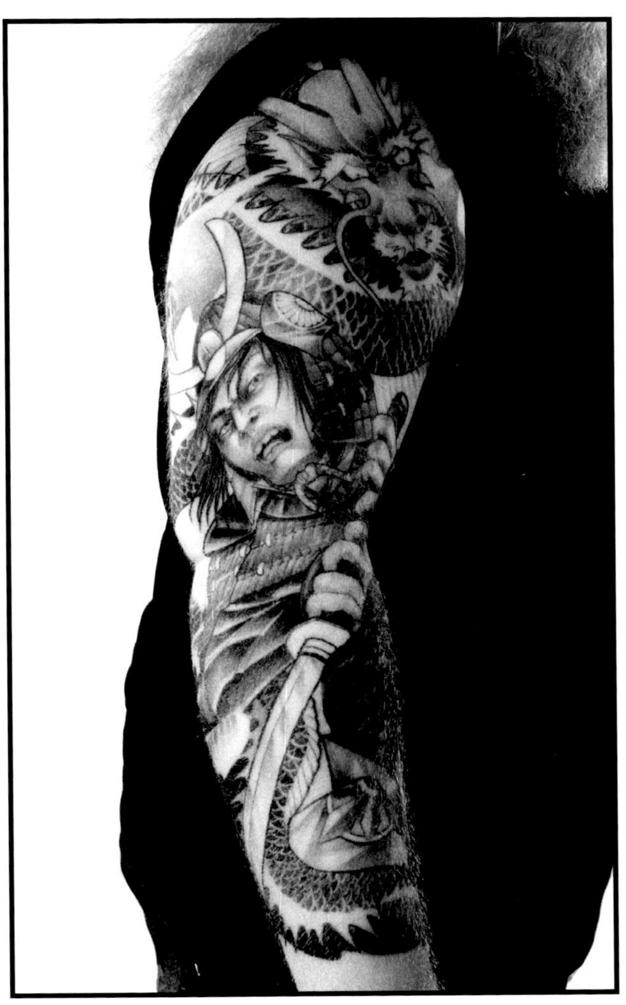

I've gotten plenty of tattoos over the last 25 years, you know, a lot of them. Stuff I got when I was younger. I've been covering them up and I always saved one arm to get one full piece instead of putting stuff together, so I went to see my friend Dave Green at Sacred Heart in Vancouver, where I live, and I told him I had a vision of a Japanese style sleeve and I was super influenced by Japanese tattoo books when I was a kid. I would see all these women tattooed from head to toe and old men tattooed from head to toe, and I just fell in love with the Japanese style of tattooing, so I wanted to get a geisha girl being protected by a warrior from a dragon. He threw it together for me and originally it was supposed to be black and grey. I decided to add some color to it after he already started it and it's pretty much my favorite piece. I've got lots of pieces from all my traveling around the world that I'm starting to cover up now and that's because I got them when I was young. I don't really feel the same way about them and they don't look the same, so I'm starting to kind of fix things up, but this is by far my favorite tattoo. It took about 27 hours to finish. My arm is about the size of some people's legs, so it took a little longer than I had expected it to.

–Byron Stroud

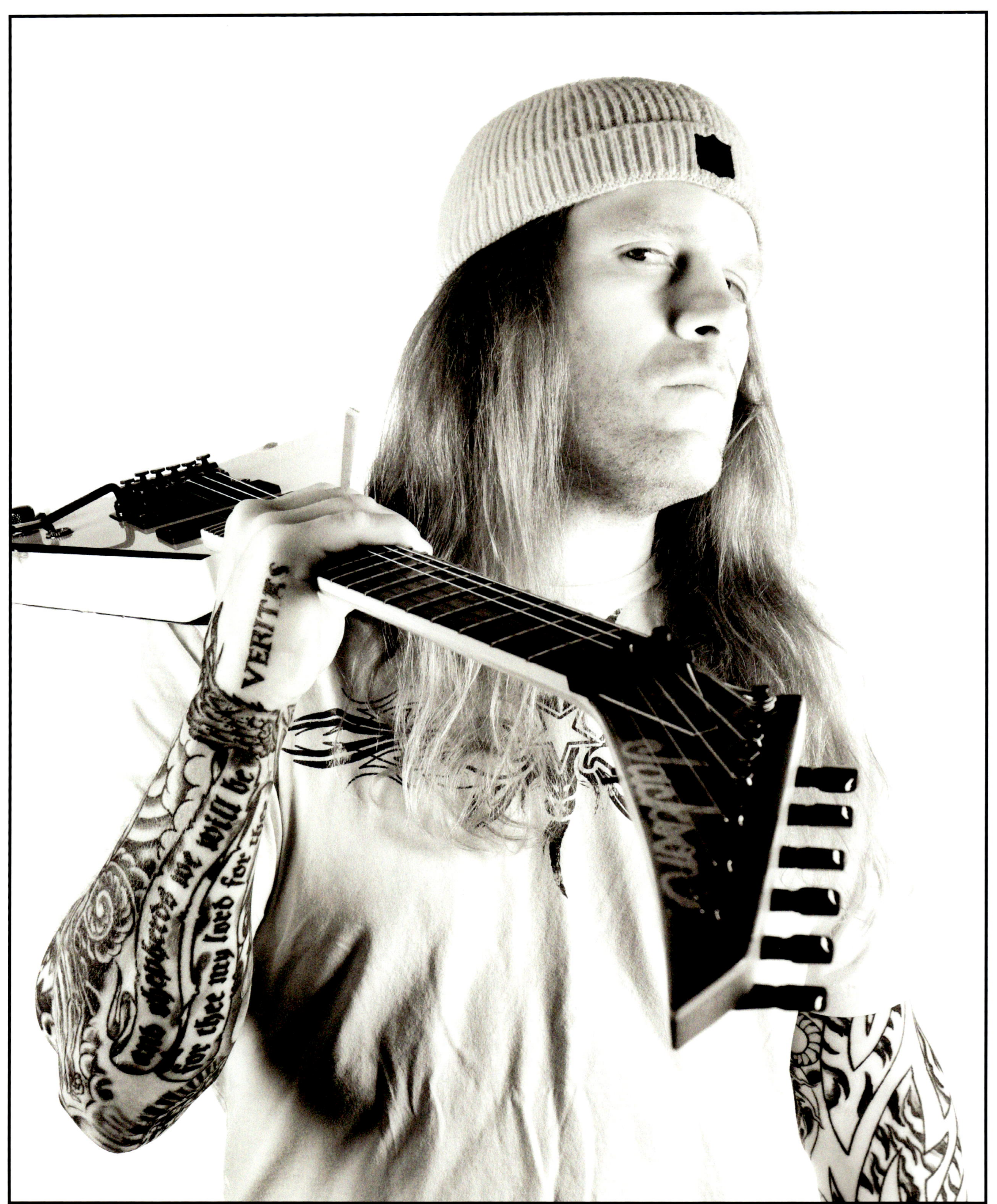
VERITAS

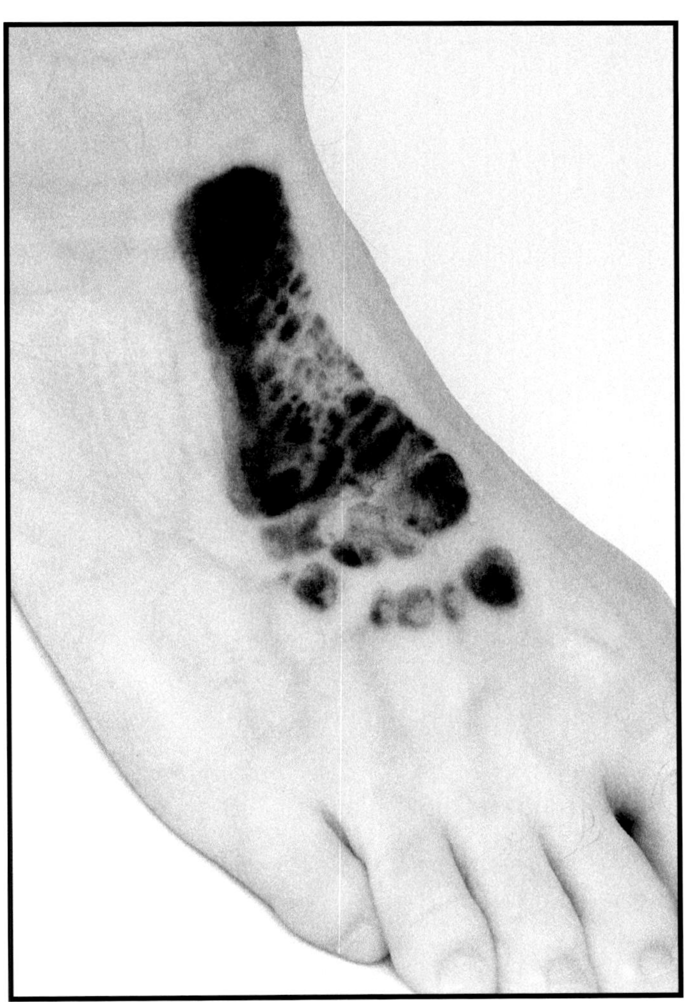

I was starting the tour cycle in 2007 for "The Blackening" and I was washing my car in the driveway. My son came out and we were walking through, transitioning from the wet driveway to a dry part of the concrete and we both stepped with our feet next to each other. I took a picture of it and I thought it was a cool photo. We were embarking on what would be a three-year tour cycle for this record and I wouldn't see him that much, so, after the first tour I rolled his foot in ink and pressed it onto a piece of paper and took it to my tattoo guy, Joe Leonard from Monkey Wrench Tattoo, and had him place it on top of my foot. That way, every step that I take away from him, he's still with me, so I'm keeping my boy with me everywhere I go.

–Phil Demmel

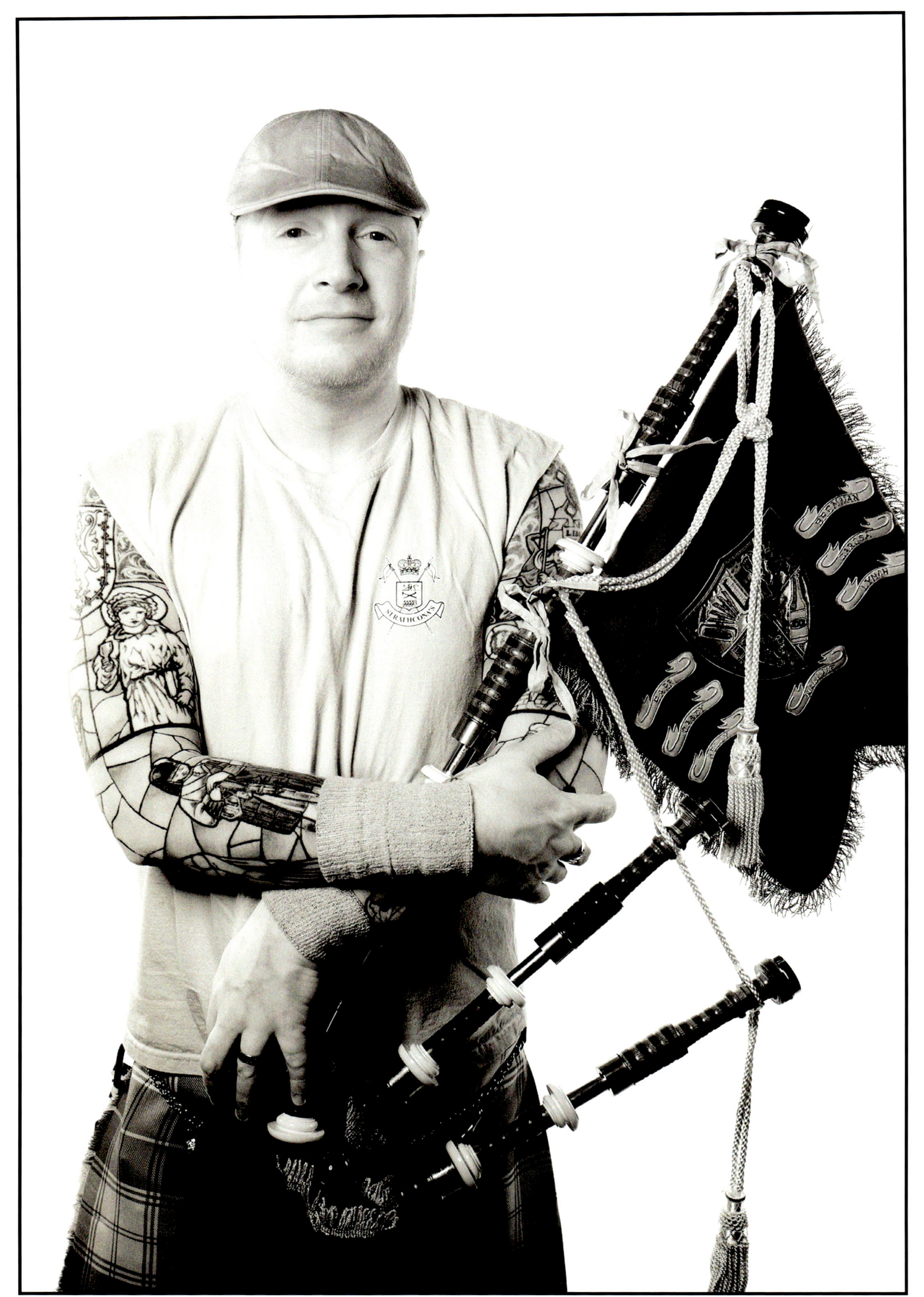
STRATHCONA'S

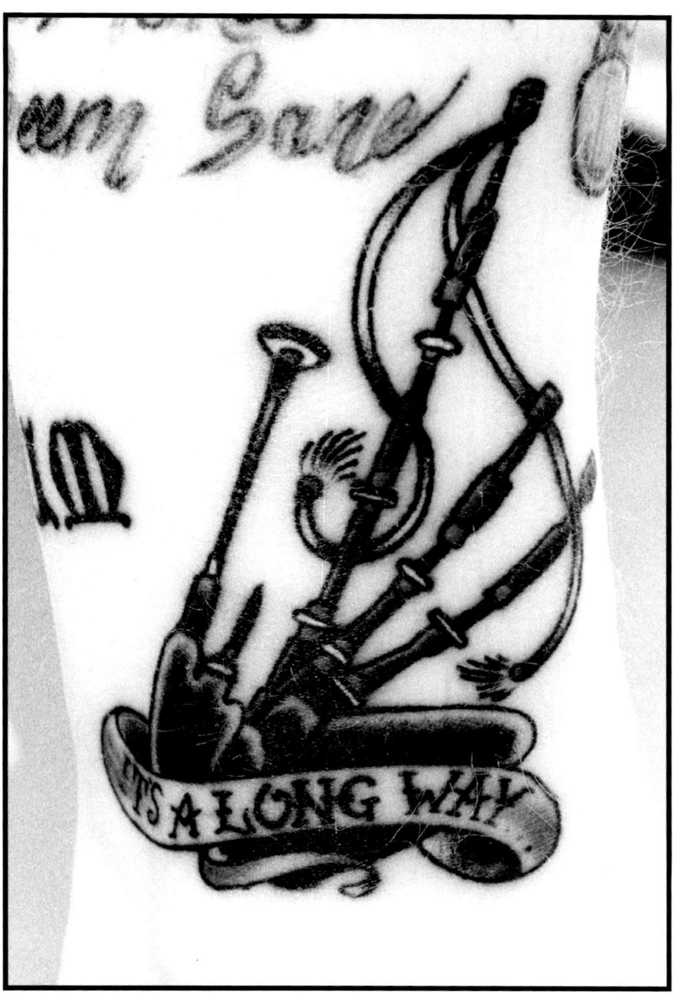

I play the bagpipes and tin whistles with the band Dropkick Murphys. This tattoo is a set of bagpipes that I had tattooed on me in Freemantle, Australia. The reason this tattoo is so important to me is, as a piper and a rock and roller, Bon Scott was a very big influence on me. I'm a huge AC/DC guy and for him to bring bag pipes to rock and roll kind of opened a door for me, obviously, to where I am now. So it was my tribute to Bon. It says underneath in a banner, "It's a long way...." Obviously the AC/DC tune with bagpipes and, again rock and roll was a very important thing in my life and it kind of runs my life…well, besides my wife. It runs how I think and what I do and I think the biggest tribute I can give to Bon Scott was that tattoo and the only place I could do it was where he is buried.

–Scruffy Wallace

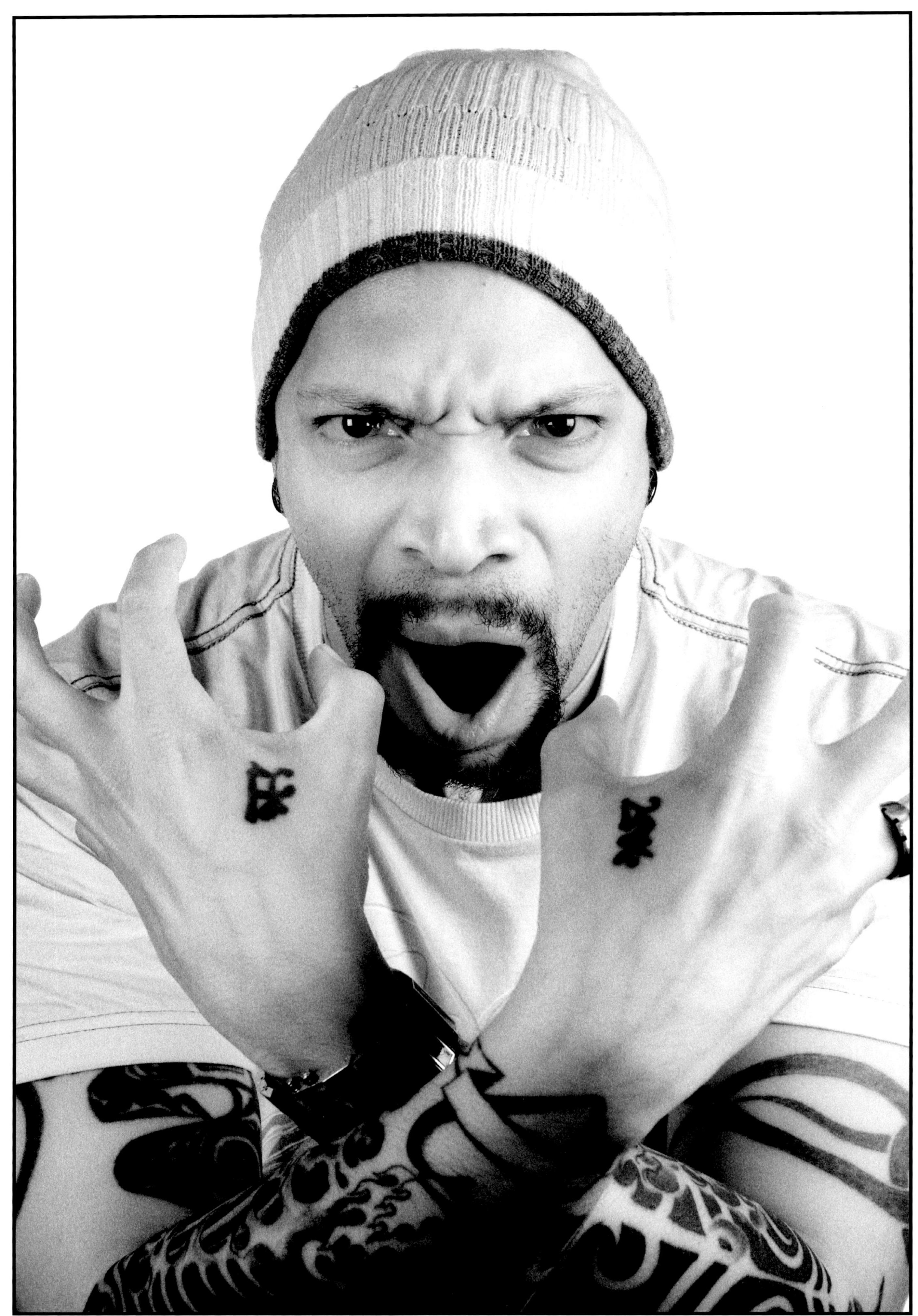

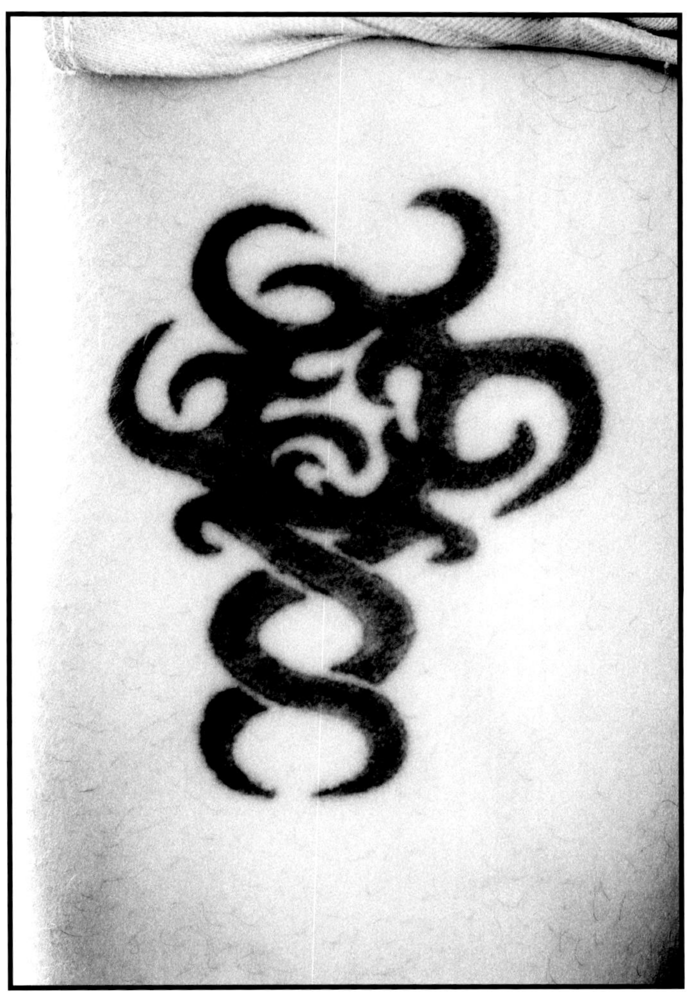

The tattoo on my leg was done by a friend of mine, David Arca, who passed away many years ago. He was a very talented tattoo artist and an amazing drummer. A group of friends of mine in Cleveland, Ohio, decided to form a skateboarding team. None of us were really that talented but we all were possessed to skate. We formed a team called the "Team Playboy Posse" and each of us had this design tattooed on the same area of our body. If you look at it one way it looks like Jesus and you look at it another way you can see Satan, it's all very abstract.

–Derrick Green

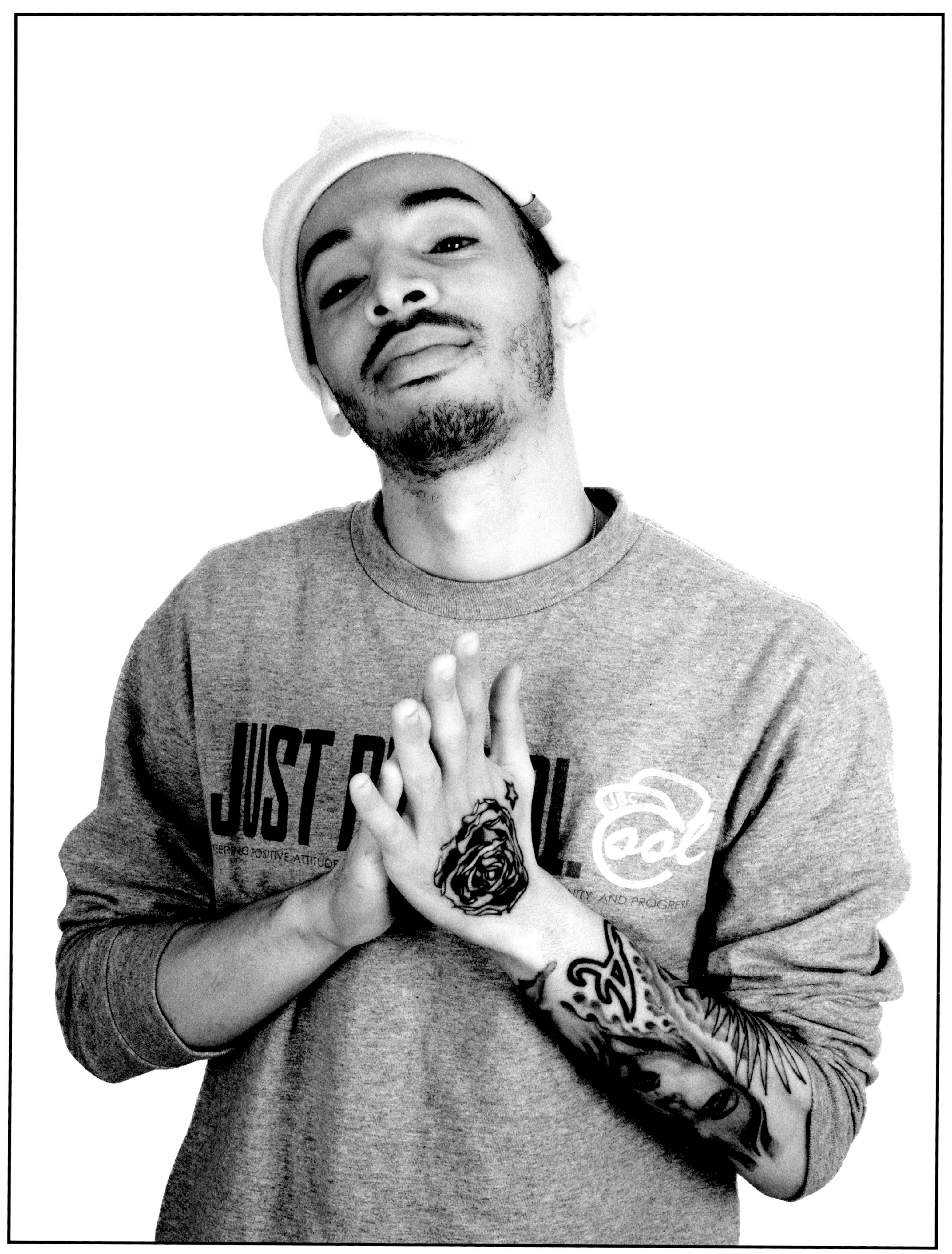
JUST

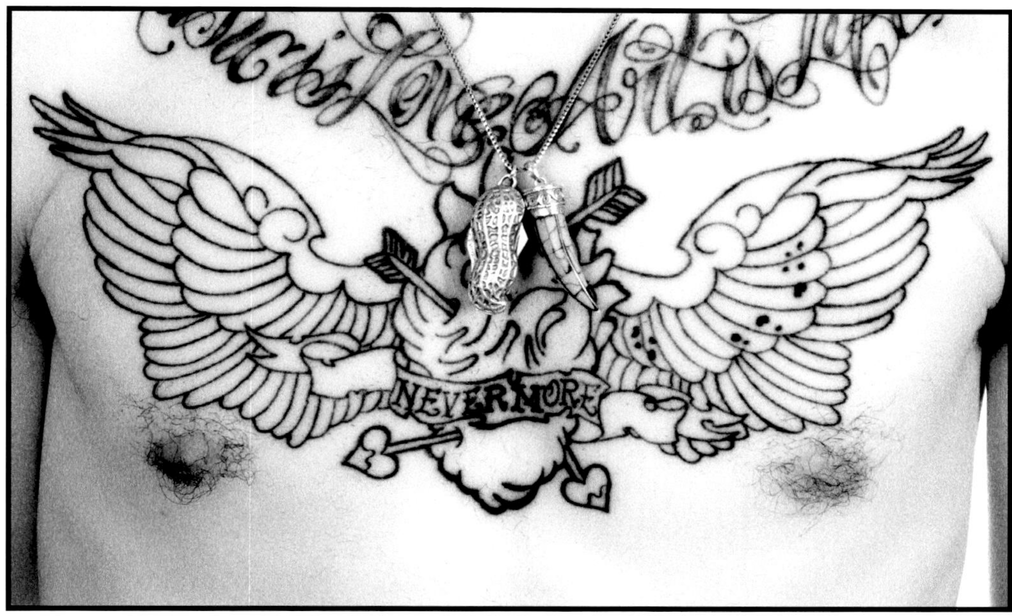

This is a tattoo I made out with my homegirl Sophie C'est La Vie, who used to work here at City Ink in Atlanta. She moved to New York, but we're real cool friends; she's like my tattoo sister. I got it during a time in my life when I was going through a bad breakup and I just felt like getting a reminder to never get my heart broken, that's why it says "Nevermore." It's a heart with piercing arrows going through it with hearts on the end of the arrows with wings on the side of the heart, so it's like even though you can be pierced by the darts of love, your heart continues to fly. I know it's not real poetic, but that's basically the whole idea of the tattoo, and I got it put on my chest so I never forget, you know? "Nevermore" means never more could your heart be broken the way it was broken, know what I mean?

–Chris McAdoo

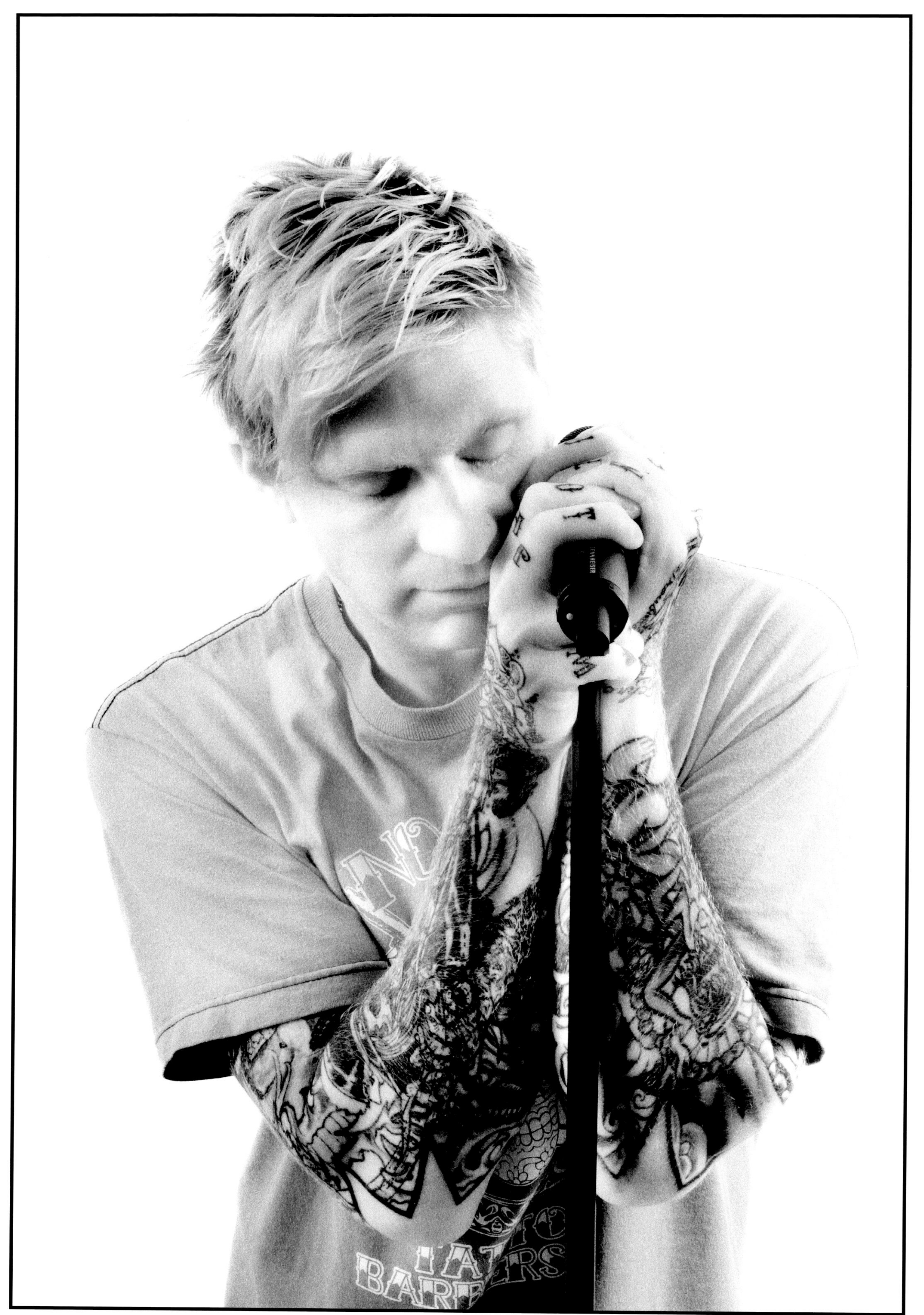

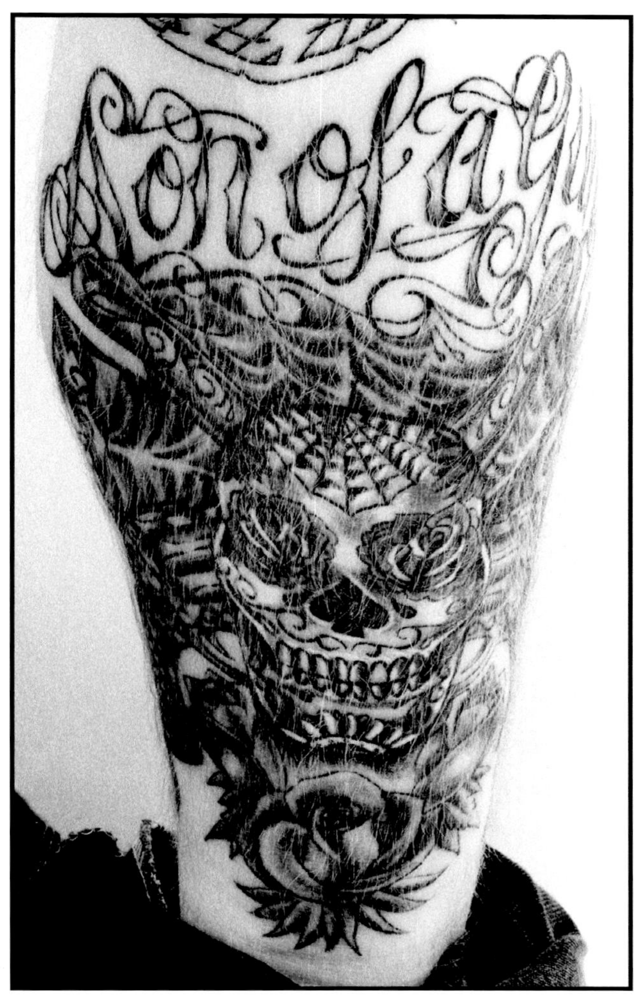

When I made the big transition from touring all the time, I wanted to do more with tattooing, not just get tattooed any more. I did a proper apprenticeship, tattooed, and was drawing like crazy. I actually moved away from my family, my wife was very pregnant at the time and I was away from them for 6–8 months working in a busy street shop because I really wanted to make that commitment to tattooing and I wasn't going to do anything like that and leave my family unless it was really important, obviously. So I did that and saved a bunch of money and said, "Okay, that's it; I'm going to open up a tattoo shop." I generally throw myself pretty heavily into things when I do them, so I came back and opened Sonofagun Tattoo & Barbershop and not just the venture but the whole experience seemed pretty significant to me so I had the logo tattooed. It's got a barber pole on one side and a straight razor on the other and I just love that old school vibe, that traditional feel of tattooing and barbering and that whole community; it's like a wonderful band of gypsies, just like touring musicians. It wasn't a crazy transition; it seemed pretty natural to me.

–Brian Byrne

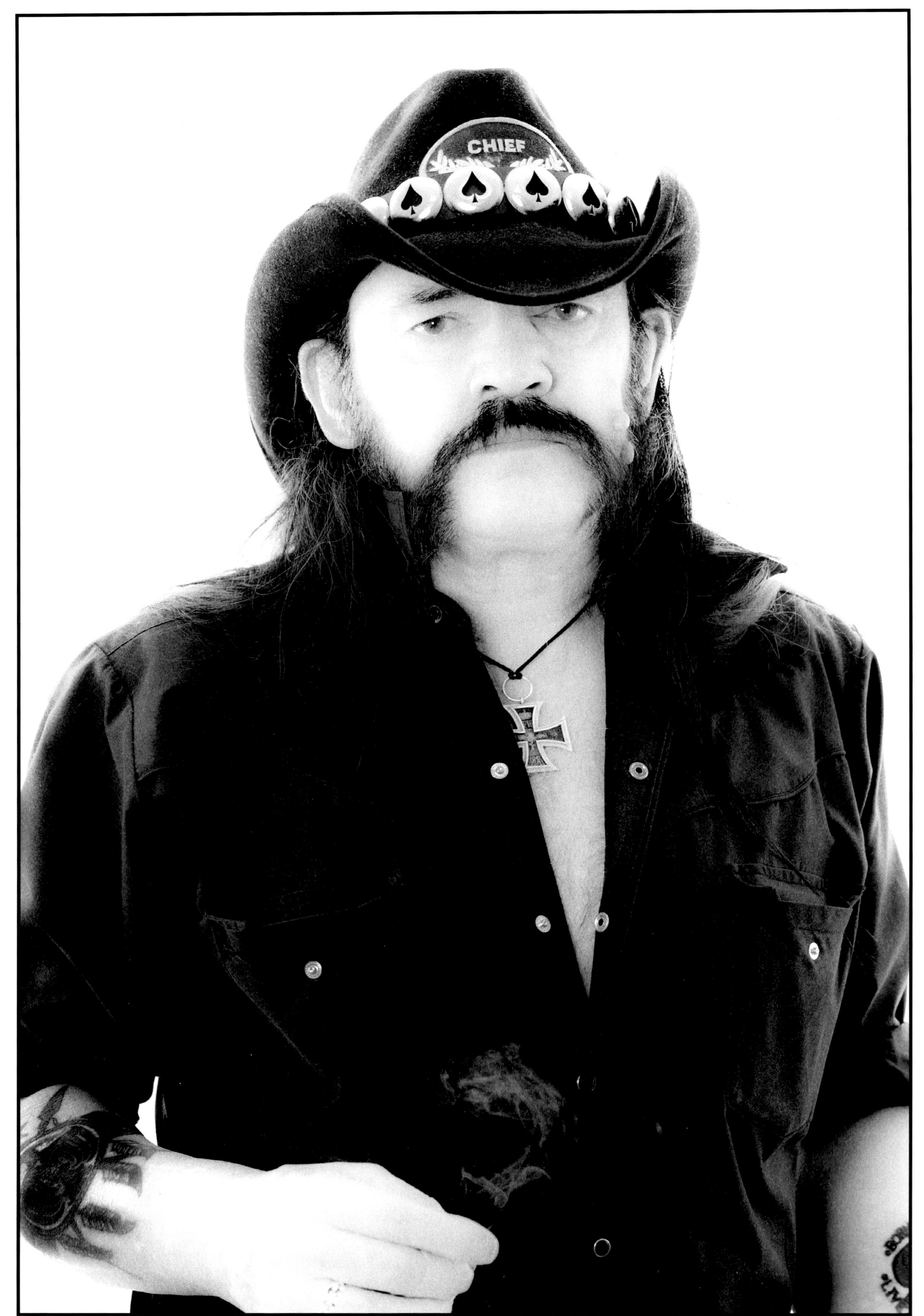
CHIEF

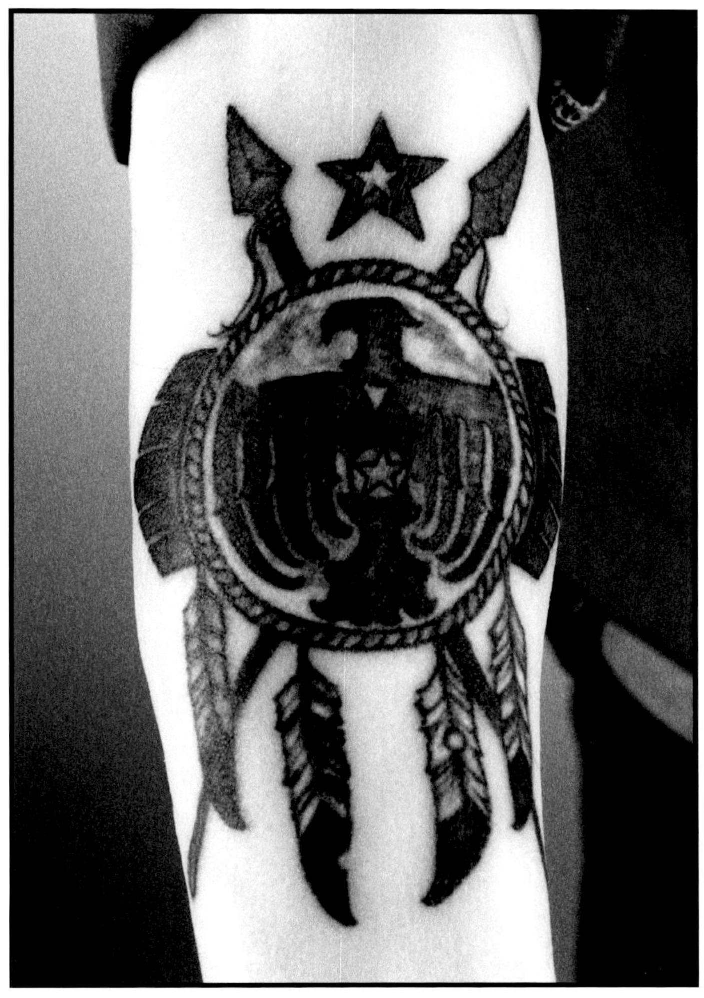

This was done a little while ago by Gill Monte of Tattoo Mania. It's covering up another one that I had, which was a Phoenix with a marijuana leaf on it's chest. It was sort of like a pizza with wings by the end of it, so I had that covered up. I think he's done a pretty good job. It's an Indian shield with spears behind it, feathers hanging off the bow, then the thunderbird on the feet. I just admire the Indian culture. The idealist fools are big with me, you know.

–Lemmy Kilmister

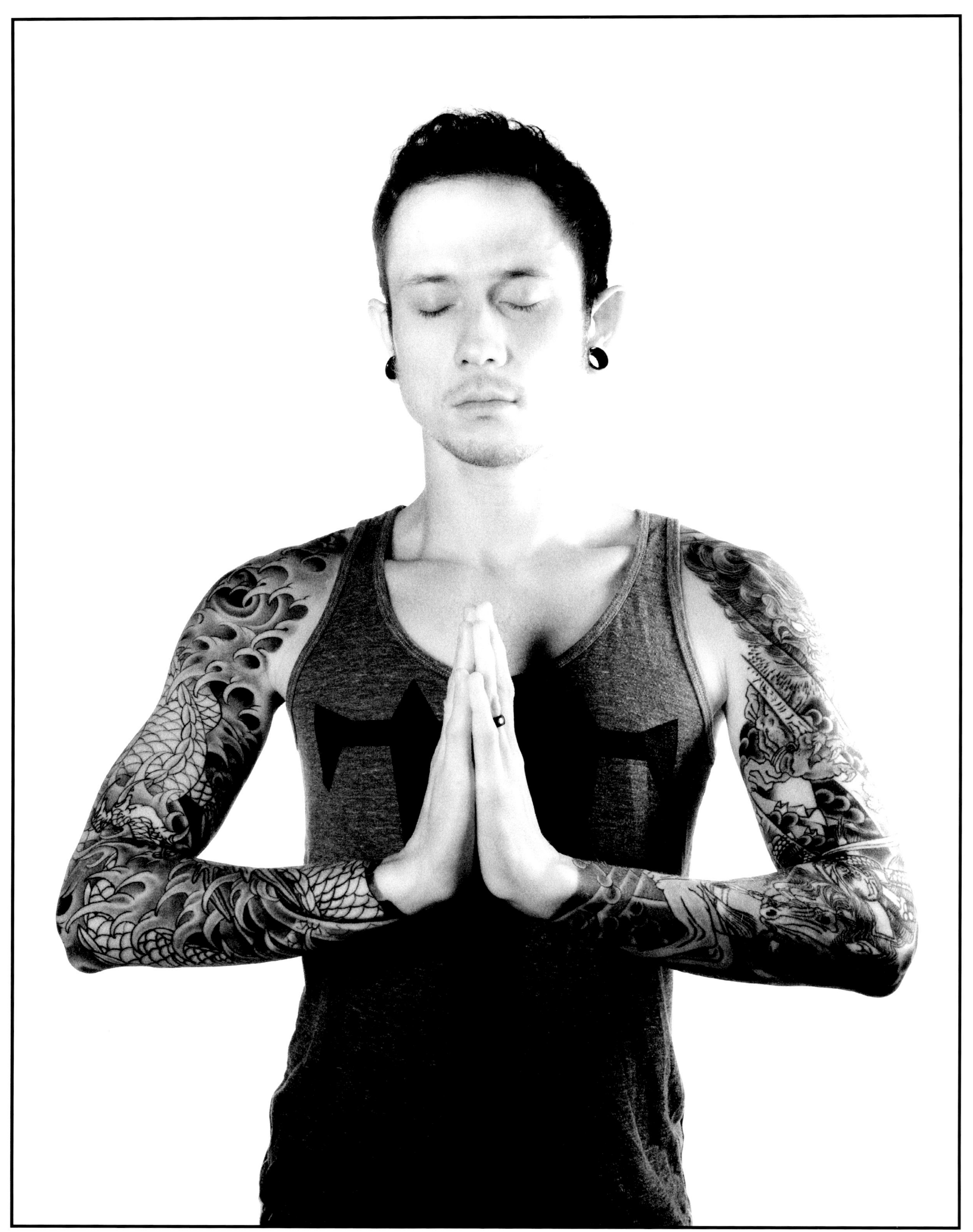

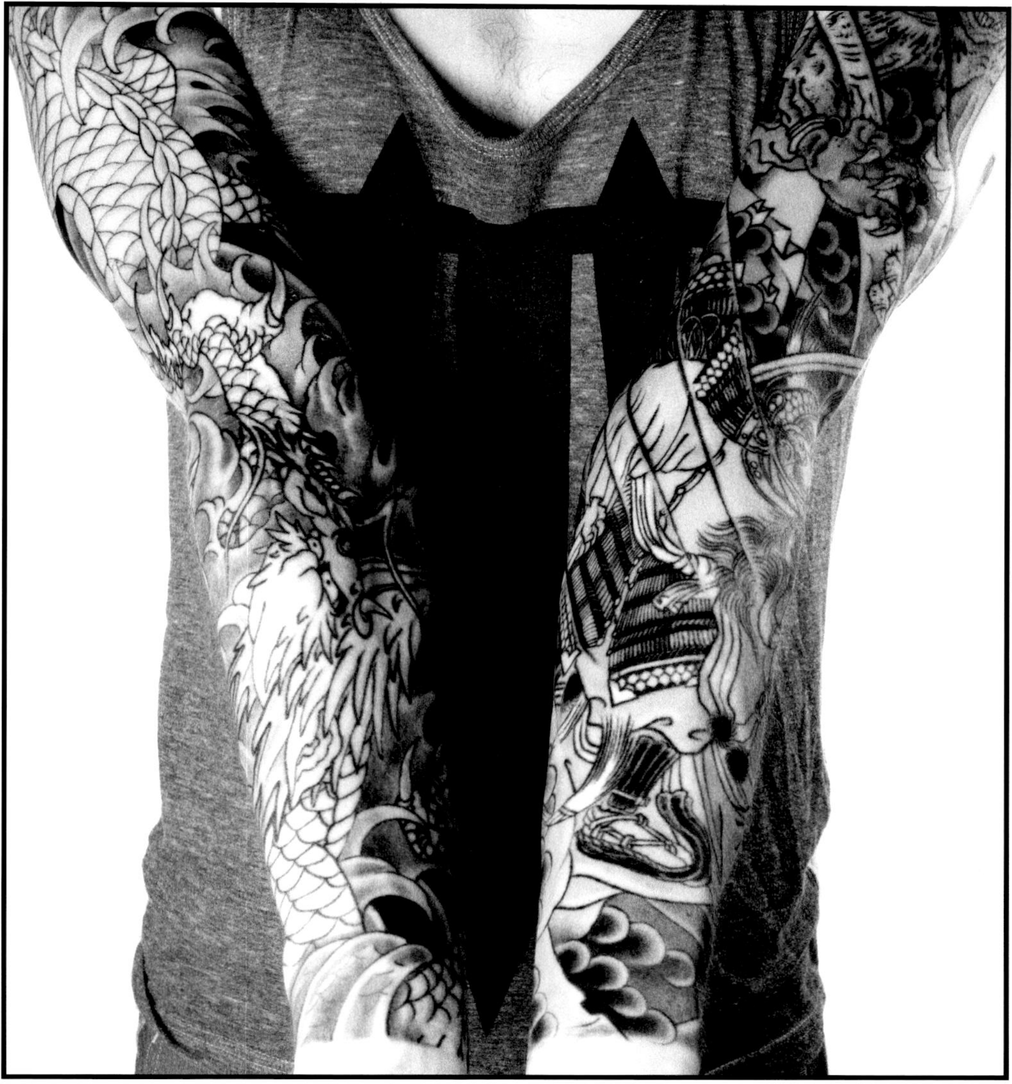

With tattoos, I decided to go with something more culturally significant. I'm half Japanese and I wanted to delve into that with the first two tattoos of my life. The very first one I got, I started the outline in 2005 with a man named Brian Bruno, who works at Tattoo City in San Francisco. I found a piece by Kitagawa Utamaro, who is a Japanese wood block carver and painter back in the late 1800s early 1900s and it was about the time our first album *Sensai* came out, so I figured that since he normally does Geisha paintings and wood block carving, the thing called the ascending dragon, it seemed to make significantly more sense to my life. I did an eight and a half hour coloring process in Tallahassee when Brian was over there randomly and I haven't seen him since. I had this feeling I wouldn't see him again in my life ever, so I decided to do the whole sitting there. The man who replaced him at Tattoo City was Kahlil Rintye, and we decided to start this piece on my left arm which is a duplicate of a piece by Yoshitoshi, another Japanese wood block and triptych artist. It depicts a samurai named Watanabe no Tsuna battling the demon Ibaraki at Rashomon Gate, which is a real place, but it's also in ancient Japanese folklore.

–Matt Heafy

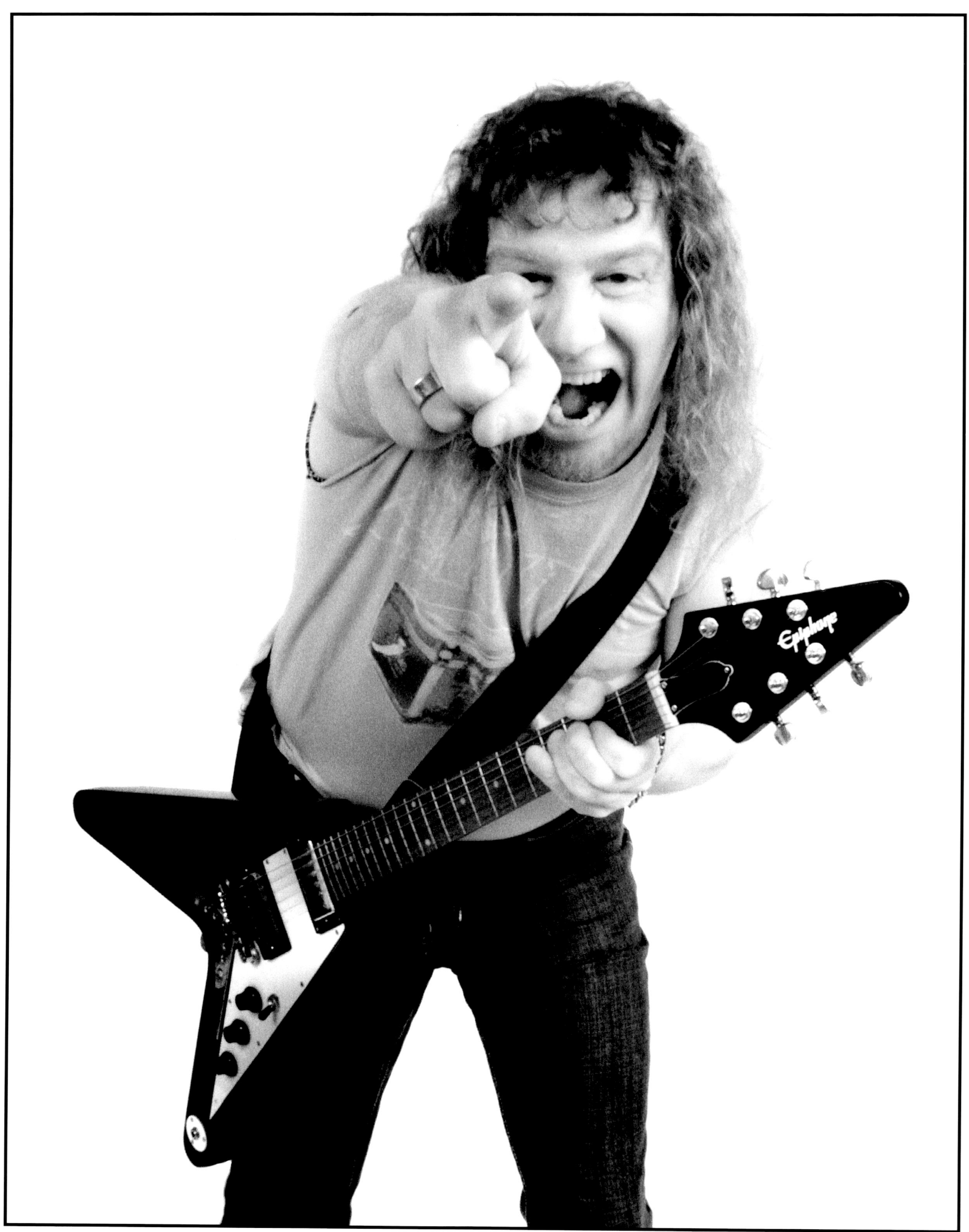
Epiphone

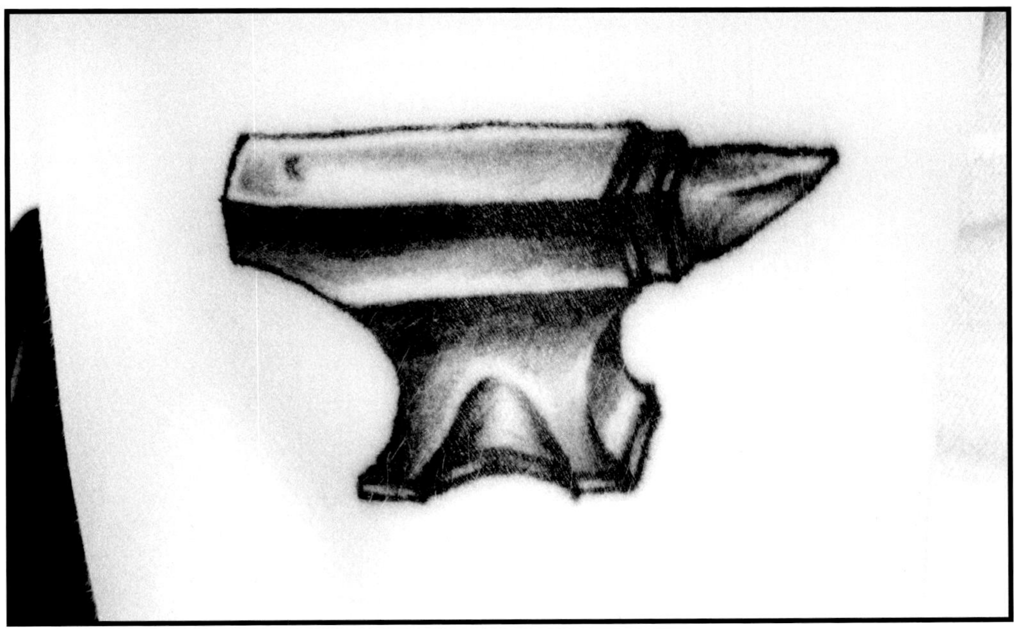

It all began with a trip to LA, but I ended up meeting my wife in Niagara Falls, on the American side, when she came to pick me up at the Buffalo airport. We proceeded to go to a tattoo shop in Niagara Falls called Fat Cat Tattoos. I had never had a tattoo and I knew that I wanted an anvil so we went on the Internet and actually used the rendering from the *Pound For Pound* album to model this anvil. The artist drew it up on a decal and put it on my arm. My wife at the same time wanted a tattoo and she got hers done after mine. She ended up being in pretty rough shape; she had some ivy done on her leg and they had done all of the black outline and she was ready to faint. She needed to catch her breath for a little bit. A couple of months after we got our tattoos we heard on the news that they had found a dead body in the basement of Fat Cat Tattoo. It's pretty mysterious; I always wondered whose body it was…!

–Steve "Lips" Kudlow

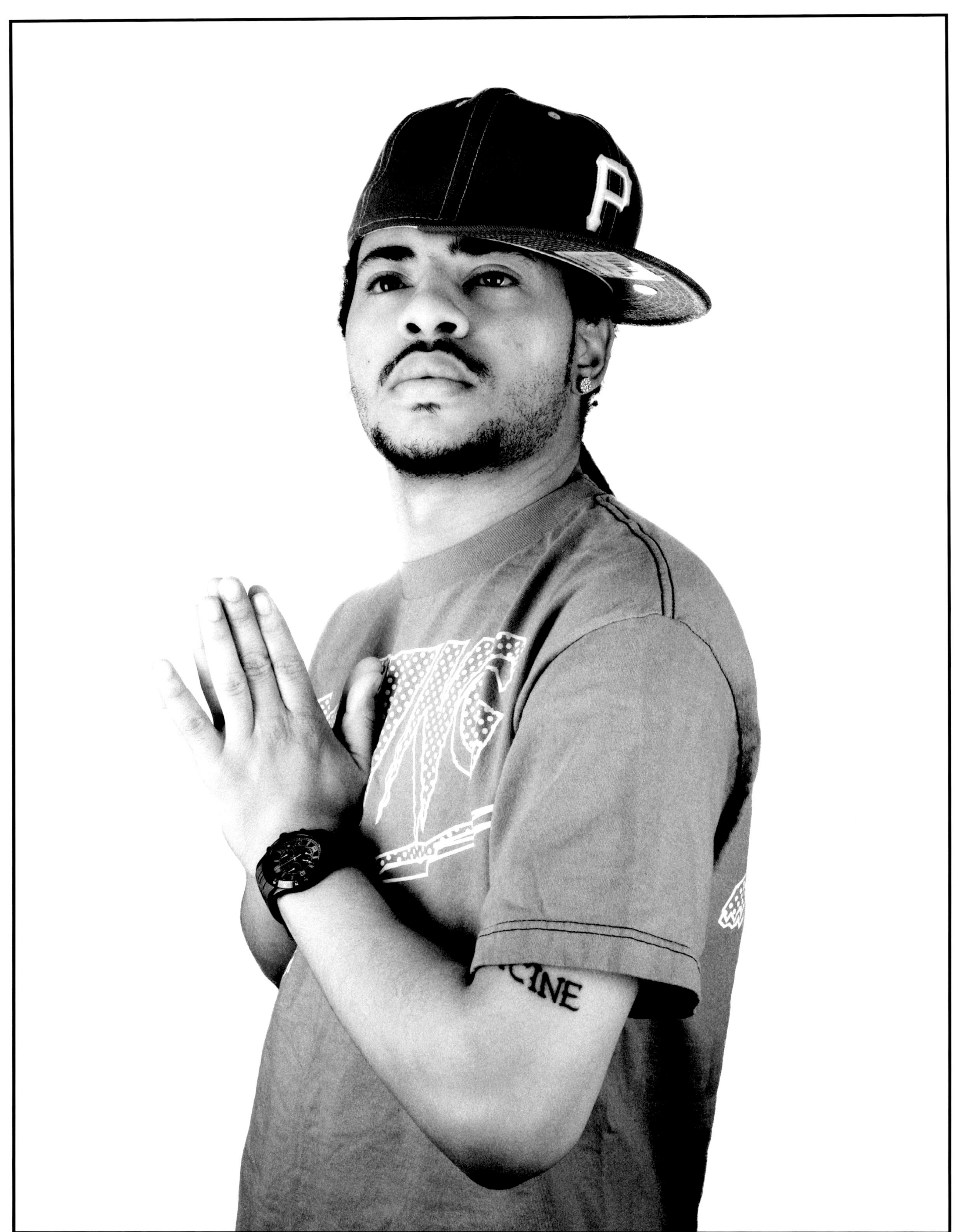

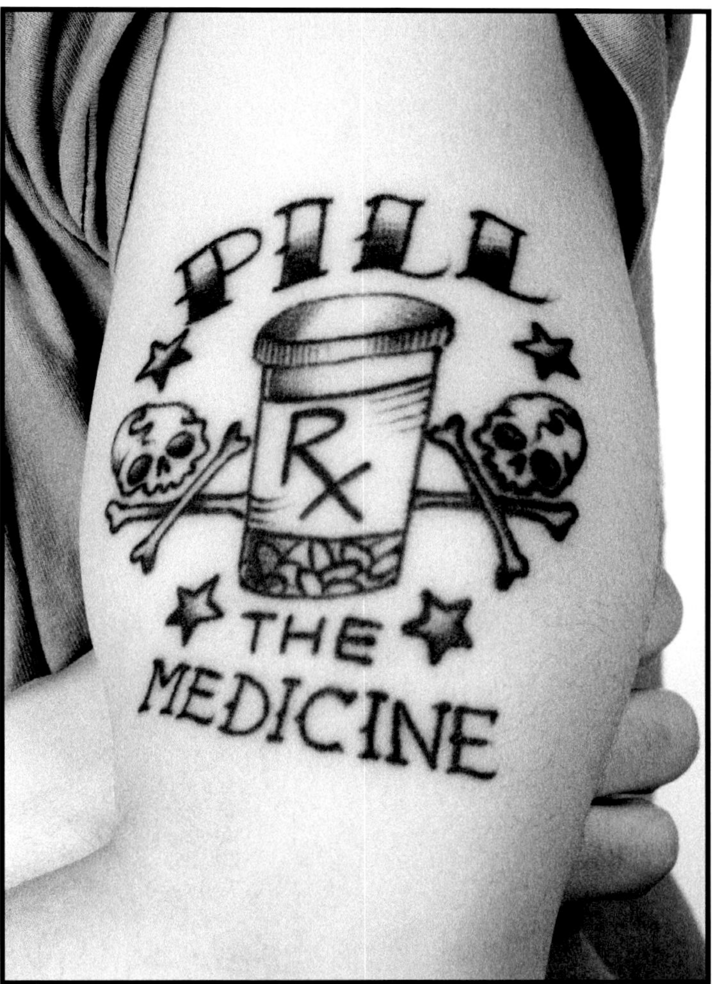

Pill

P-I-double-L, this is the story
of the tattoo Pill, The Medicine.

It came about one day when I was doodling in my notebook I normally write my raps in. I probably was about 17–18 and I decided that I wanted my first album to be called *The Medicine*. My name is derived from being in football, and as I got more popular around the schoolhouse as a rapper, I kinda manifested into Pill being the medicine, the cure for rap cancer. So when you see the bottle, that's supposed to be the medicine, the Pill, the cure for rap cancer and so I started doodling, started drawing. I was like, "Maybe I should make this come to life one day on my arm," and so a couple years later, when I got more serious with the rapping, I decided to get it on my arm. I drew this and I took it up to the Liberty Tattoo. I drove up there and I hollered at a guy by the name of Bill. He got the paper, doodled it, ya know what I mean, came back and laid it down.

–Pill

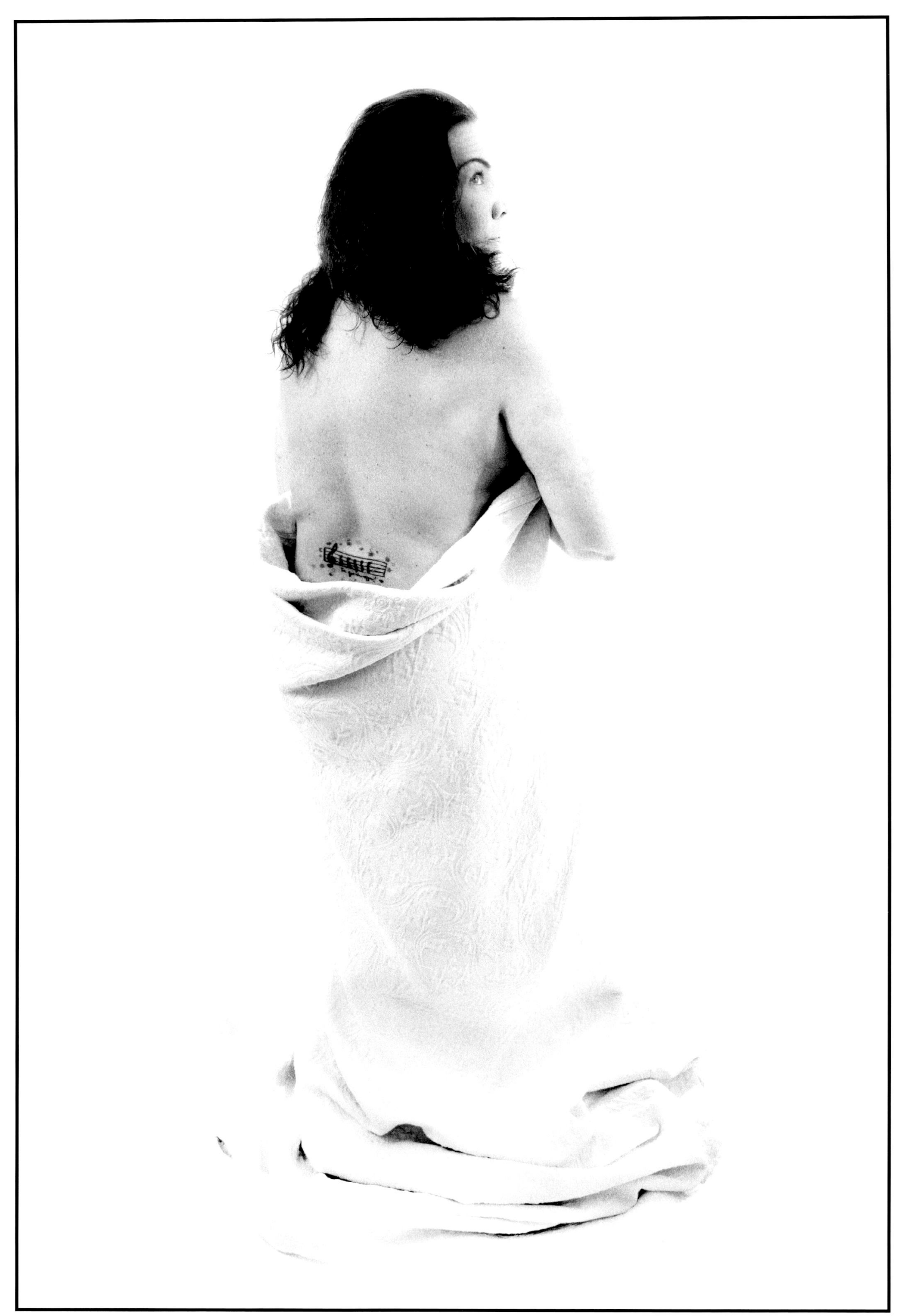

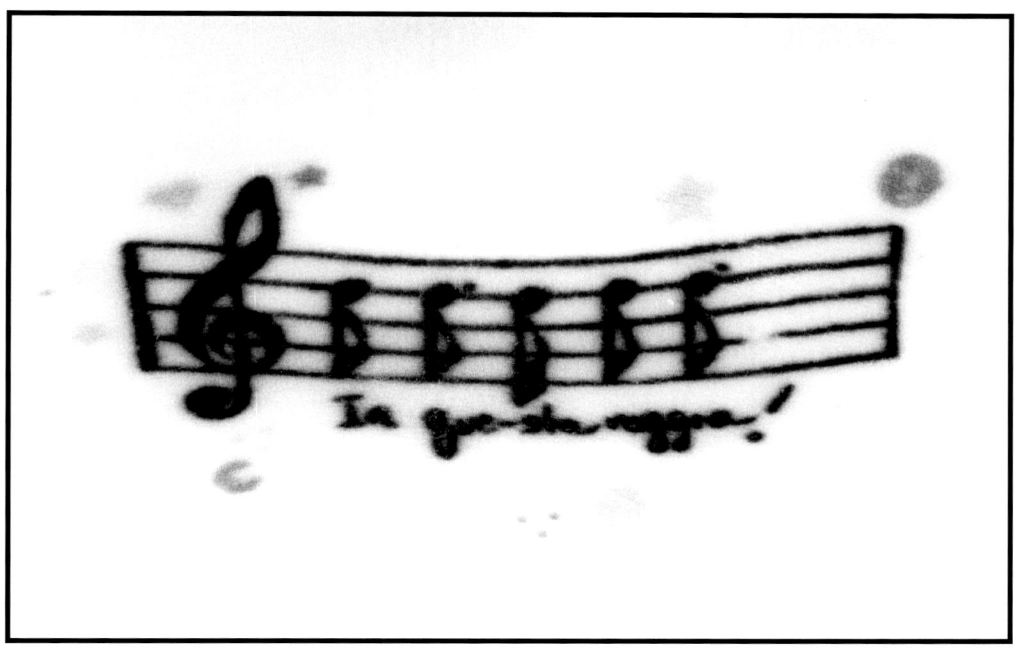

I had gastric bypass surgery after September 11, 2001, when I lost seven very dear friends. I lost about 150 pounds, then I started singing Turandot at The Met, which became my signature piece. The first line of Turandot is: "*In Questa Reggia*" which means "In this Palace." The tattoo on my back is the first phrase of Turandot's big aria: "In Questa Reggia," which is how the character Turandot, the character I sing, starts the opera. It's the most beautiful aria, and for so many people it's so difficult to sing but for me I just found a niche with it and it really worked for me, and the tattoo took on a life of its own. The tattoo has a lot of meaning for me; first of all, it's the piece that I've sung well over 100 times and has brought me a lot of success and a lot of joy to sing and also it signifies this palace, this new body that I have. There's also another side to it: The character goes on to talk about what happened in the palace, which was a lot of brutality, she talks about her ancestor who was raped and tortured, and a lot of horrible things that had happened and how she's going to overcome it, and that is also part of my story, of overcoming a lot of tragedy and hardship, and so it reminds me of all of those things. That is to me why this tattoo is permanent and powerful and I believe that because ink is permanent it should be something that you want to live with for the rest of your life, and so everything that I have on my body is something that when I'm 90 or 100 I will look at and I will feel comfortable with.

–Andrea Gruber

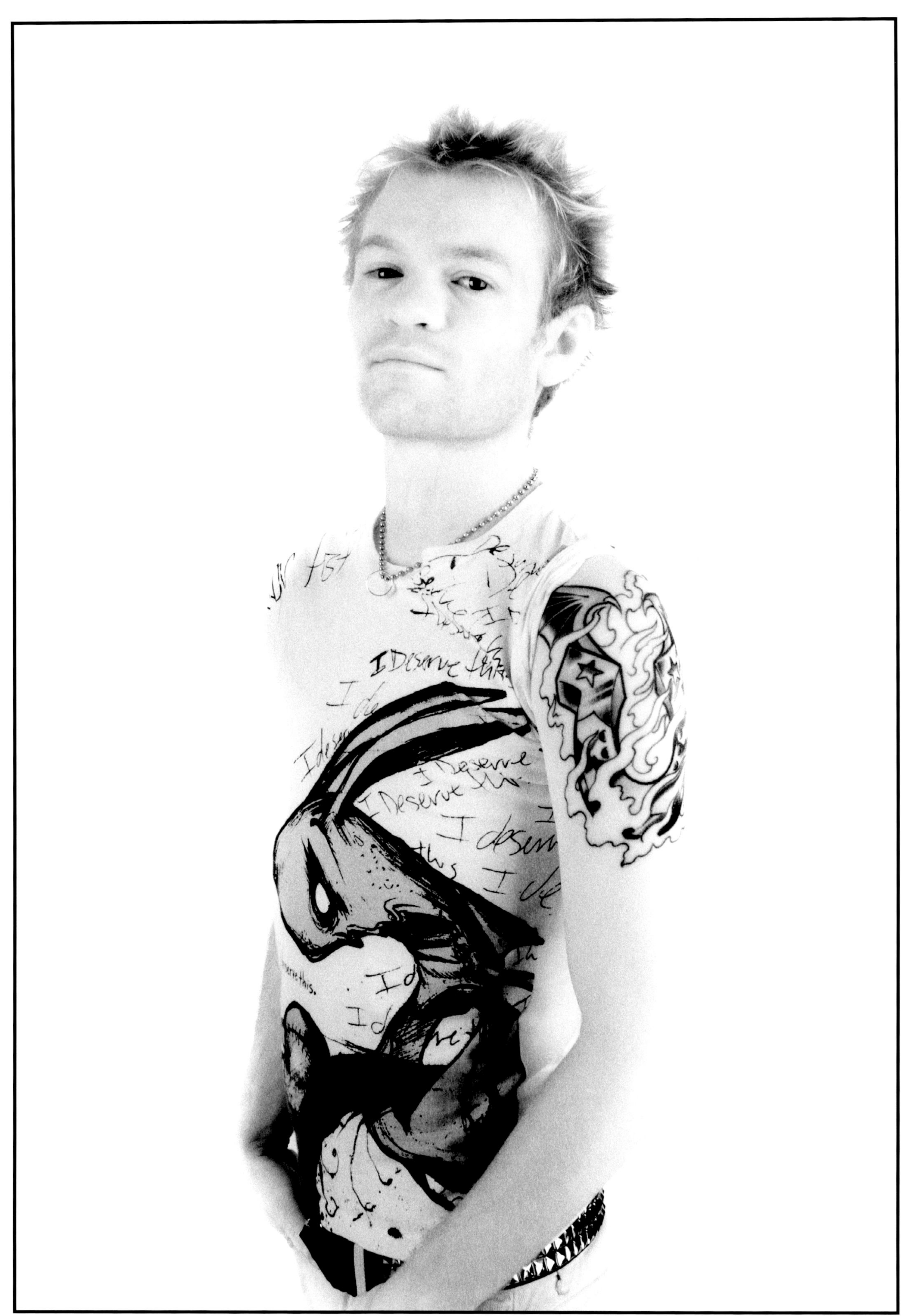
I Deserve

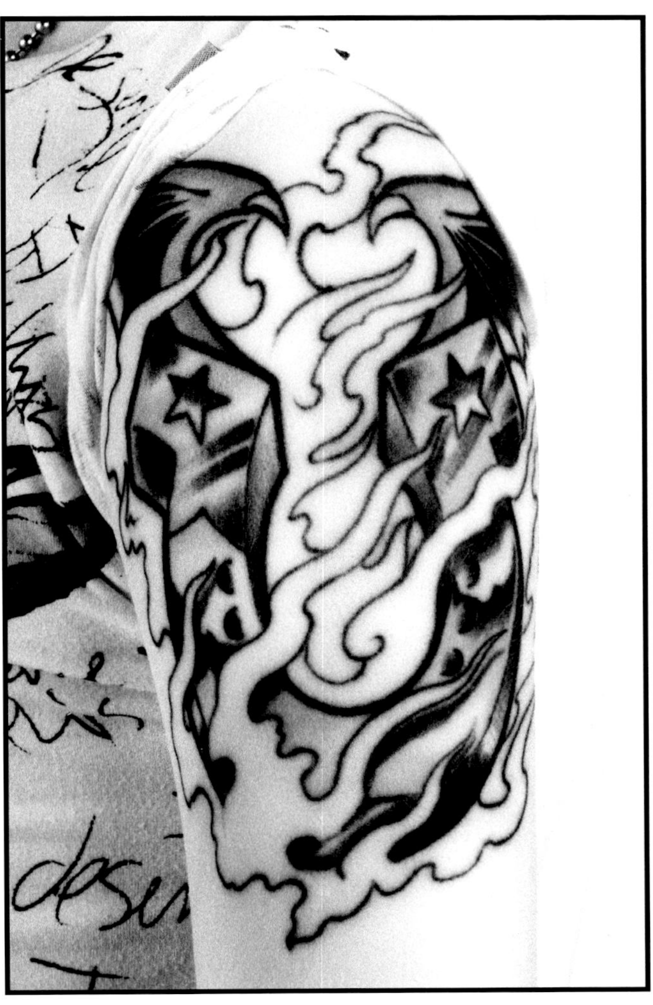

I had only ever had one tattoo before and I was not really like a tattoo guy. I remember I made a joke; we were in a casino and I was with Cone and I was like, "I had this really big bet," and I was like "if I win, I'm going to get a tattoo of a horseshoe." And then I won. I can't remember how much it was, maybe like a thousand bucks or something like that, and then he was like, "So you gotta get a tattoo now." So I thought about it for like six months and then I had a friend of mine kinda draw it up and then we just did it in his house, in his living room. It took about five hours. It's the biggest tattoo I have, and kind of is the reason I don't have any more; it's not good after five hours!

–Deryck Whibley

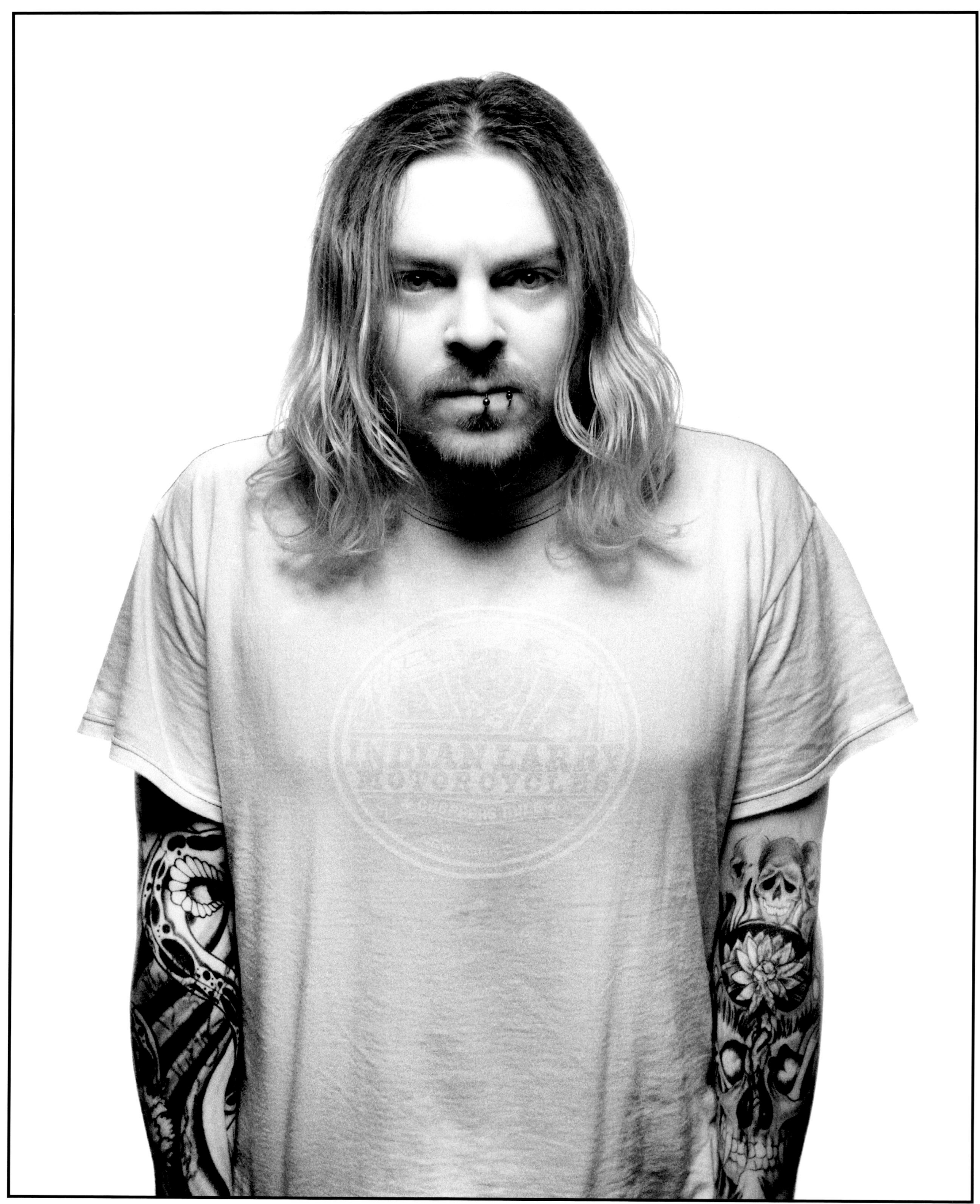
INDIAN LARRY
MOTORCYCLES

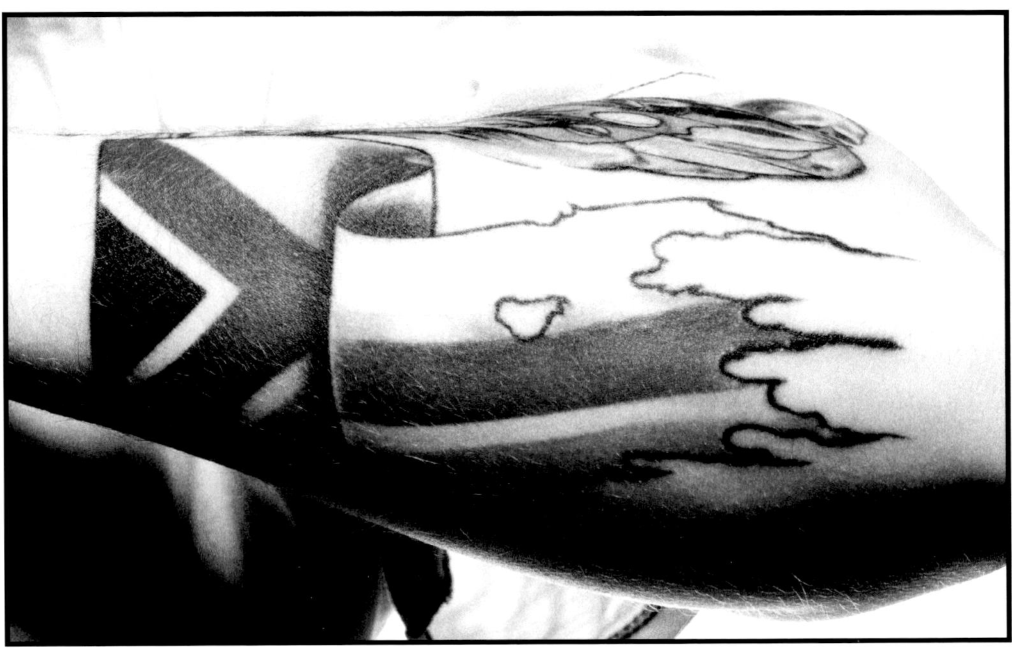

This tattoo is of my country's flag and I originally wanted just a little tiny one to sort of represent them. The tattoo guy, his name is Mike Parsons, he decided, "Well, you have this whole forearm," so I ended up saying "Well, go ahead." He freehand sketched it and I kind of wanted it to be a war flag because of things I've been through to get to where I am today. You know, it's been a battle, like anything. To be successful, I guess is a real battle, so I think it represents basically where I'm from, what I've been through, and the fact that the flag is still flying where I'm hopefully still going to go.

–Shaun Morgan

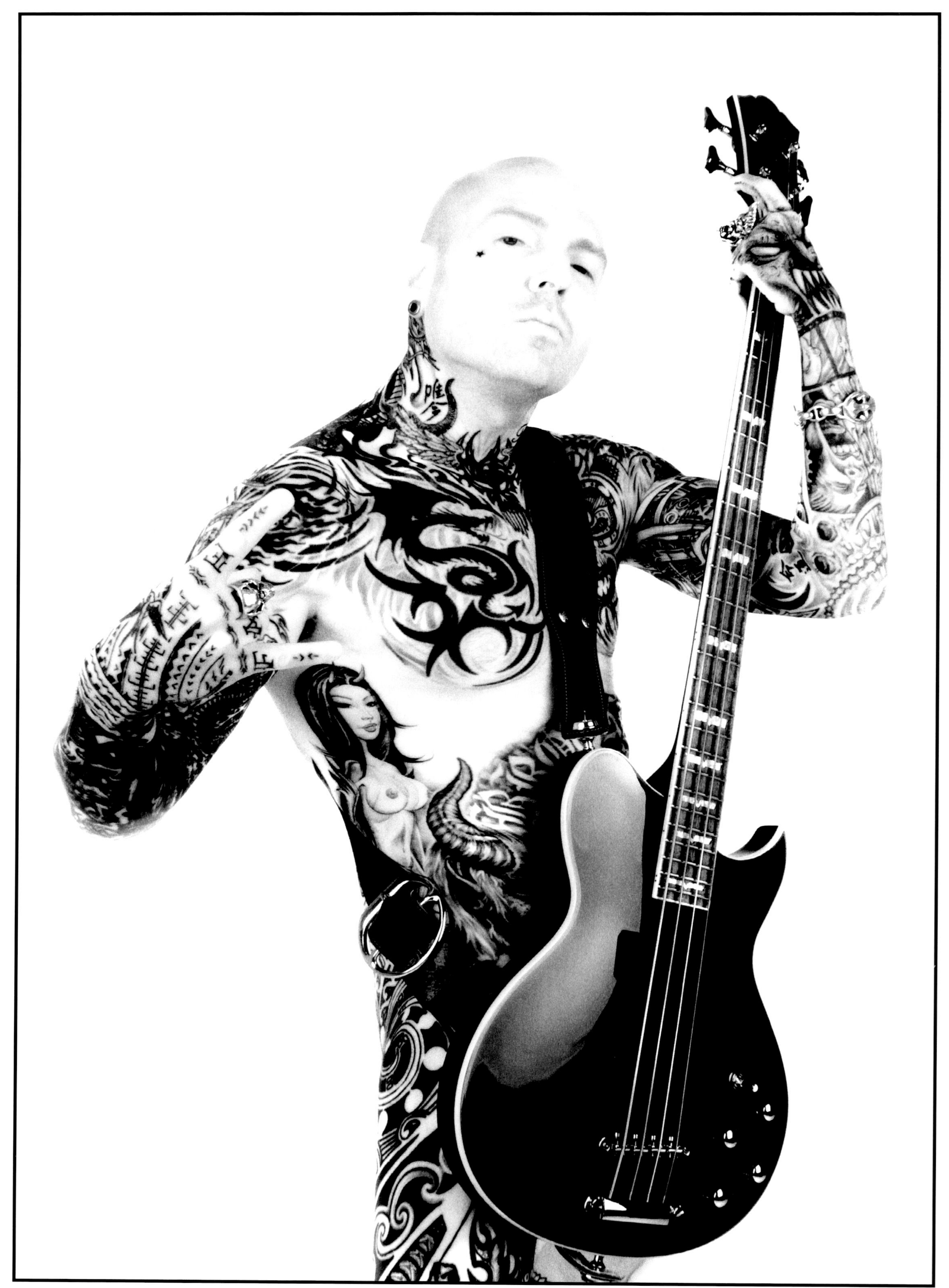

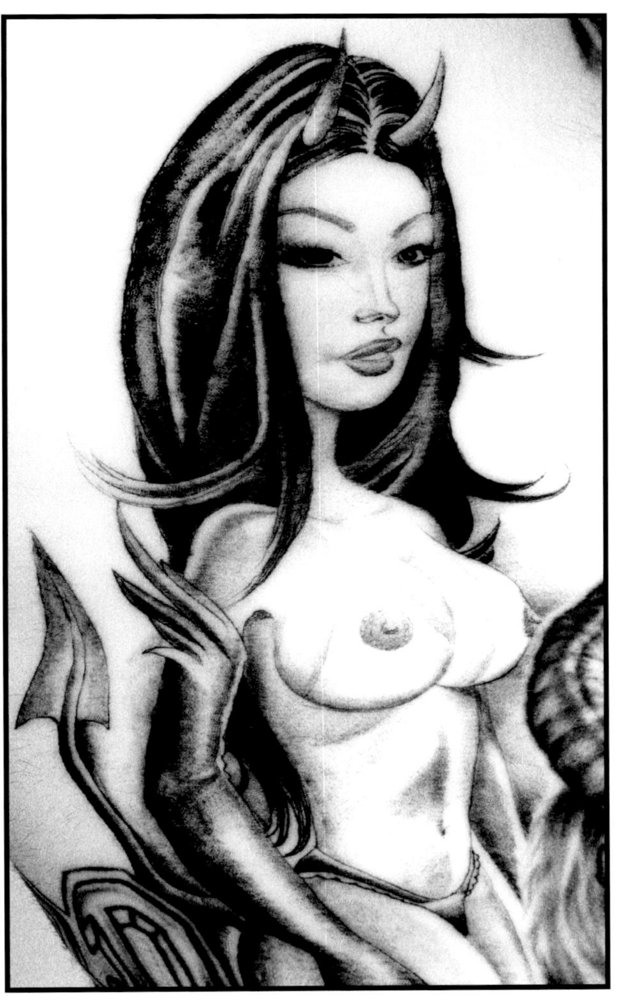

I've always...since I was a teenager...I've always felt the push between good and evil and I've always felt that when people have the ability to be good, they have the equal and opposite ability to be pulled over to the dark side. I find my life to be a dichotomy where it all comes into play every day. A lot of my tattoos represent the push and pull; I've got a great devil and angel on my stomach from Paul Booth and I wanted to do a portrait of my wife, but I didn't want to do a literal portrait because I was never a fan of the literal portrait because it marks a stamp in time of what somebody looked like. I more wanted a kind of fantasy impression and I chose Mr. Cartoon who is an old homeboy of mine who I have known since he first started tattooing, since before he tattooed, to do my wife, the most beautiful woman in the world, Tera Patrick, as a devil bitch. I'm trying to decide who's going to do the other side, whether it's going to be Jack Rudy or Kat von D or Tim Hendricks. Those are three people I'm definitely going to get tattoos from in the future. One of them is going to do my Tera Patrick as an angel. For me, my body is my temple, and I'm painting the walls.

–Evan Seinfeld

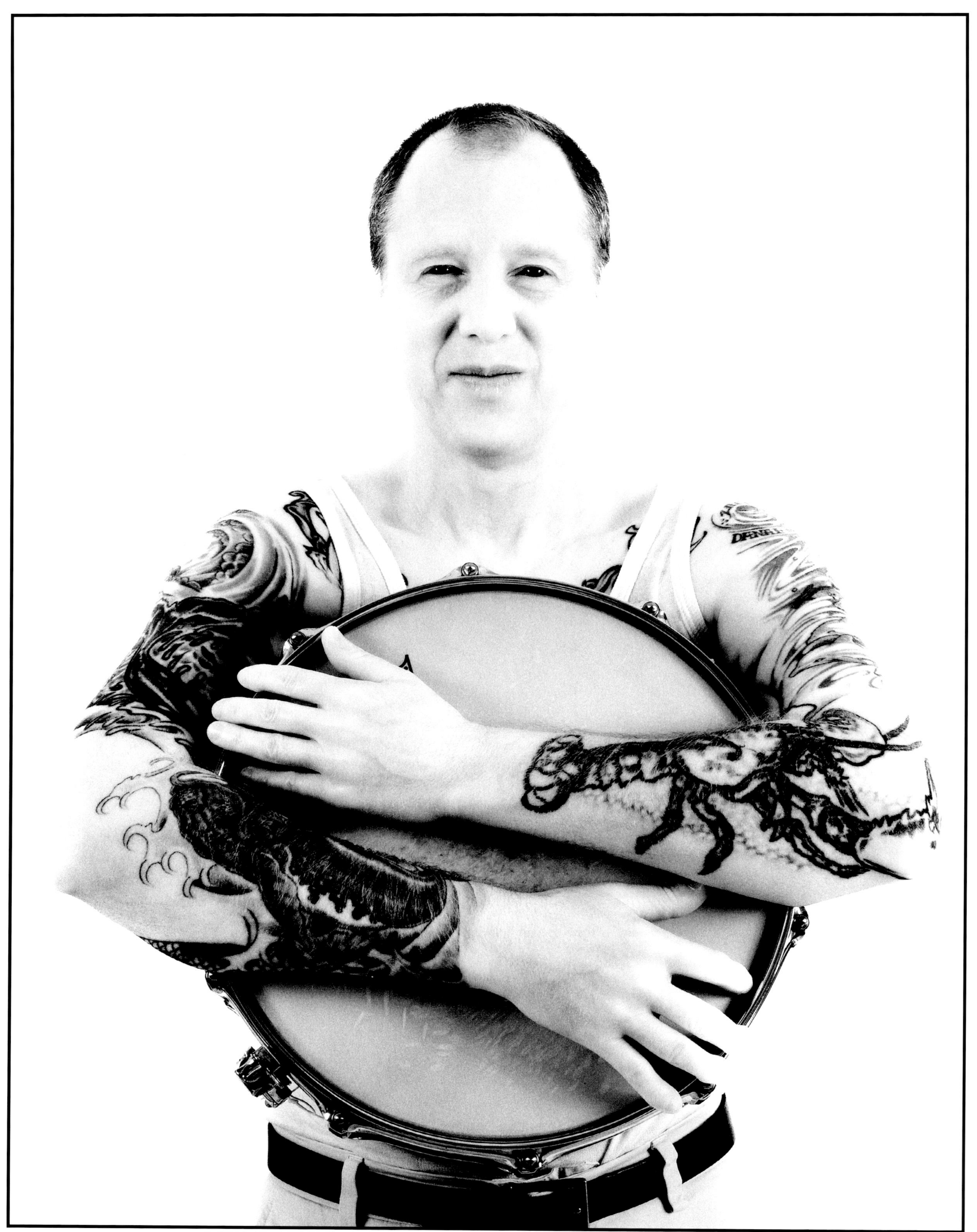

It was the winter of 1988, and I was on my first European tour with the Red Hot Chili Peppers and three of us were booked to get tattooed by Hanky Panky in Amsterdam. We were in Paris the day before, and this was my first tattoo and I hadn't figured out exactly what I wanted and my first idea was to get a big tattoo of Bozo. So in Paris I was trying to find images of Bozo and I went into a couple of comic book stores and they were like, "Que est Bozo?" No Bozos here, so I didn't get the Bozo. I had no idea about tattoos, this was my first tattoo and I didn't know that you could shrink any image or take any piece of art and have it re-interpreted; I thought you had to get it exactly as you were getting it. I asked around and found out that you could do that. I had a shirt with the Sea Shepherd logo which had a really cool whale and dolphin design on it, but it was huge and I didn't think you could do it and once I found out you could, I went with that as my first tattoo, and since my whole body is a sea life theme, I went with it. After that I got ten years worth of sea life tattooed on my body. It was pretty good that I didn't get Bozo, or I might have had ten years worth of clowns and pictures of Bozo. I might

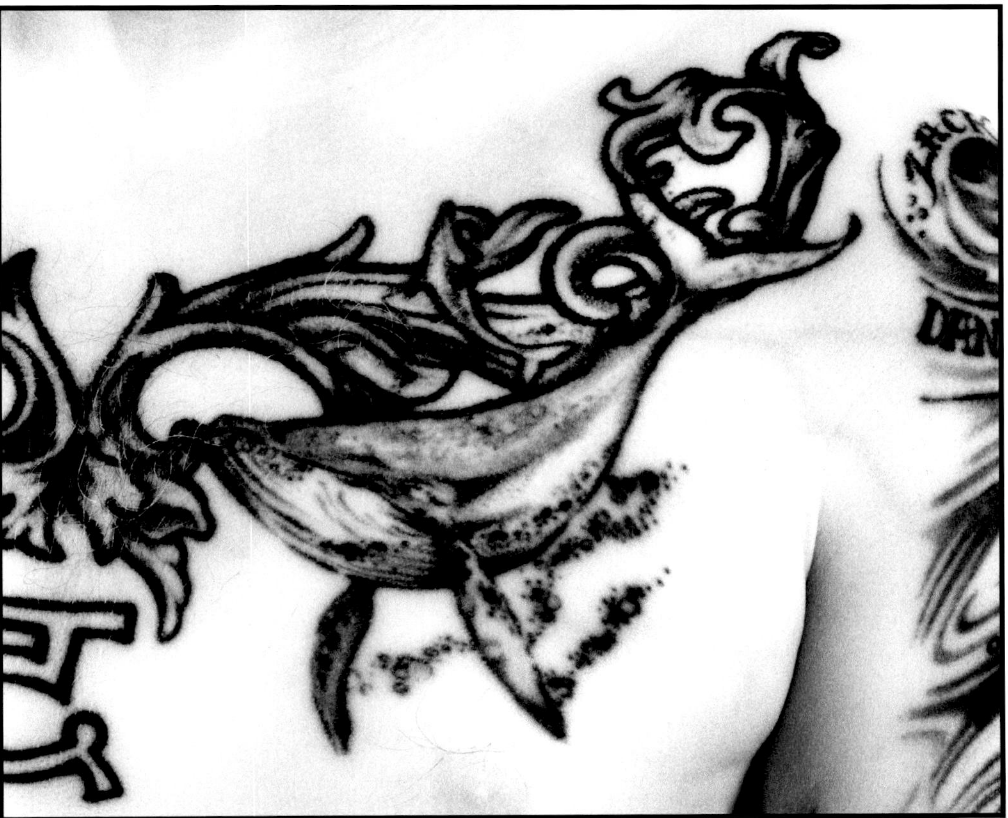

have gotten into the circus theme, and that wouldn't have been too bad, but still. I don't know, right now I don't think that would have been the best choice. I've always loved dolphins and whales. I felt a closeness to them. I had strong feelings about what people did to them. I love whales and the mystery of them; they're just these huge creatures that we don't understand. They roam this vast sea. For me I think my love of it came because there was always a sense that as human beings we have a society, we have homes, we have a lot of complex things that we deal with, and when I was younger I always looked at dolphins and whales—and I don't know their life —but I always looked at it as simpler and seemingly freer. Now that I'm a little bit older, I don't think that I know that much, but when I was younger I thought perhaps naively because I'm not a dolphin or a whale and I don't know what they're up against on a daily basis, how they have to adapt but I just loved them and...I don't know…maybe I was a dolphin in another life; that's what I would tell myself back when. That went with the sea life theme. It's beautiful, it's pretty.

–Jack Irons

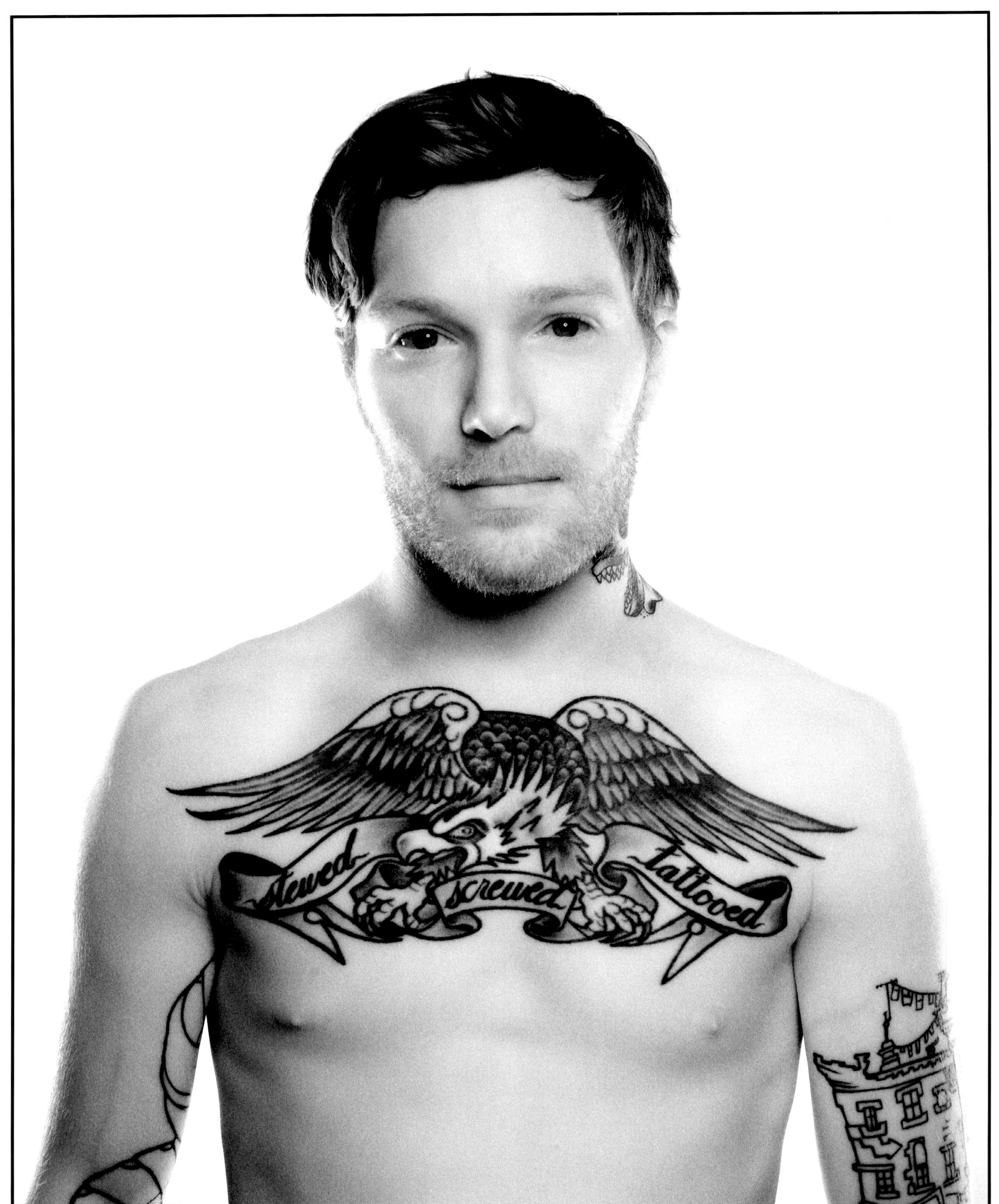
Stewed
Screwed
Tattooed

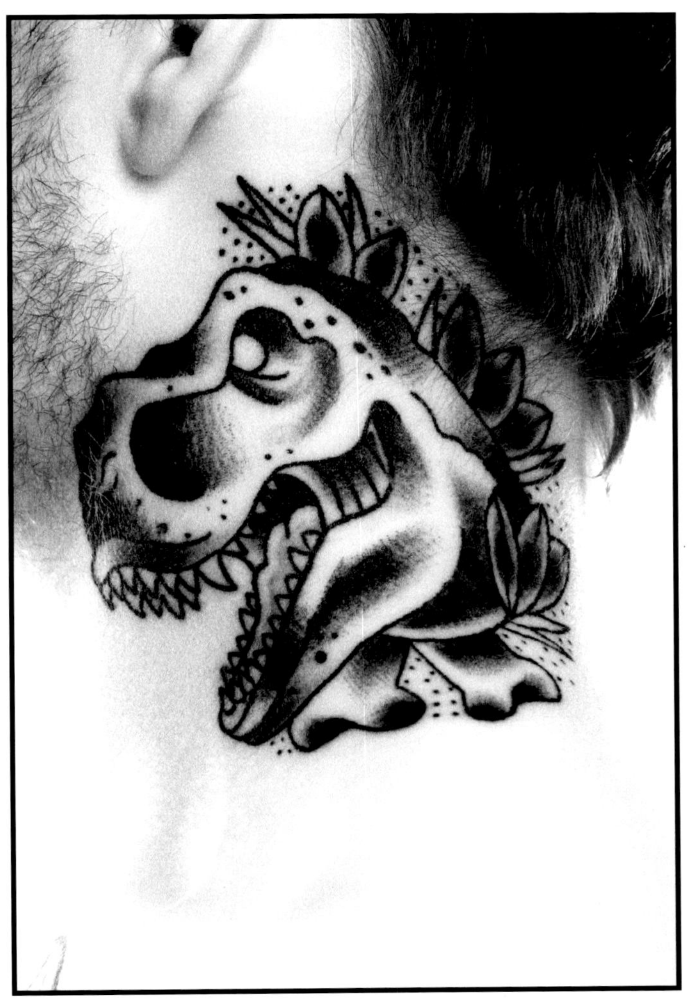

As a small boy, as a little guy, I was obsessed with dinosaurs. I always just had an obsession with anything prehistoric and now I have a 2½-year-old little guy named Mason who is my pride and joy. He's my everything and he has taken a liking to dinosaurs himself. Every time he sees my neck or if he sees a dinosaur, he's always with the big, "Rraawwrrrr!" He loves that sort of stuff. You know what, I love seeing him smile and if I'm able to bring that to him every time he looks at my neck, then I'm a proud papa. Dinosaurs are way cool, so why not get one tattooed on the side of your neck? T-Rex! A guy named Franz Stefanik, who tattoos out of Anchor Studios in Burlington, Ontario, did it.

–Johl Fendley

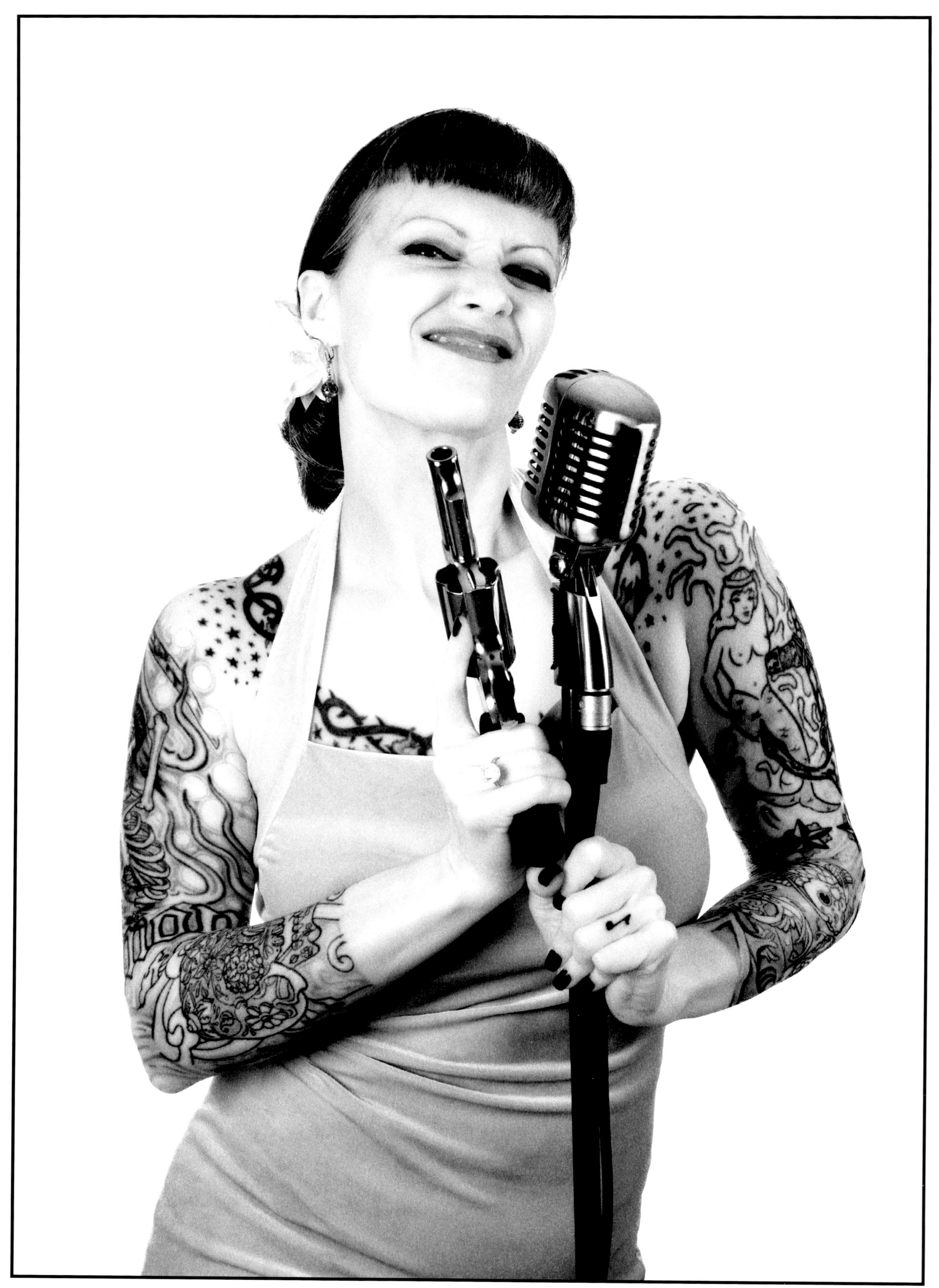

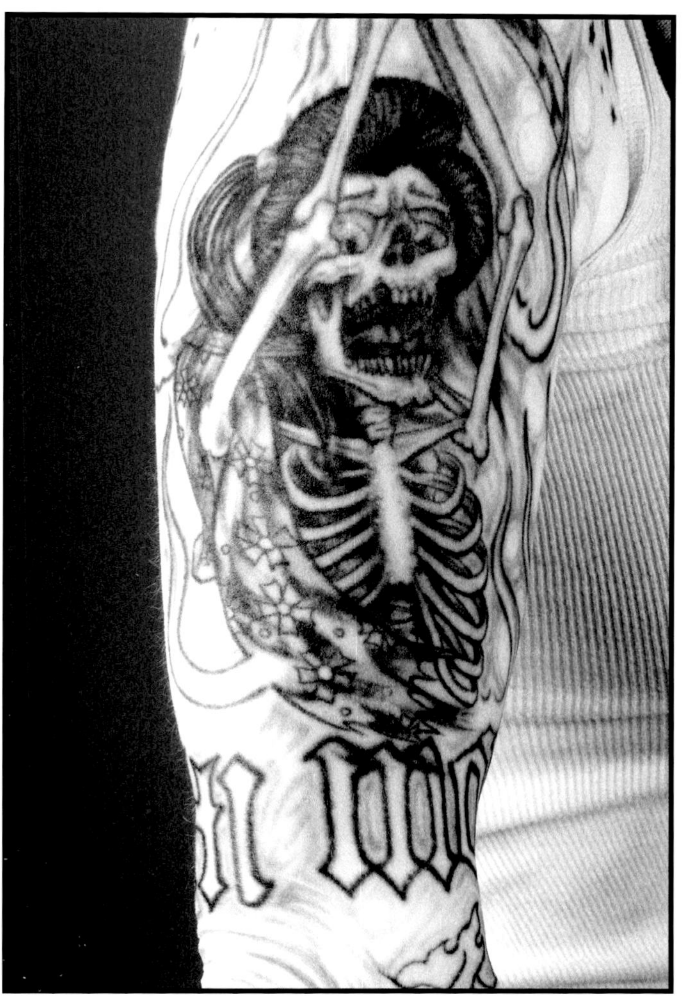

My first tattoo is a big, scary skeleton that I got when I was 17 and I was living in New York City and it was like 1982 and girls weren't getting tattoos so much back then, and it was illegal to get tattoos in New York City. I had always had an obsession with tattoos and had always been kind of just cuckoo about them and piercings and stuff. It was inevitable as soon as I was old enough to get one that I would go, and I went out to Long Island and I brought a sketch of what I wanted. I wanted this big, scary skeleton, wielding a bloody dagger and I wanted "Hi Mom" written underneath and she would not do the "Hi Mom," and I just had to kind go with the flow and get what she would do, so she changed the design quite a bit and did the tattoo and then a few years later, I had to go and get somebody to do the "Hi Mom" underneath, and luckily it was Jamiee Toreho in San Francisco and he thought it was hysterical. He was very happy to do it and so that's my first tattoo.

–Bernadette Seacrest

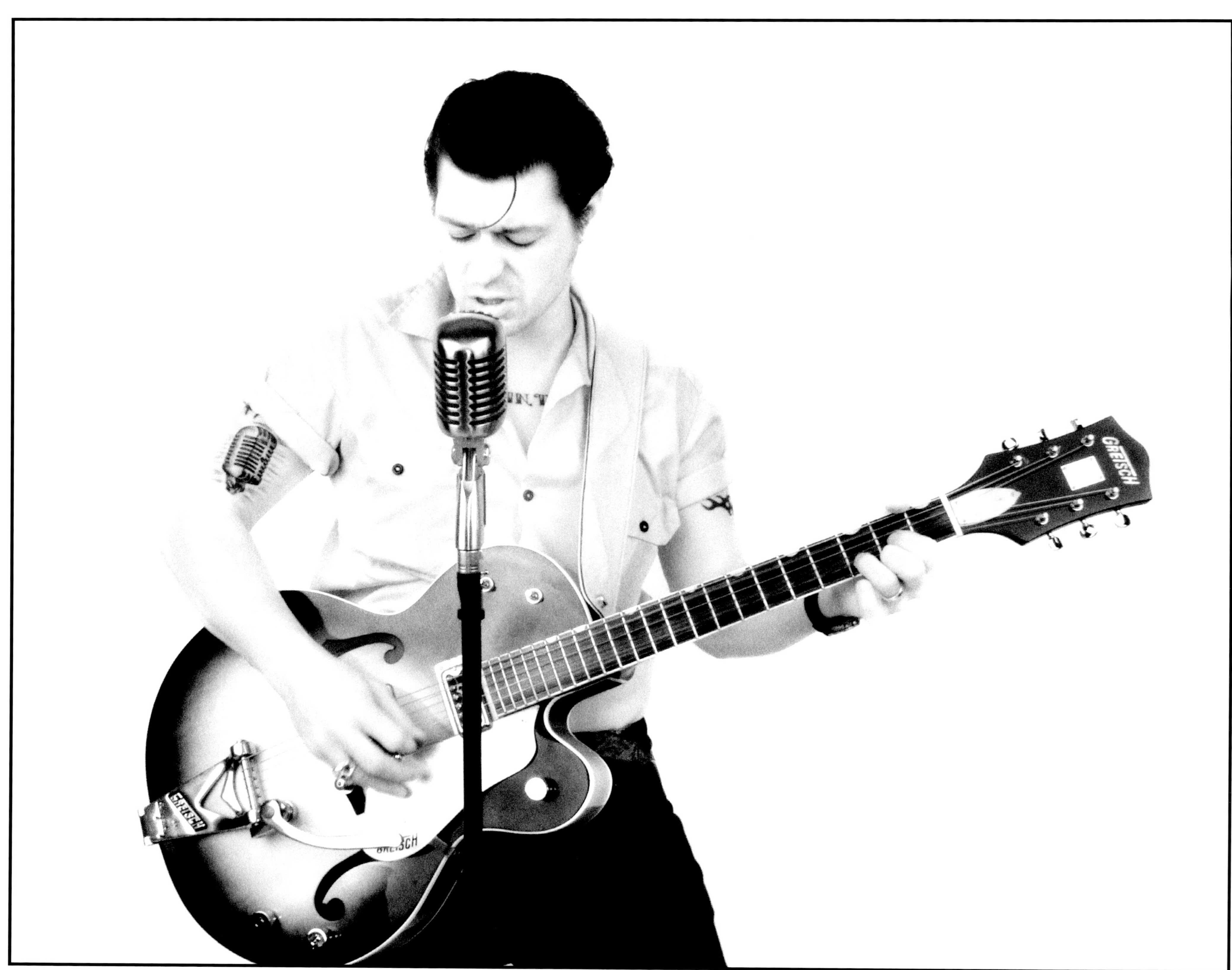
GRETSCH

I guess my favorite tattoo is always the last one. They are all meaningful in some way, but the current favorite is the Shure 55 mic on my right arm. They're real old school technology, and it's the mic I use onstage, so it makes a lot of sense that way. It helps that it's such a cool looking old thing, and makes a pretty classic rockabilly tattoo. Tattoos are pretty widespread through the rockabilly world, and, like you would expect, it's largely a celebration of '50s themes. So you see a lot of similar stuff—old Sailor Jerry designs, Wurlitzer style jukeboxes, pin-ups, like that. People really want to put these kinds of pictures in their skin to show how much they love this stuff, and identify themselves with the rockabilly sub-culture. It's really an insider thing, like the old sailor and jail tattoos. Jimmi Hellbent was the artist for the mic, and at the time he was also playing drums in my band Christian D and the Hangovers. Having one of my musicians as my tattoo artist made for a pretty cool experience. I don't have that many tattoos, really. I see 20-year-olds these days that have full sleeves; when I was a kid it wasn't so popular. It used to be having ink was a pretty bad-ass thing, it was much more rockers, bikers, punks, and sailors. It's pretty acceptable now to have tattoos, and I think that takes some of the romance out of it somehow. Of course, that isn't to say I'll be stopping anytime soon! It's really cool that you can wear your heart on your sleeve (literally!) through tattooing, and it's one of the only things I know of that you pay for and then you keep forever—that kind of permanence is a rare and beautiful thing in this old world.

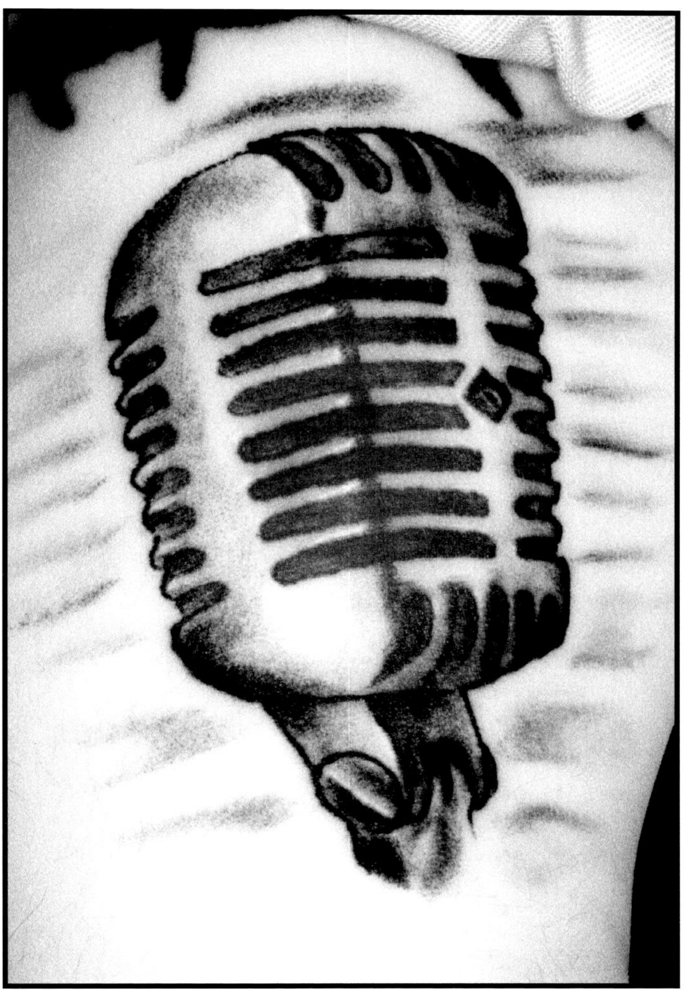

–Christian D

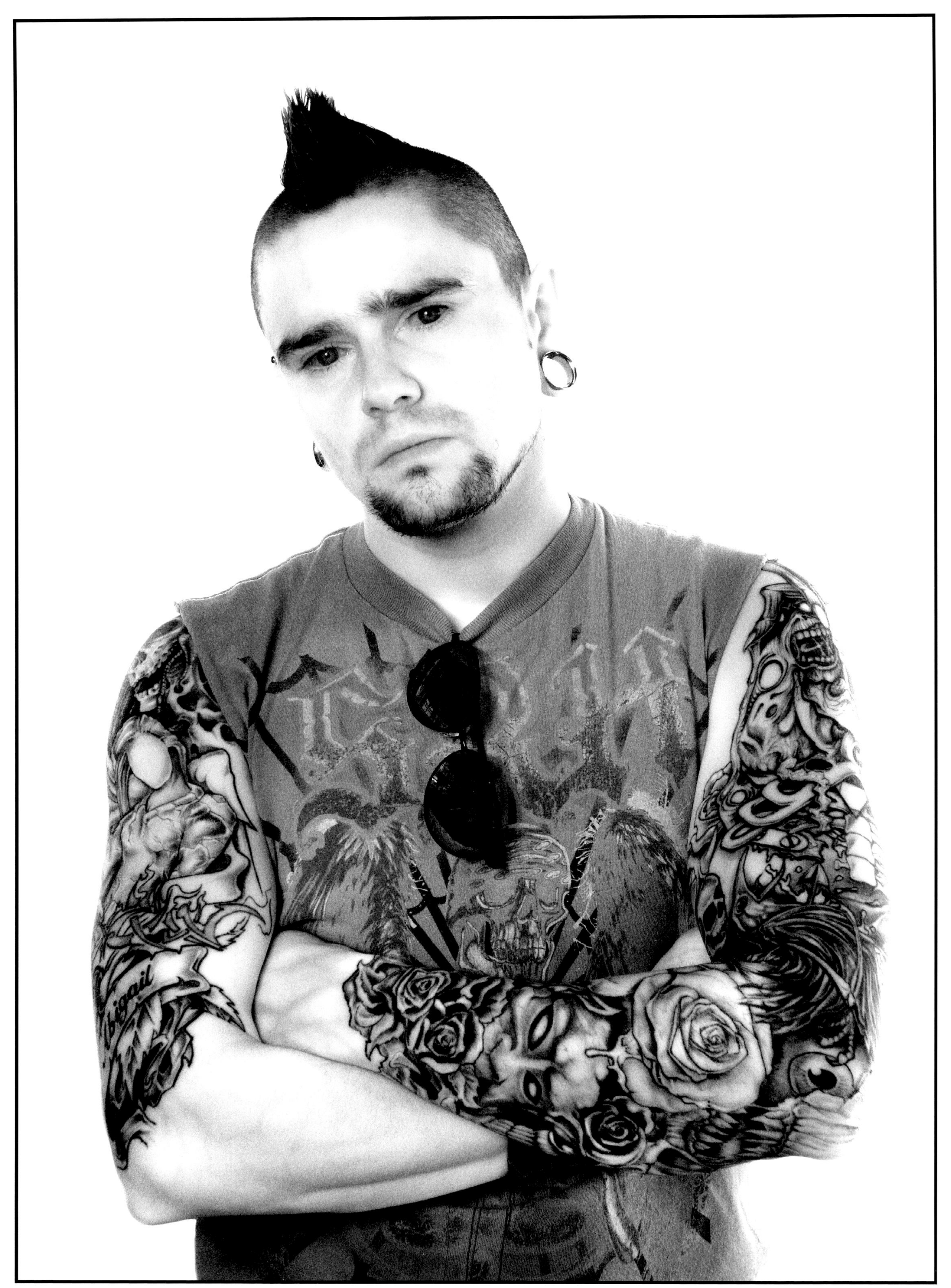

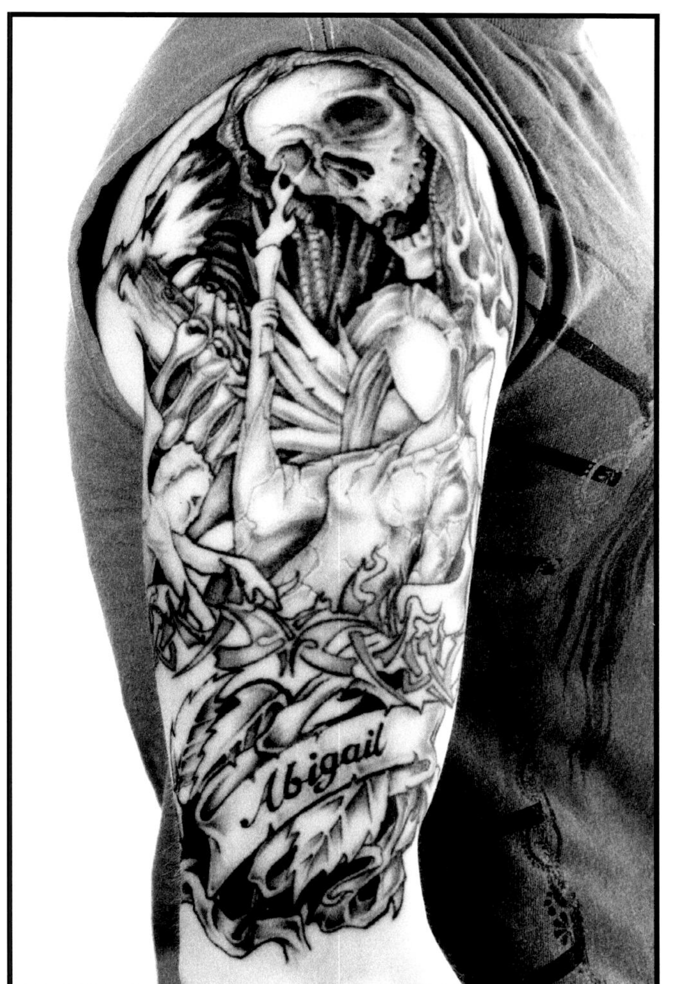

I was on tour with Guns N' Roses years ago, before my first child was born, my daughter. Her name is Abigail. My father got sick with cancer the same time she was due to be born, so I had to fly home from the Guns N' Roses tour, deliver my daughter, and then bury my father a week later. I had this tattoo to show that; the grim reaper symbolizes the cancer and the disease, taking my father away and then there is a pregnant, faceless angel giving me my daughter, which is Abigail, all in the same week. It was pretty rough.

–Jason James

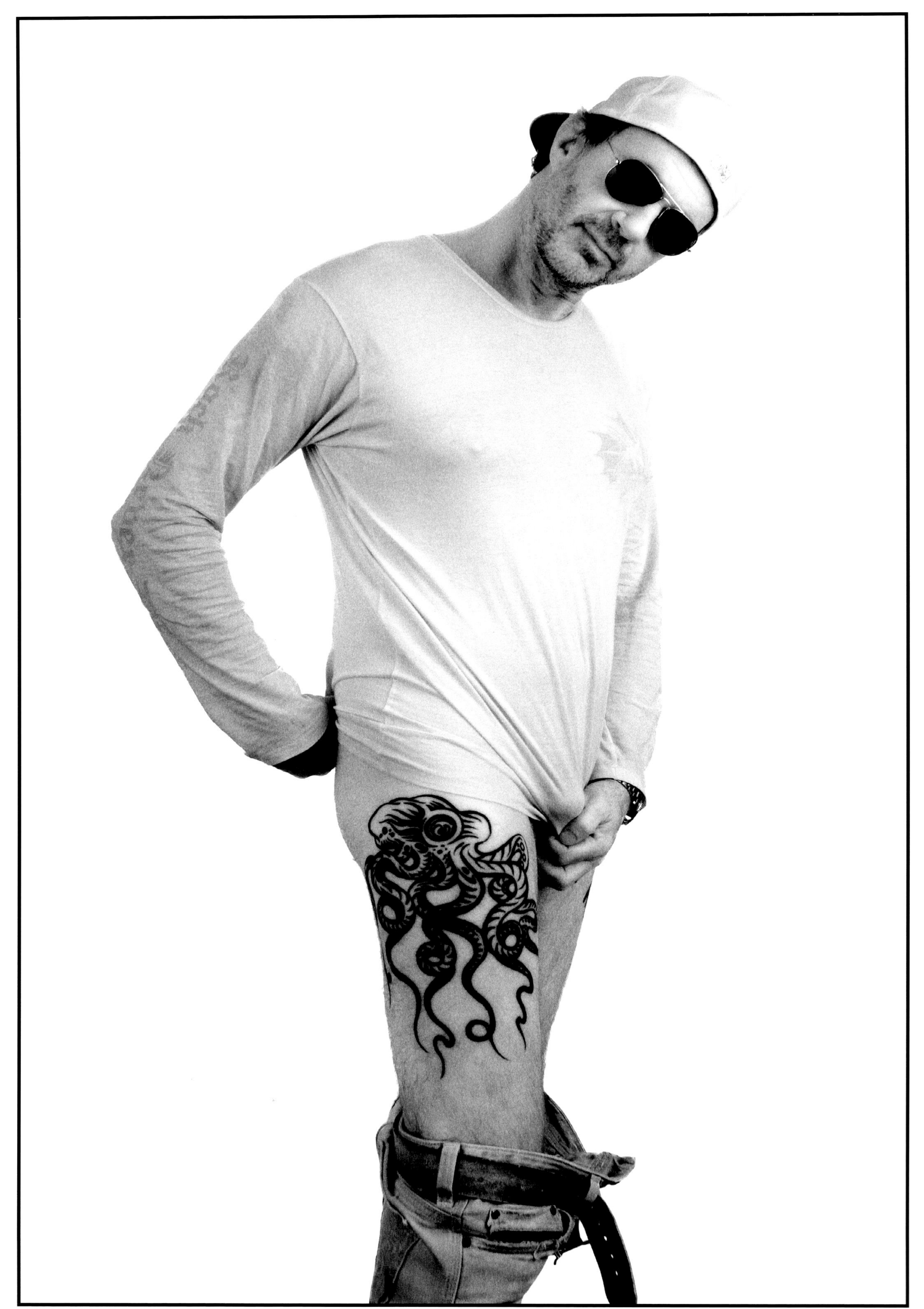

I got this tattoo in 1991 by Henk Shiffmacher, aka Hanky Panky, a very famous Dutch artist, painter, tattoo artist in Amsterdam. I was on tour with the Chili Peppers and we were playing in Holland, and I had gotten a couple of tattoos from Henk but I wanted a really big piece and thought it would be great to get one on my leg. I'm a big fan of scuba diving and undersea life and that wonderful world down below. I told Henk I want an octopus, can we draw something up, a really cool tribal octopus? He said, "Yeah, yeah, yeah" and drew something up and I get to his shop and he's all ready to tattoo me. About a month or so earlier I had a hernia operation on the right side, down in the groin area and I had jumped out on tour a little too quick, so it really didn't have a good chance to heal so it was still kind of an open wound, so to speak and playing the drums every night certainly didn't help it heal. So he's shaving my leg, getting ready and I see the tattoo thing and I'm thinking that's going to be awesome. He's getting ready to tattoo me, he's got the gun out, I've got my pants down and he looks and he sees the little bandage and he says, "What's that?" So I tell him I just had a hernia operation and it's just healing

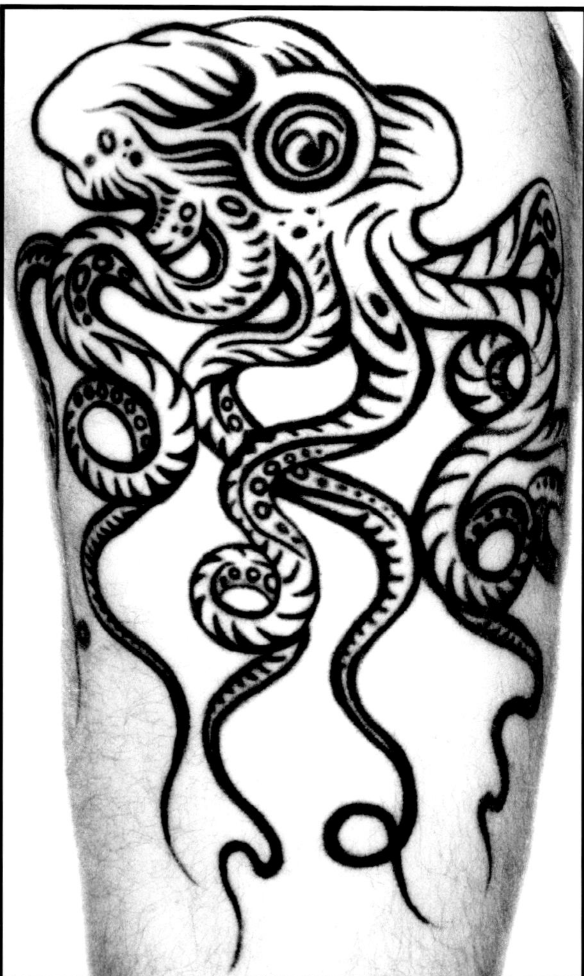

you know, it's no big deal. He says, "Well, let me see it." I open it up and he looks at it and he goes, "Oh my God, that's like an open wound. If I put that much ink into your leg right there, it's gonna blow up. Your leg's just going to get infected and you're probably going to get gangrene and they're going to have to cut your leg off." I was like, "No, no. It's okay." I was so excited to get the tattoo, that I was like, "I don't care, it's fine. Don't worry." He's like, "I can't. I can't do it. I can't. I can't. It's not safe." I was all ready to get tattooed and I didn't. I was so disappointed. Of course I had to wait until it healed, and I came back and he did it, and I think it's my favorite tattoo. I just love it. And whenever I take my pants off, in the privacy of a partner, they always get a real surprise to see what's going on…down below.

–Chad Smith

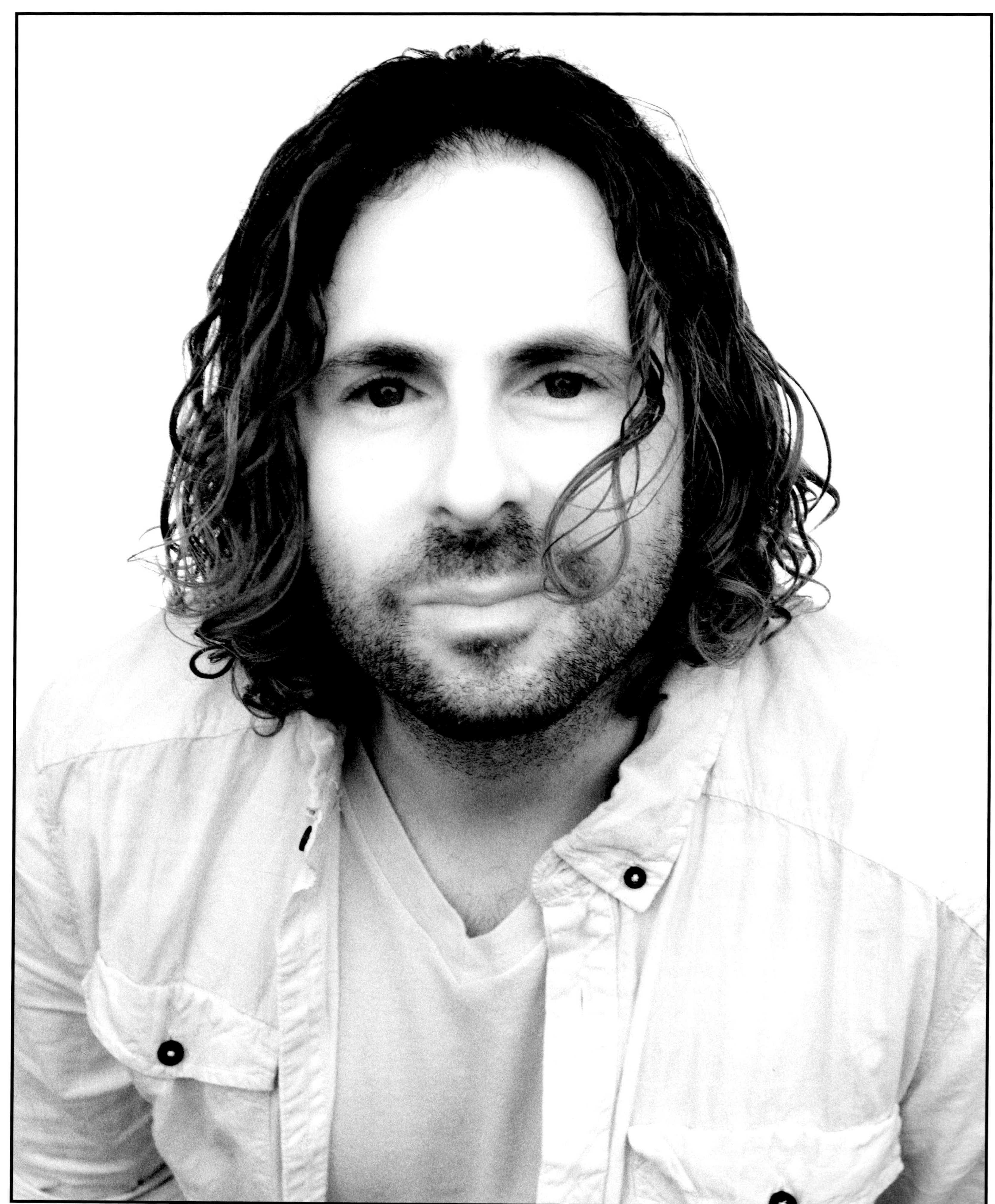

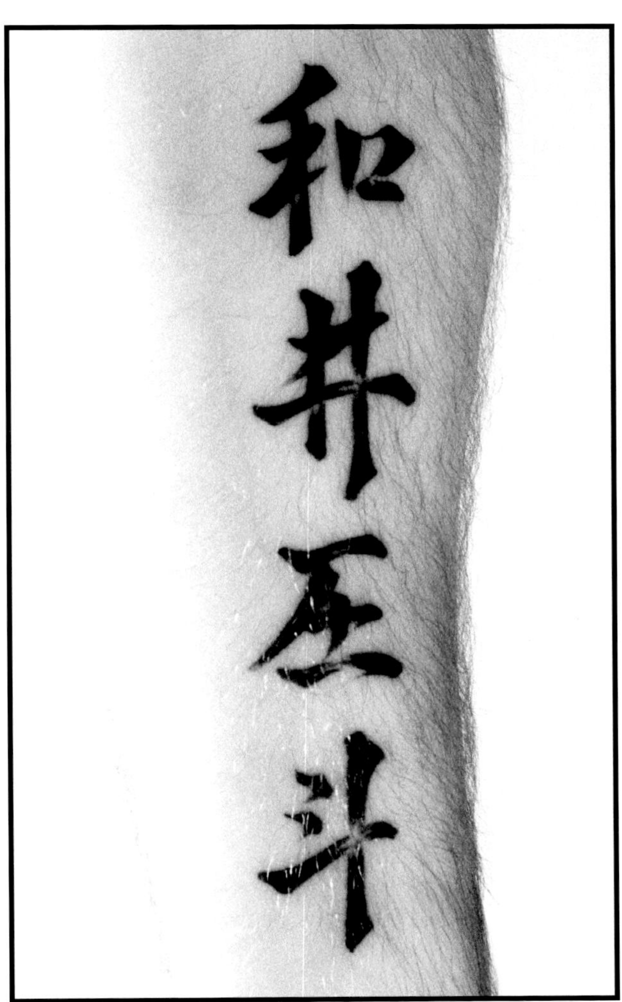

I got this done in Tokyo by a guy named Mikala, who I believe is a third- or fourth-generation tebori style tattooist. I searched him out over the net, contacted him and when we were in Japan, I was able to go to the shop and have my first tattoo done there. It's my son's name, Wyatt. It's done in traditional tebori style; you lay down on the table and he makes his own stick and I think there was probably eight needles in it. He basically just lays it on his thumb and just pokes it. He actually outlined the whole thing with a gun first. Actually that hurt worse than the tebori style, which I thought that was kind of strange. But it was very exciting. Even trying to find the place in a cab, having Japanese writing translation obviously, but we made it there, wrote it down, started to work and it was done in like 1½ hours. It was just a great experience and for my first tattoo, I was pretty stoked to get it done there and in traditional style. I would definitely recommend it to people to do that tebori style.

–Tony Polermo

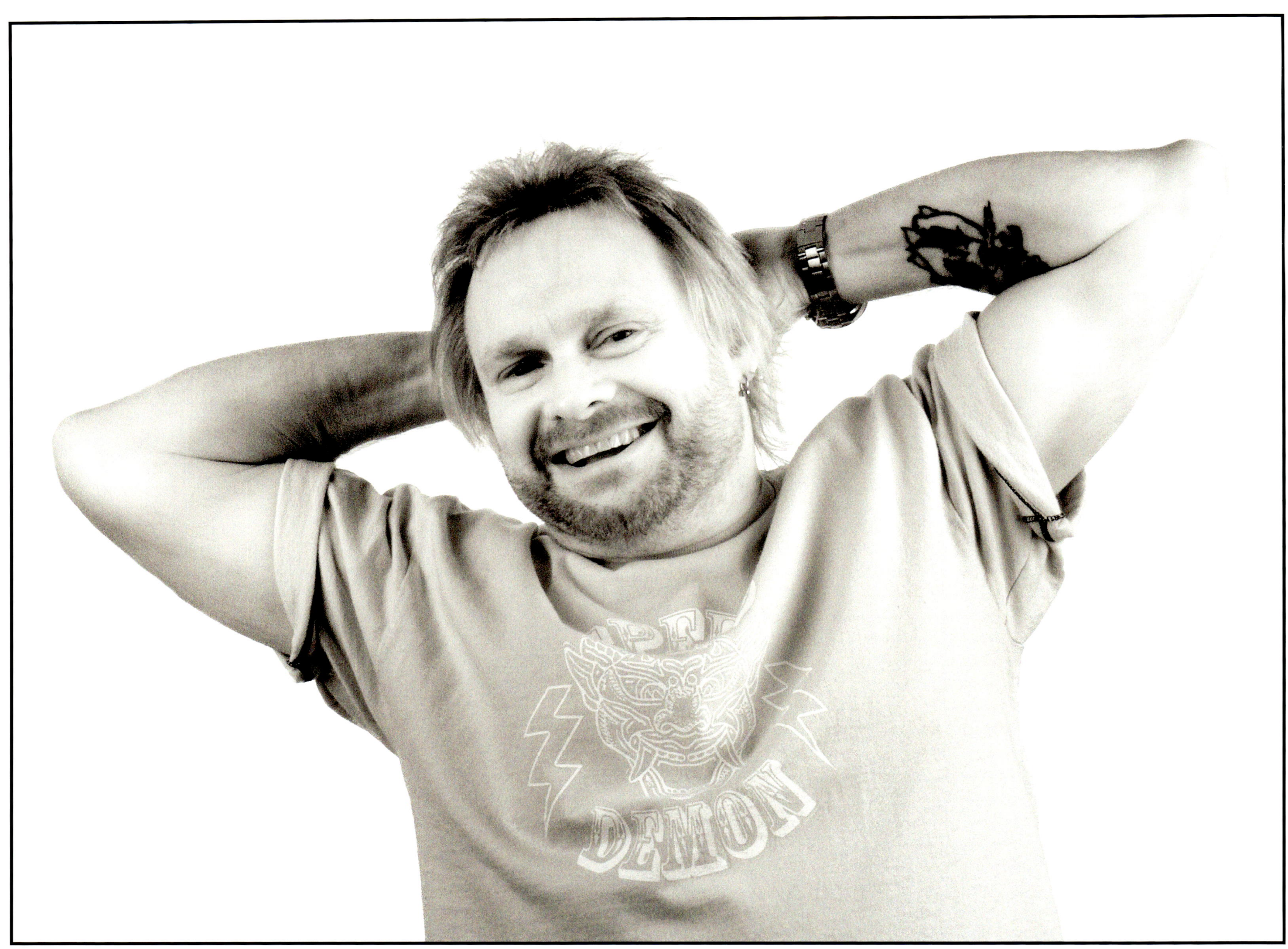
DEMON

I have a little chili pepper man that's exiting my arm. He's a habanero chili, blowing flames out of his mouth. The first time I actually saw a picture of this was on a bottle of hot sauce by a company called Ring of Fire out of San Diego, California, while we were shooting a Van Halen video for a song off of our *Balance* album, "Don't Tell Me What Love Can Do." They had this bottle of hot sauce at catering and I really liked the hot sauce, and I really liked the bottle. I looked at the picture and I thought, "Fuck man, that's a cool looking picture. I'd like to do a tat of that some day," me being a hot sauce connoisseur of sorts. It looked only appropriate, so the catering people gave me the bottle, this was in about 1994. A couple of years later, probably around '97 or '98, I had kept the bottle in my pantry at home and I pulled it out; I was going to put this tattoo as a little thing on my ankle, but my wife actually talked me into putting it on my arm saying, "Hey you know people will really be able to see this thing while you're playing bass if you put it on your arm." So I got the tattoo done and some friends of the owners of the company that I had gotten the image from, the Ring of Fire people, saw my tattoo on my arm, got a hold of the hot sauce company and they started sending me hats and t-shirts. Pretty much right after that I contacted them and we started to develop what would become the Mad Anthony hot sauce line. Crazy stuff, but I likes it...I likes it HOT!

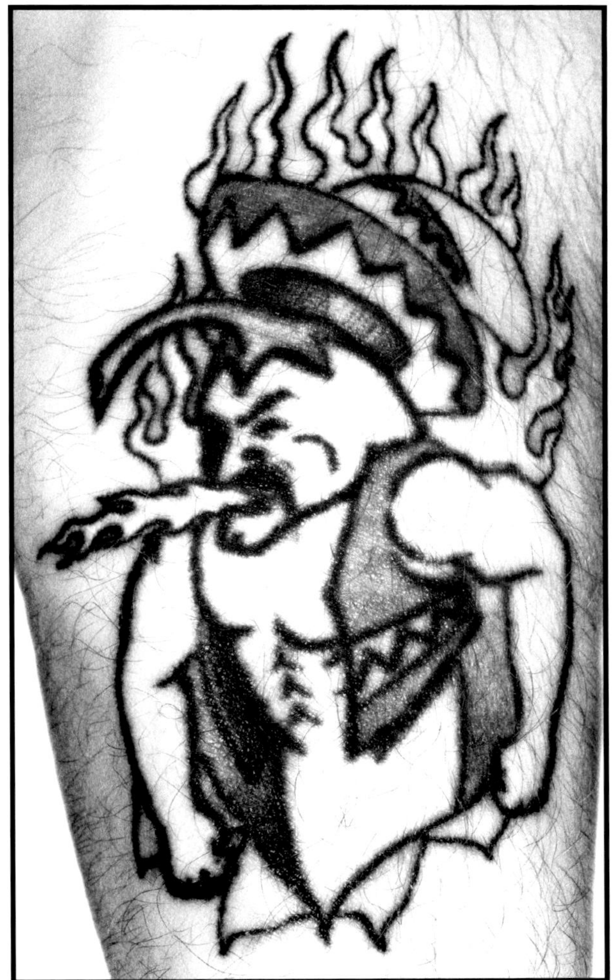

–Michael Anthony

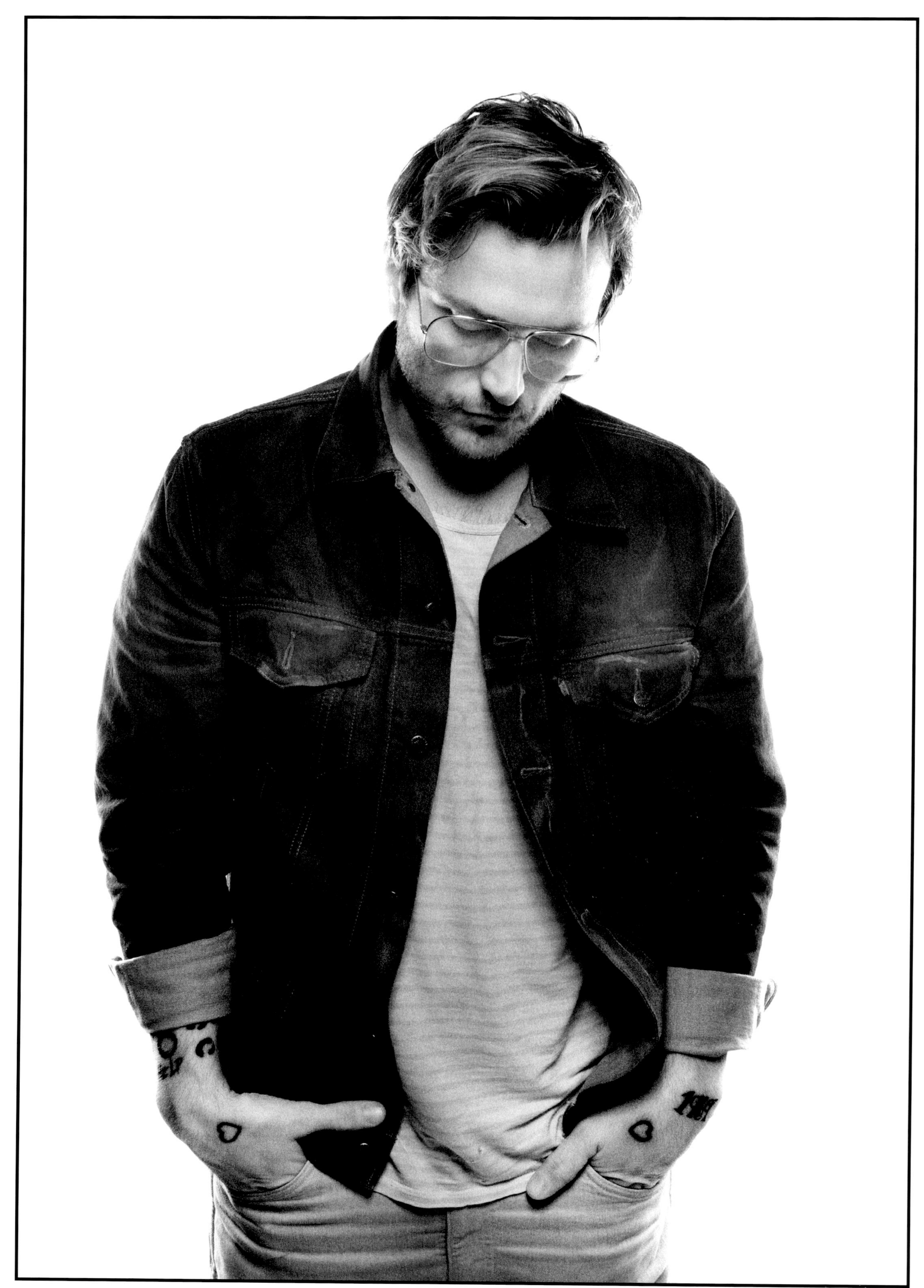

I think of the more interesting tattoos I have, it's not even that it's interesting so much as the story that surrounds it. When I was going through a pretty bad divorce in my younger years, too early to be getting married, in the early '90s I guess, I really was looking for something to speak to me musically, lyrically. I was so crushed from it and I had a hard time getting out from this dark hold, this dark period and I started really getting into Elvis Costello. I was very much a late bloomer actually by the early '90s, because he'd obviously been around since the '70s. I went back and really focused on his catalogue a lot and really got super engulfed in everything he did and man the guy, you know, he could tell a love story and a bit of a breakup story like nobody else and really inspired me. So, of course, I get his likeness tattooed from *This Year's Model* on my inner arm here, which is all fine and great, but nobody told me that you really probably shouldn't get a tattoo of someone's likeness on your body, that's still alive, because one day, you're going to run into them in a dark elevator at midnight in a hotel in Hollywood, with just the two of you on the elevator and of course, I fan-boyed out and freaked out and was like, "Oh my God, oh my God,

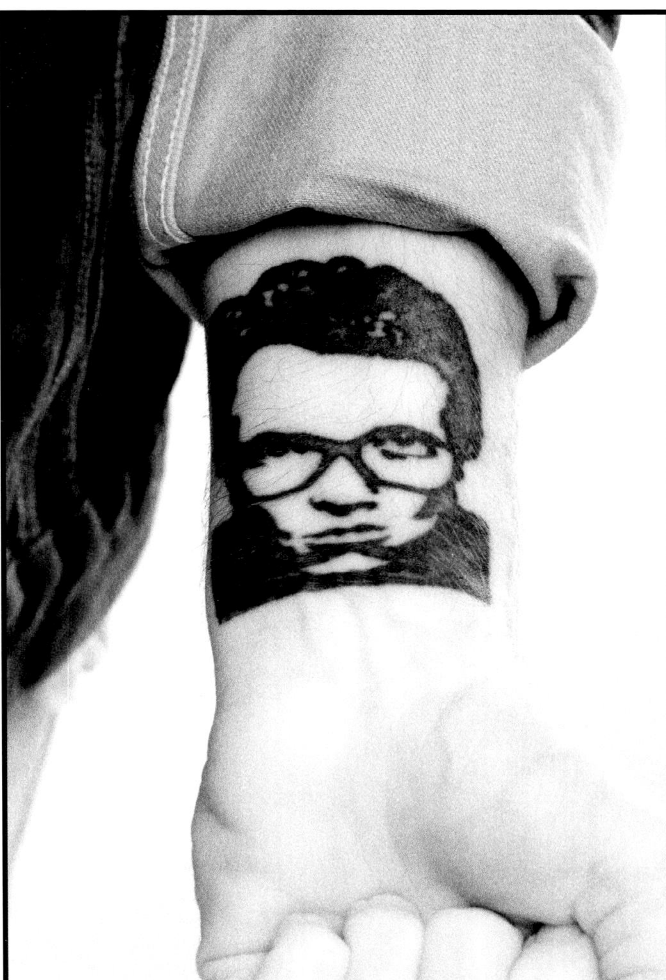

oh my God" and started pointing to my tattoo. He turned around hitting the stop elevator button going, "Yeah, yeah, that's great" and so I thought to myself, um, you know, I'll never really be able to bro down with Elvis Costello now and be buddies. I'll be the weirdo with the tattoo of his face on my arm. But nonetheless, I'm still pretty proud of it and it will always be there. Can't cover it up now.

–Butch Walker

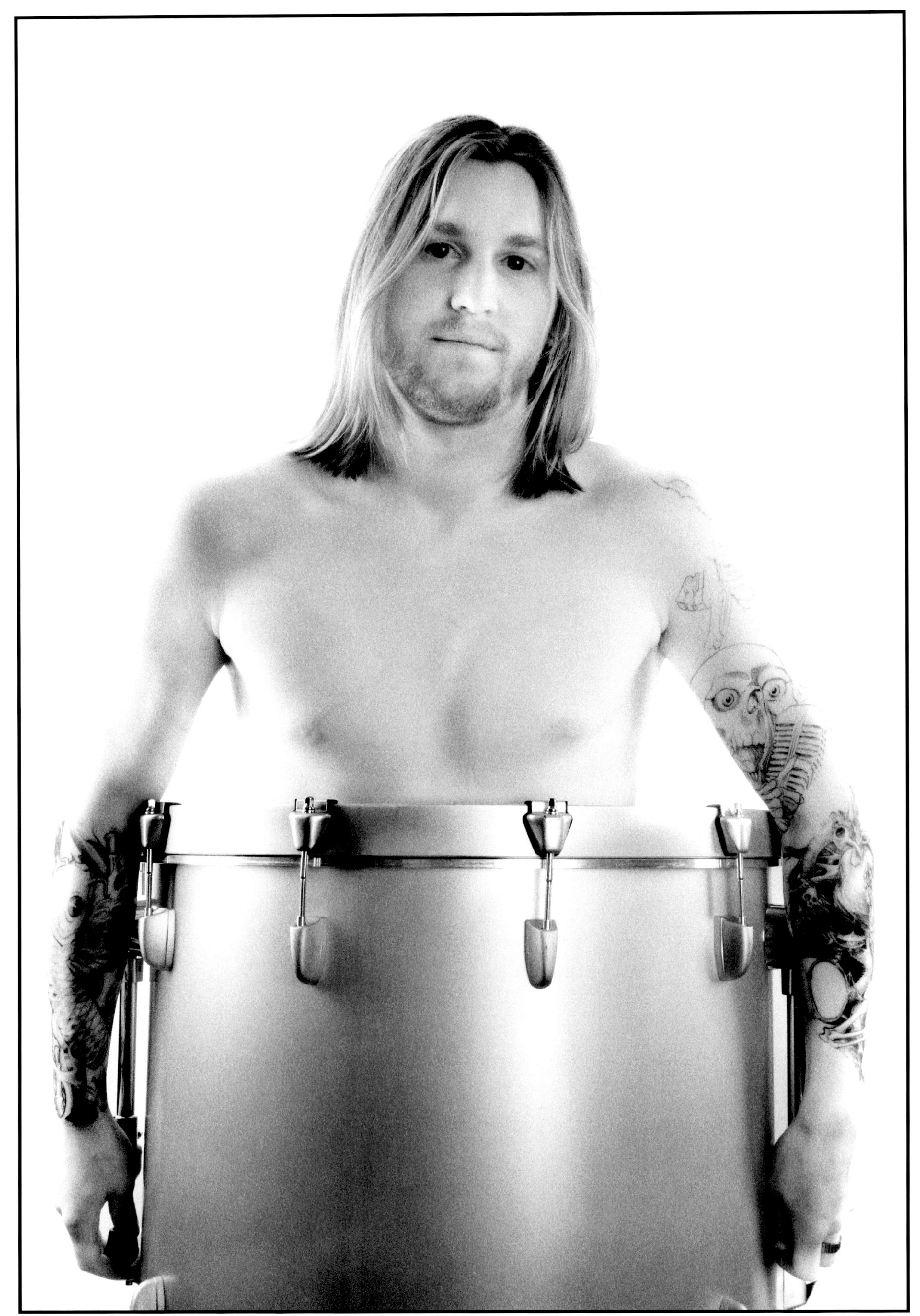

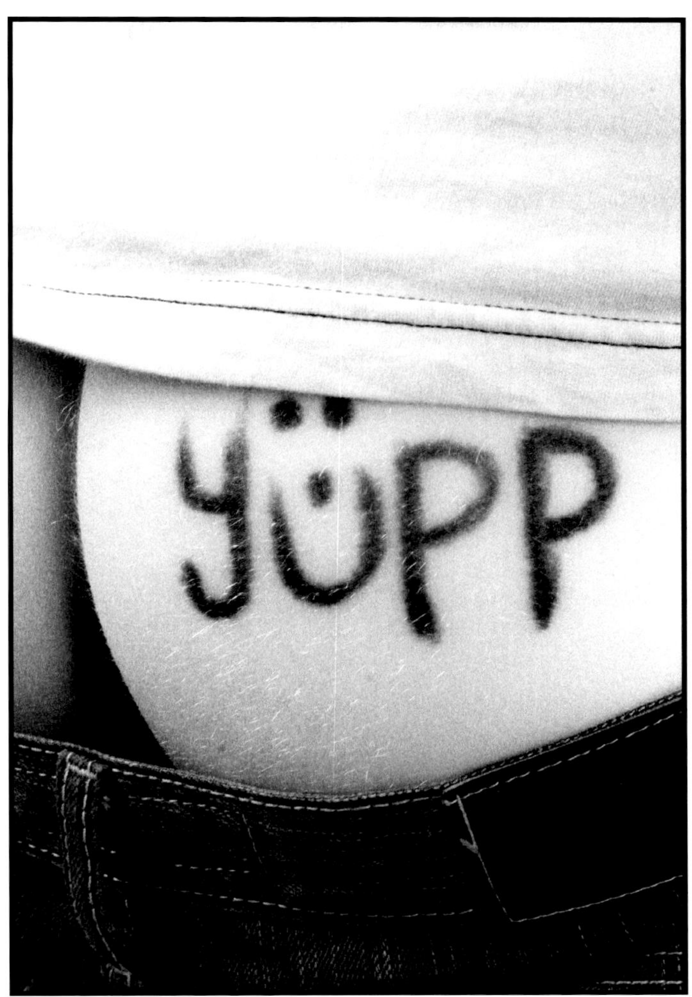

The “Yupp!” tattoo. Well the whole idea was that when the band got signed to a major label, we’d all get a tattoo on our ass, kind of commemorating the signing. We got signed and I agreed to step up first. Our guitar player Dan got a tattoo gun off eBay and I let him do it. He did a total hack job.

–Dustin Steinke

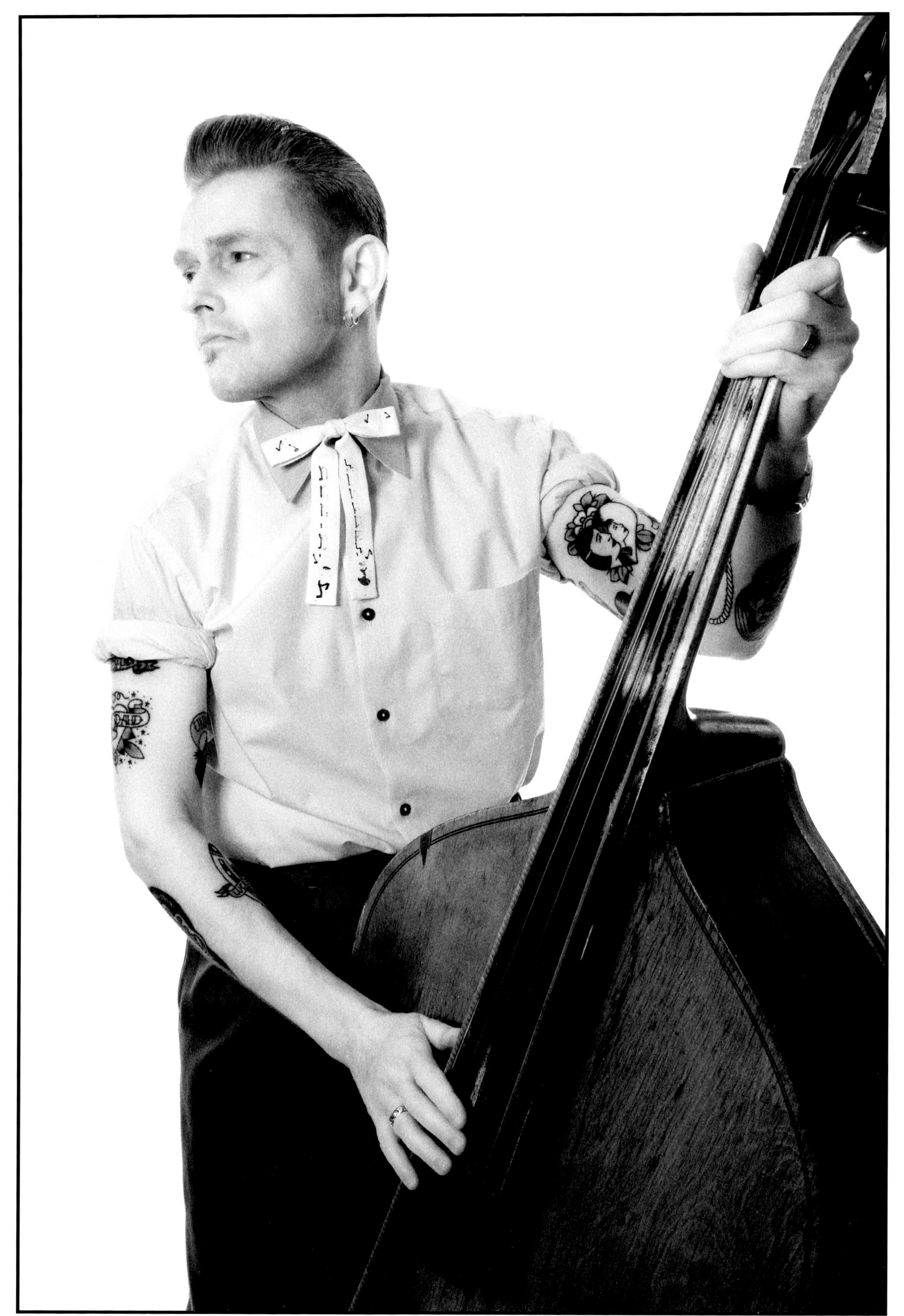

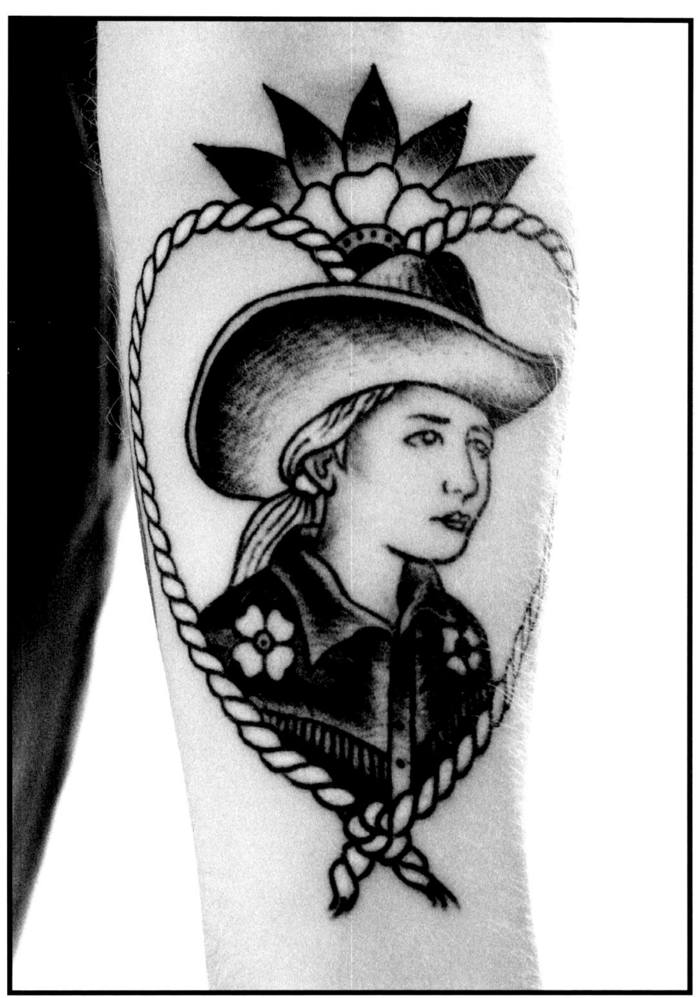

This is Josephine, my daughter. I had it done on my birthday, October 15, and the following day, my mother was admitted to emergency at Scarborough General Hospital. She didn't want to go to emergency because she was afraid she wouldn't get out, and eventually she didn't; she passed away November 7, but seeing the tattoo of Josephine, it really made her happy. She liked seeing it and it made her smile for a little bit. The other thing is my dad is not a big fan of tattoos and it made her happy to see him get a little upset about it. She liked stuff like that.

–Steve Good

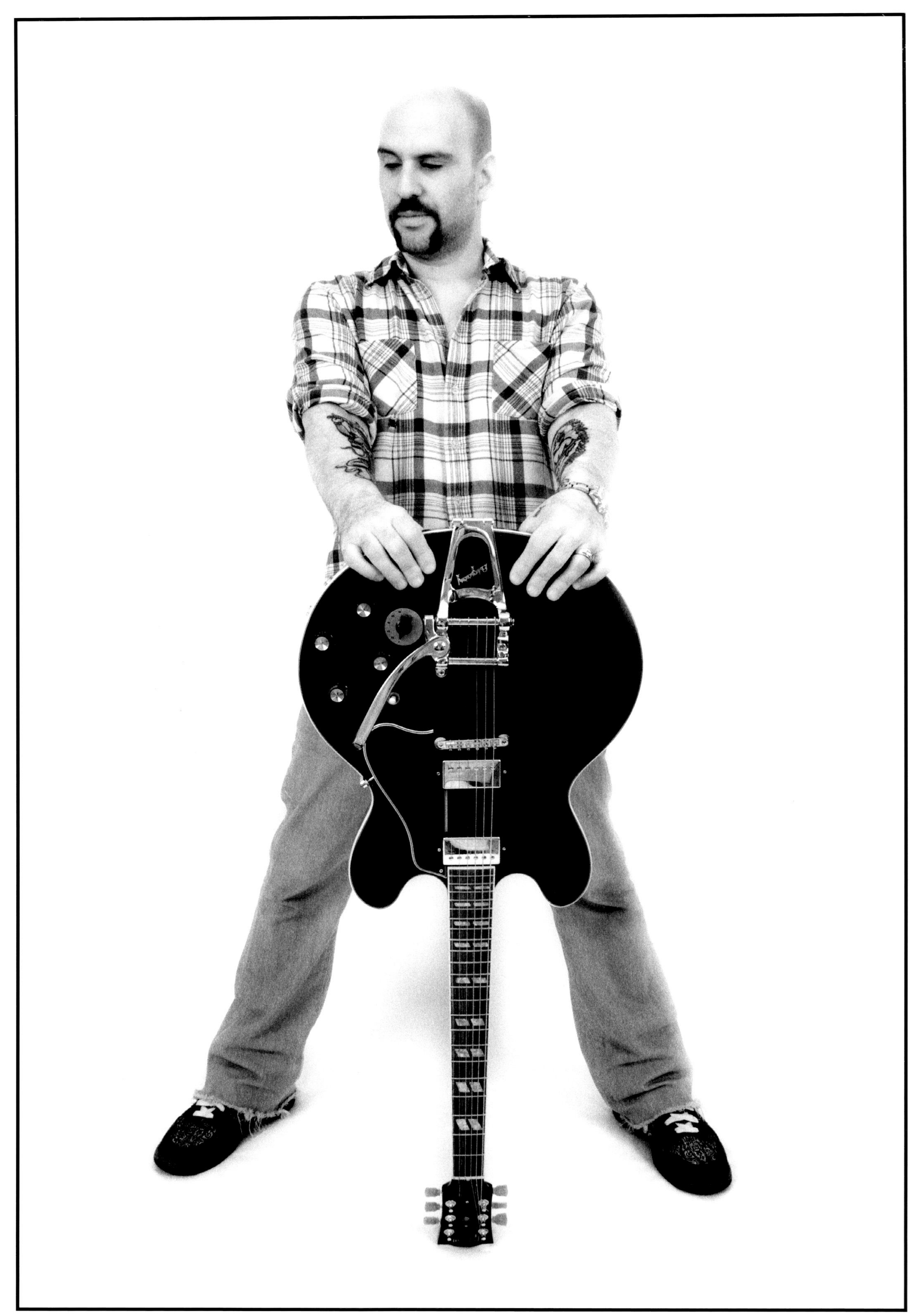

I'm telling you the story of this tattoo: my wife's name. Except for my mother's maiden name on my wrist, I've never had a tattoo of anyone's name. We started dating in 2002 right when Velvet Revolver was first getting together and through all of that, at which point I was totally broke and working at the rehearsal studio where we would rehearse. I would work 9–2 and Velvet Revolver would rehearse from 2–6. I was building sets at the time to make a living to pay rent and stuff, but I couldn't take any jobs because I was afraid that if I did that I would lose the Velvet Revolver spot. So I started working at the rehearsal studio for $13 an hour doing cartage and fixing the studio across the way. I started dating my wife and she's awesome. She was really great because, you know, I had nothing and she didn't care. For me it's just really cool to know that from where we are now with a house and two cars and two kids and some nice things, it's nice to know that we started together with nothing and that we came up together. We got married when we were mixing the first record, and she had never been out of the country. Velvet

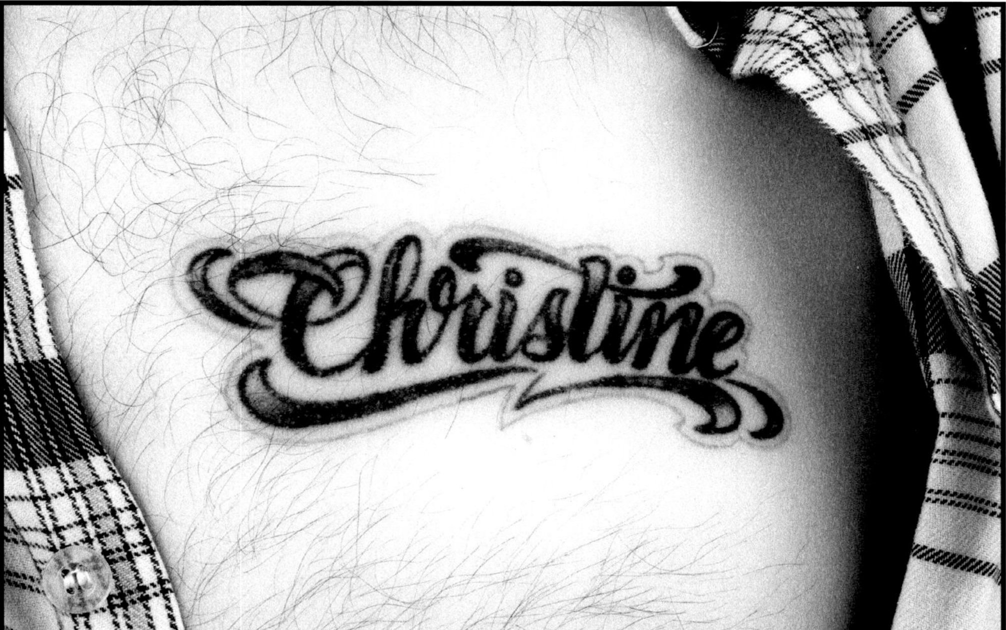

Revolver travels in style, so we got to see the world together. We got to experience all of these things together as a team. I got a tattoo of her name on my chest when we had been dating about five months. I didn't tell anyone. I just went and did it on my own. It was done by Frank Ball, a tattoo artist here in LA who I think just has a really good style for writing. I totally surprised her; I didn't tell anyone. I had the bandage on my chest and had my shirt on and we were talking and she kind of saw it and felt it and asked, "What's that?" I said, "Oh, it's a tattoo" and she kind of knew; the color went out of her face and she kind of freaked out for a second and then she saw it and she got all emotional…this is my memory. She might have a totally different story, but she's not here. Every time for a year and a half that I would see her brother or her friends or her parents or anyone we knew, she would make me take my shirt off and show it off to everyone. But hey, you know what? I haven't had to cover it up and we're still married with two kids and there you go.

–Dave Kushner

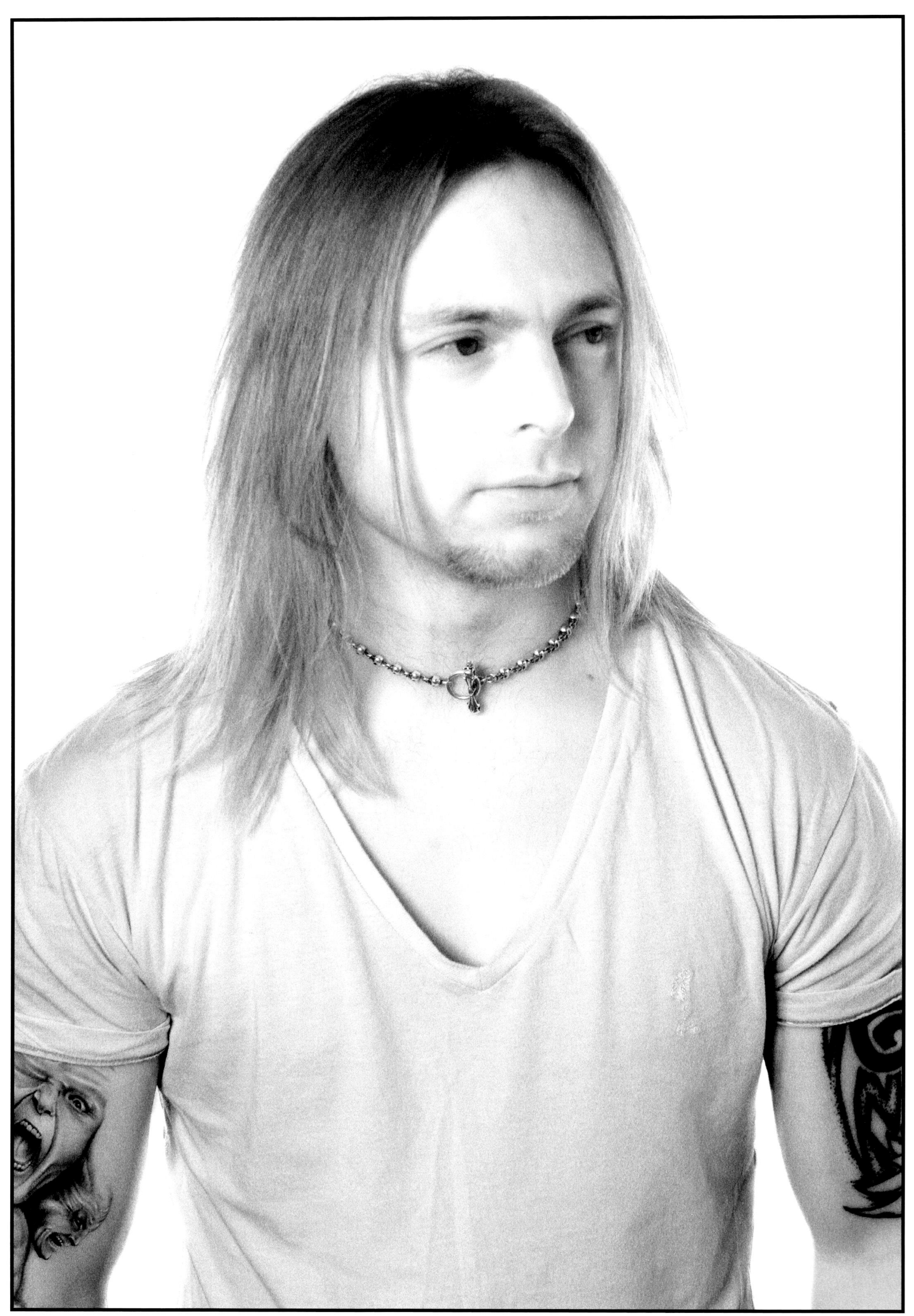

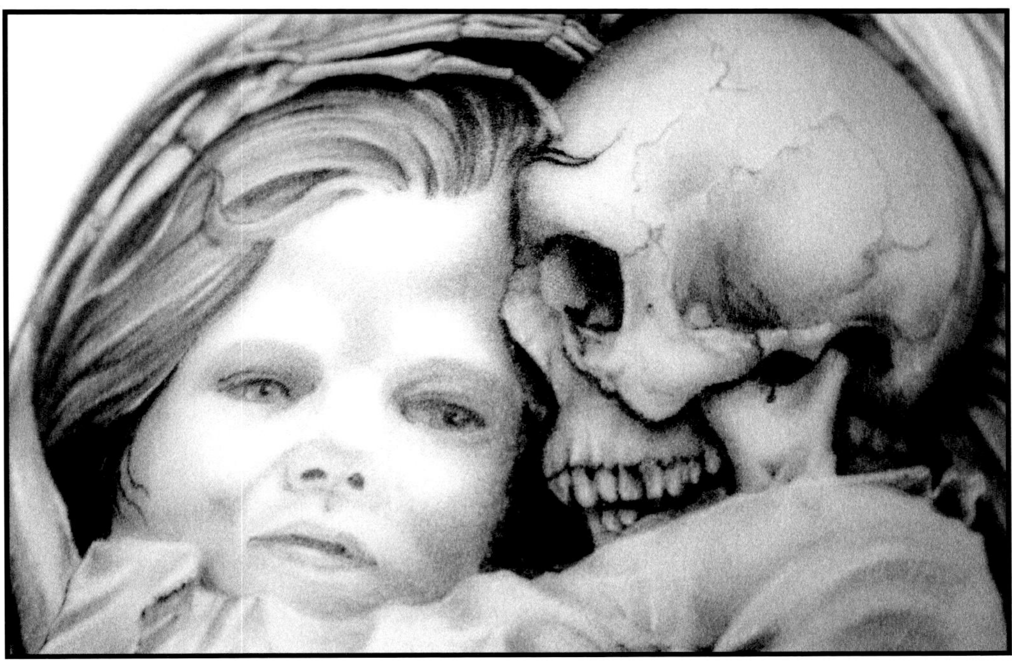

My sleeve is still a work in progress. My favorite artist is Laurie Lipton. My tattoo guy and I put this together. It's a collage of some of her work and I incorporated a lot of little personal touches in it. I became a dad about a year and a half ago, so I wanted something that kind of represented what I felt was an unconditional love for your child. That's what I tried to make the sleeve really about, and I've got stuff like his name in baby blocks, his date of birth and stuff, so it's a bit of a personal twist. It's black, white and grey; I didn't want any color, and I love it. I think it's amazing with the fine details. It took such a long time to get to this stage and there's still a lot to go, but it'll definitely be worth it.

–Matt Tuck

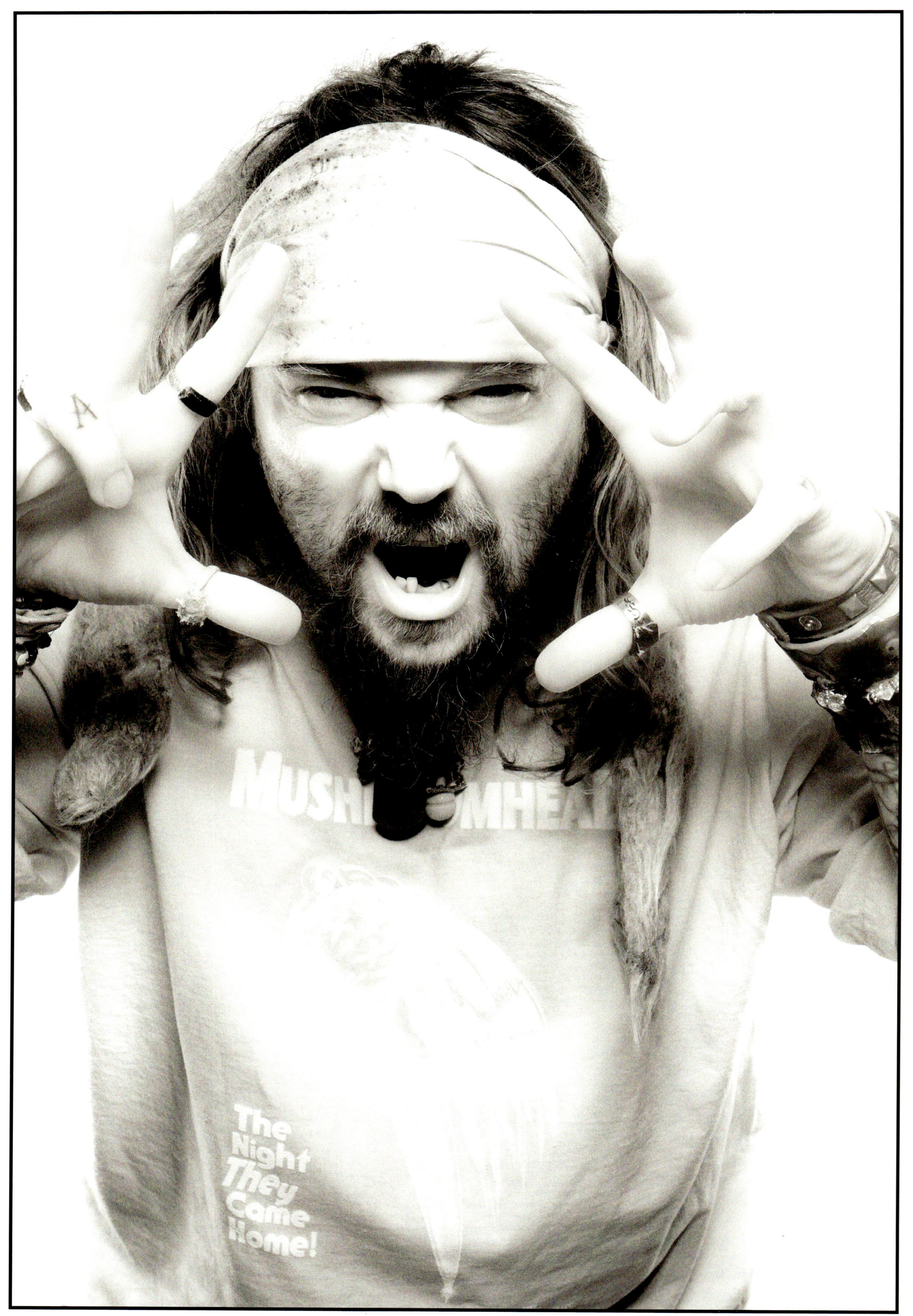
The Night They Came Home!

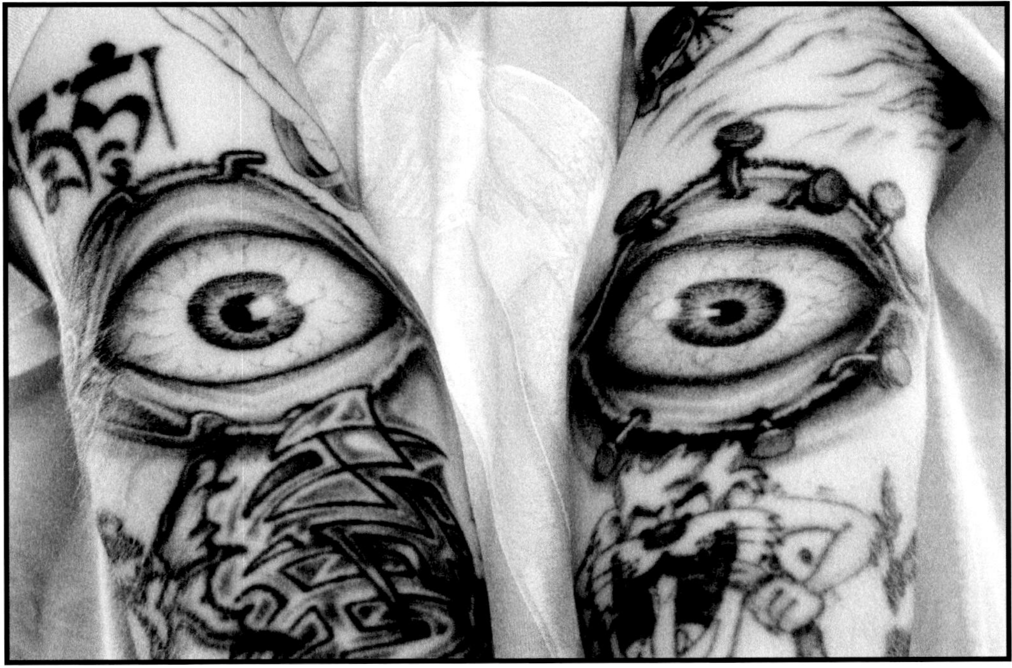

This piece is an idea based on the movie *A Clockwork Orange*, which I've watched many times. I'm a big fan, especially the part when he's making the guy watch a lot of movies and he grabs his eye and they're poking it open and they get like metal things going through the eyes, so that was the idea, but we added effects like nails; he has nails holding the eyes open and one has some kind of metal clamp. This one is more like *A Clockwork Orange*; he has the metal clamp which was what was used in the movie. The tattoo was done by Paul Booth who is an awesome tattoo artist. A lot of his work is really dark, even people consider him evil and satanic or whatever. We're good friends. Our friendship goes back all the way to the Sepultura days. I did that when I was in Sepultura. My idea behind it was even if I was not looking at the crowd, my eyeballs will always be facing the crown when I play the guitar. So I'm always watching the crowd no matter what.

–Max Cavalera

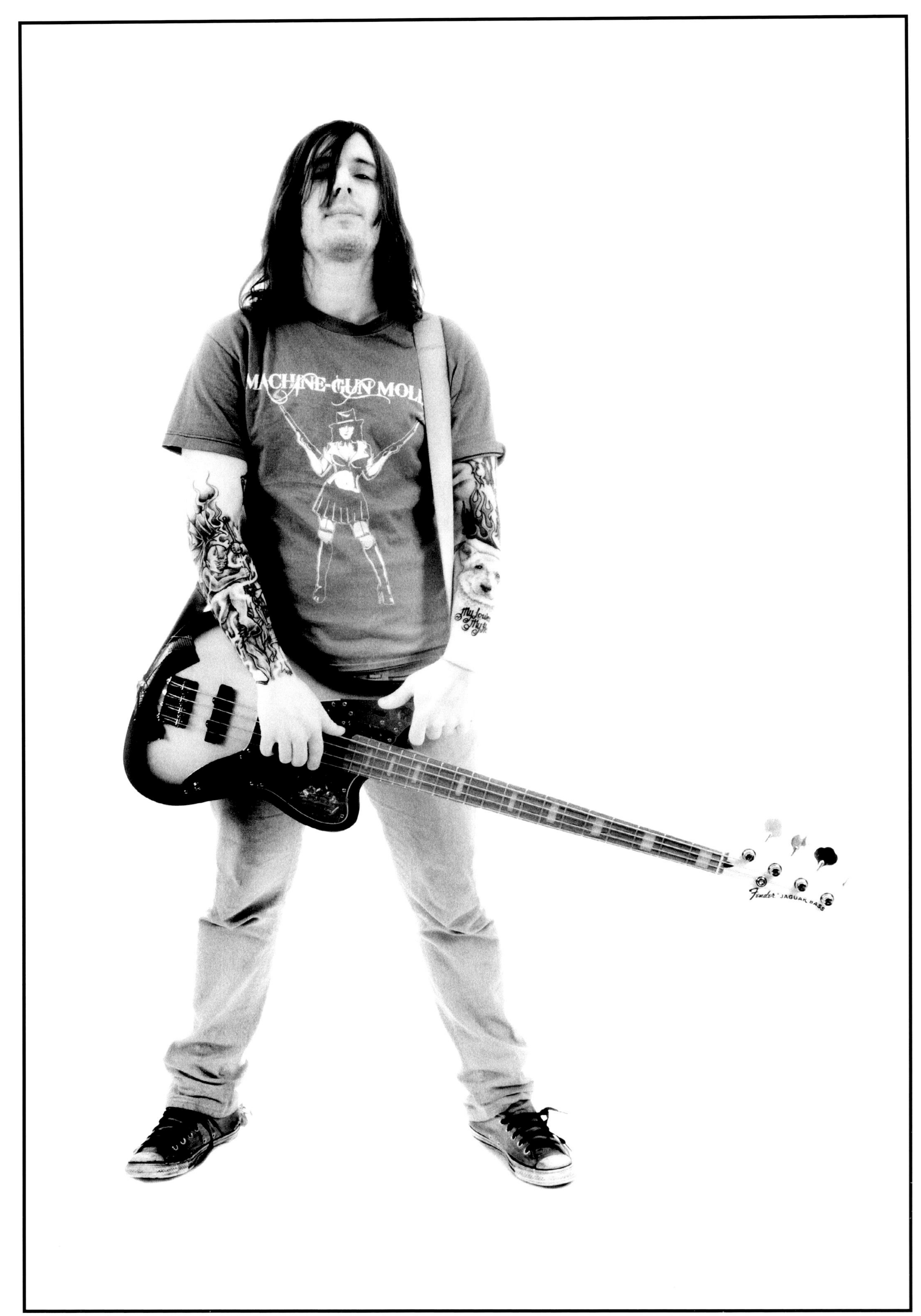
MACHINE-GUN MOL
Fender JAGUAR BASS

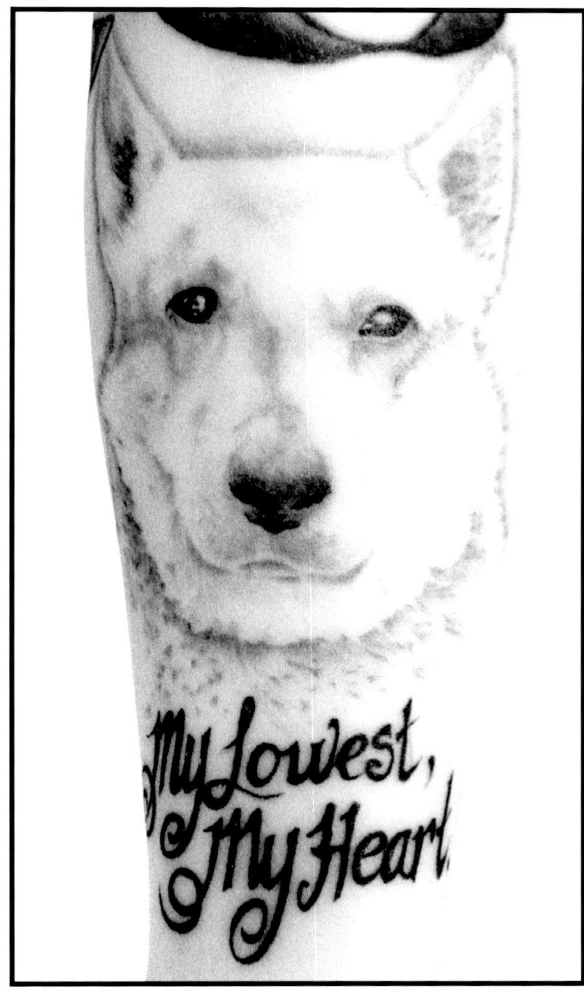

This tattoo was done by Kelly Rothschild, a good friend of mine who owns Machine Gun Molly. Mylo is the dog pictured in my tattoo. I had him for a good 11 years; his whole life from when he was about four months old. Needless to say he was a huge part of my life. Throughout his whole life I had been planning to get Mylo tattooed on me, but I never had time. When he passed away it seemed more than appropriate to get him done on my arm. I've always been into photography so I had taken a lot of him and found a really good one that I took to Kelly and she did him up for me. I had him cremated and had some of his ashes mixed in with the ink so I could always have him with me not only on my arm but also have him with me in me, and it means a hell of a lot to me. The text, "My Lowest My Heart," he was a big part of my life and he was included in a lot of my songwriting and a lyric from one song was "My Lowest My Heart" signifying that Mylo is with me at all times: my lowest times, my best times, and he really represented my heart. He was the most innocent creature. If you take those words, they can also be spoken as "Mylo is my heart." It's not a sad thing to me; it's a happy thing, a celebration.

–Anthony Bleed

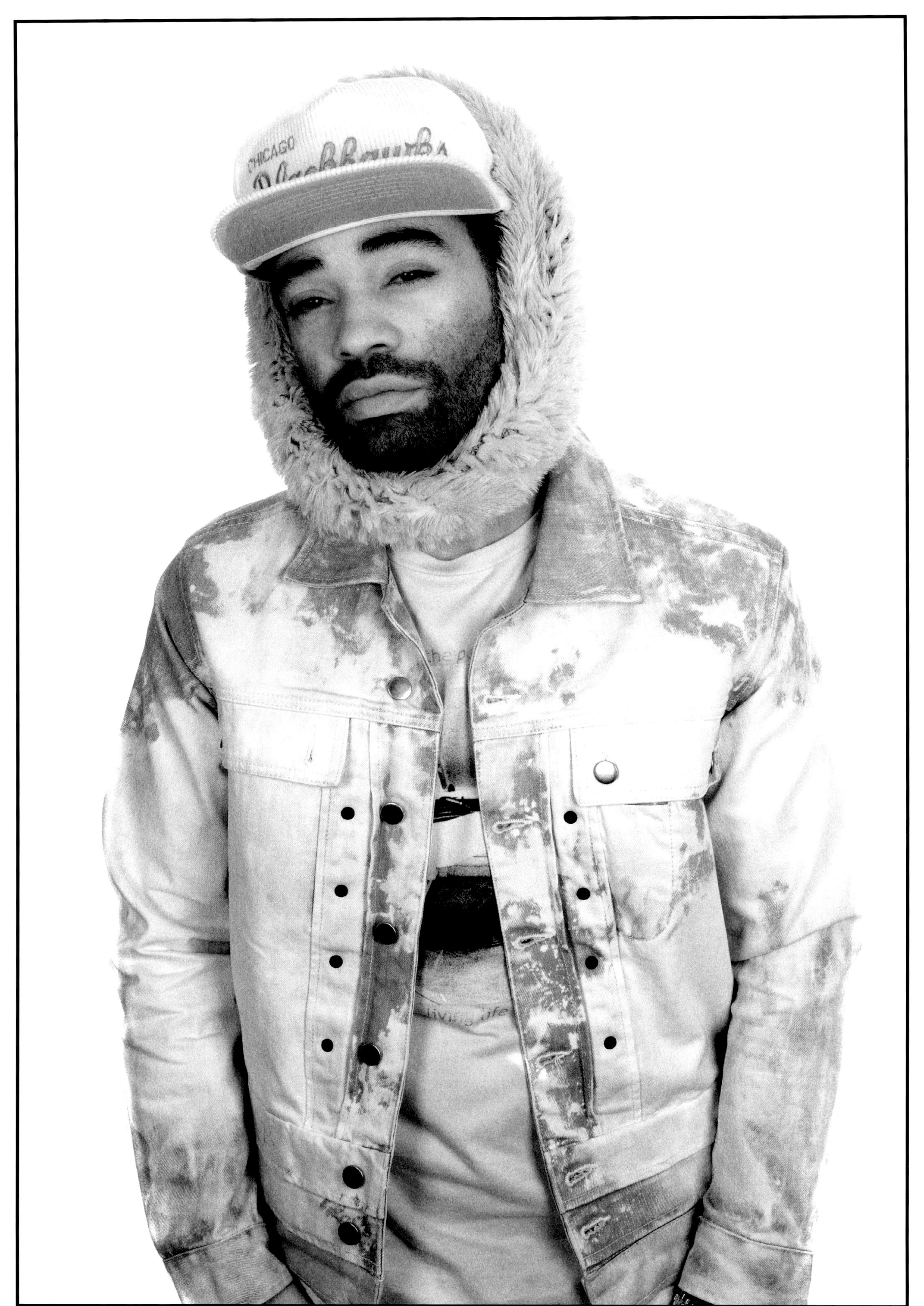
CHICAGO

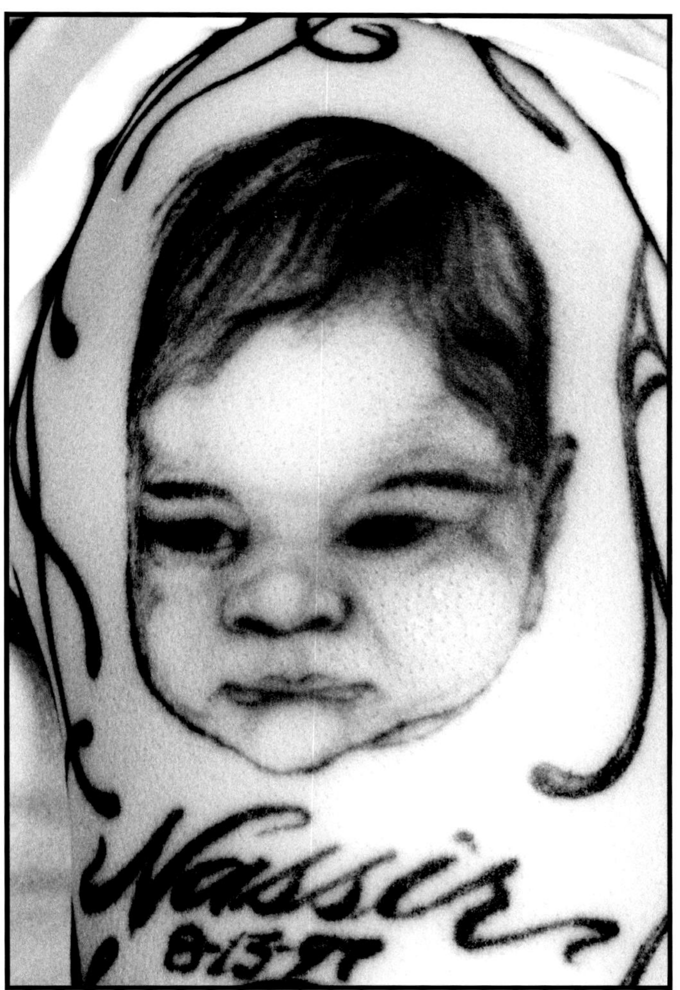

First son, first tattoo, first—period, you know? I got this 13 years ago, dude that works in here [Atlanta's City of Ink] did it. That's about it man, nothing more to it, I just wanted something meaningful if I was gonna get it on me, it's gotta mean something and I had a son, you know. First son, I just wanted a legacy.

–Mr. Bangladesh

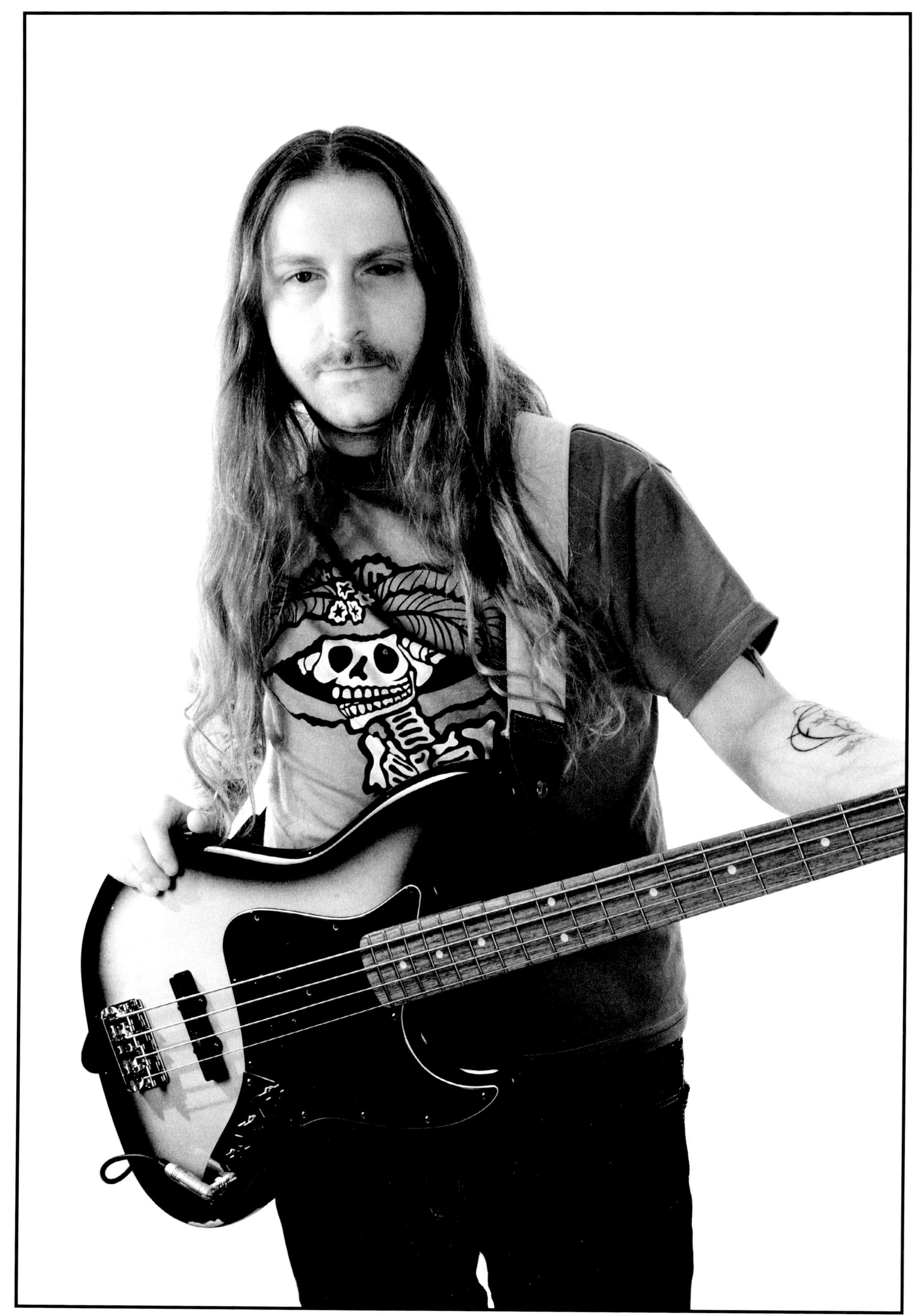

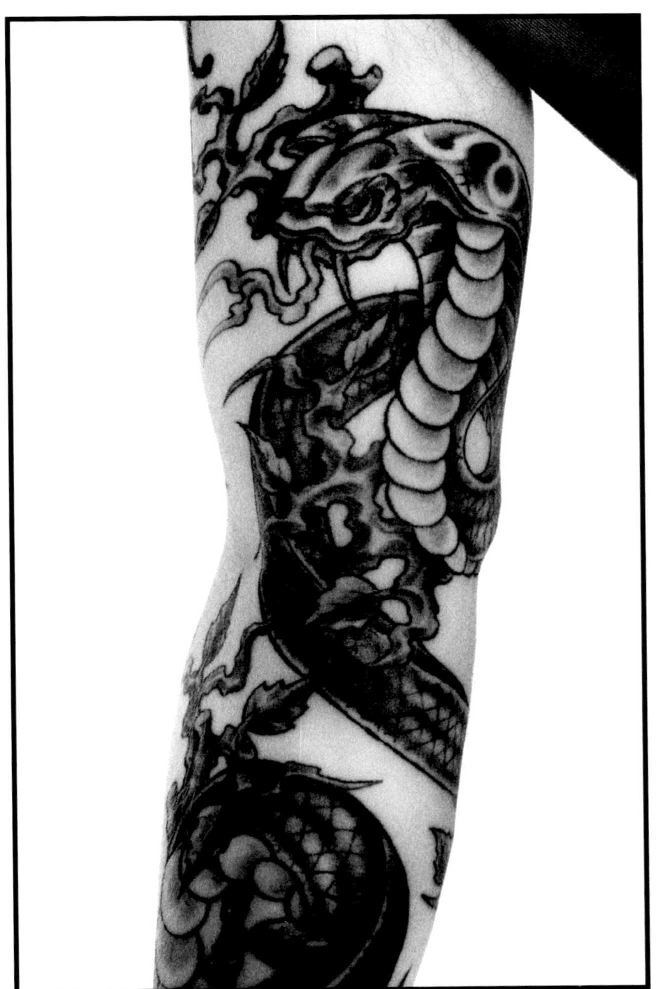

I did the tattoo in 2004. I think it was during the recording of our album Ghost Reveries. I gave the tattooist the idea and he just did it freehand. It felt cool at the time, kind of a change, a symbolic change at that point in my life and it's a cool tattoo.

–Martin Mendez

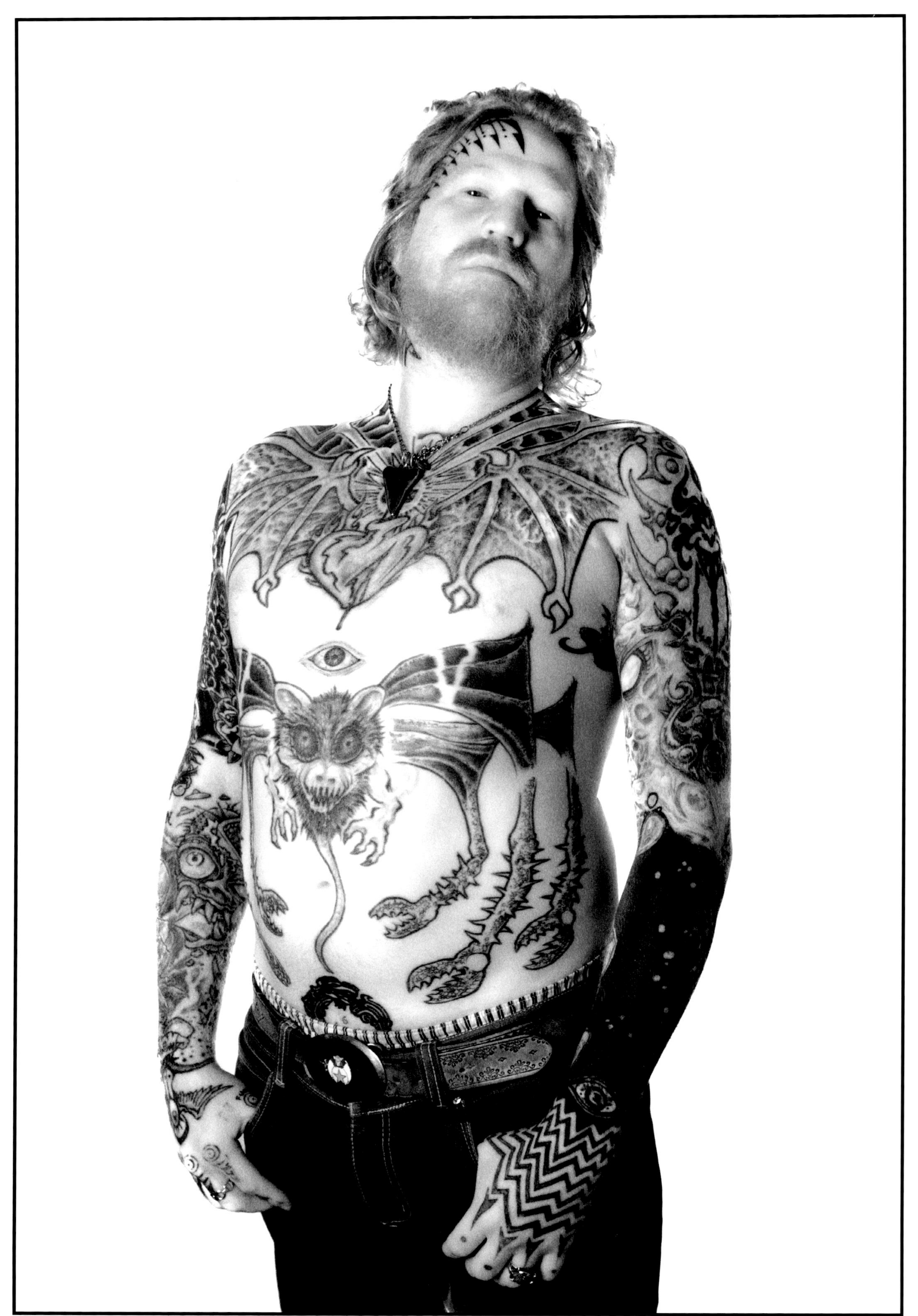

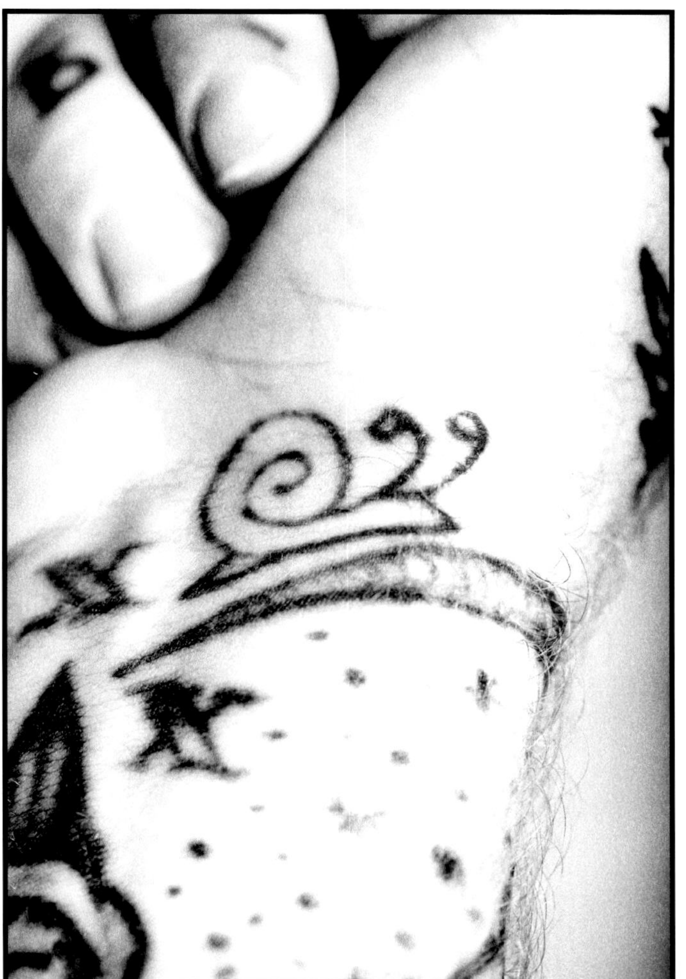

The reason I got this snail tattooed on my wrist on my right hand is because I usually play guitar way too fast and I get ahead of myself. I got the tattoo there so that when I look down and I get excited it teaches me to slow down and have patience and be more methodical with my thoughts and not rush into things. You know…look before you leap!

–Brent Hinds

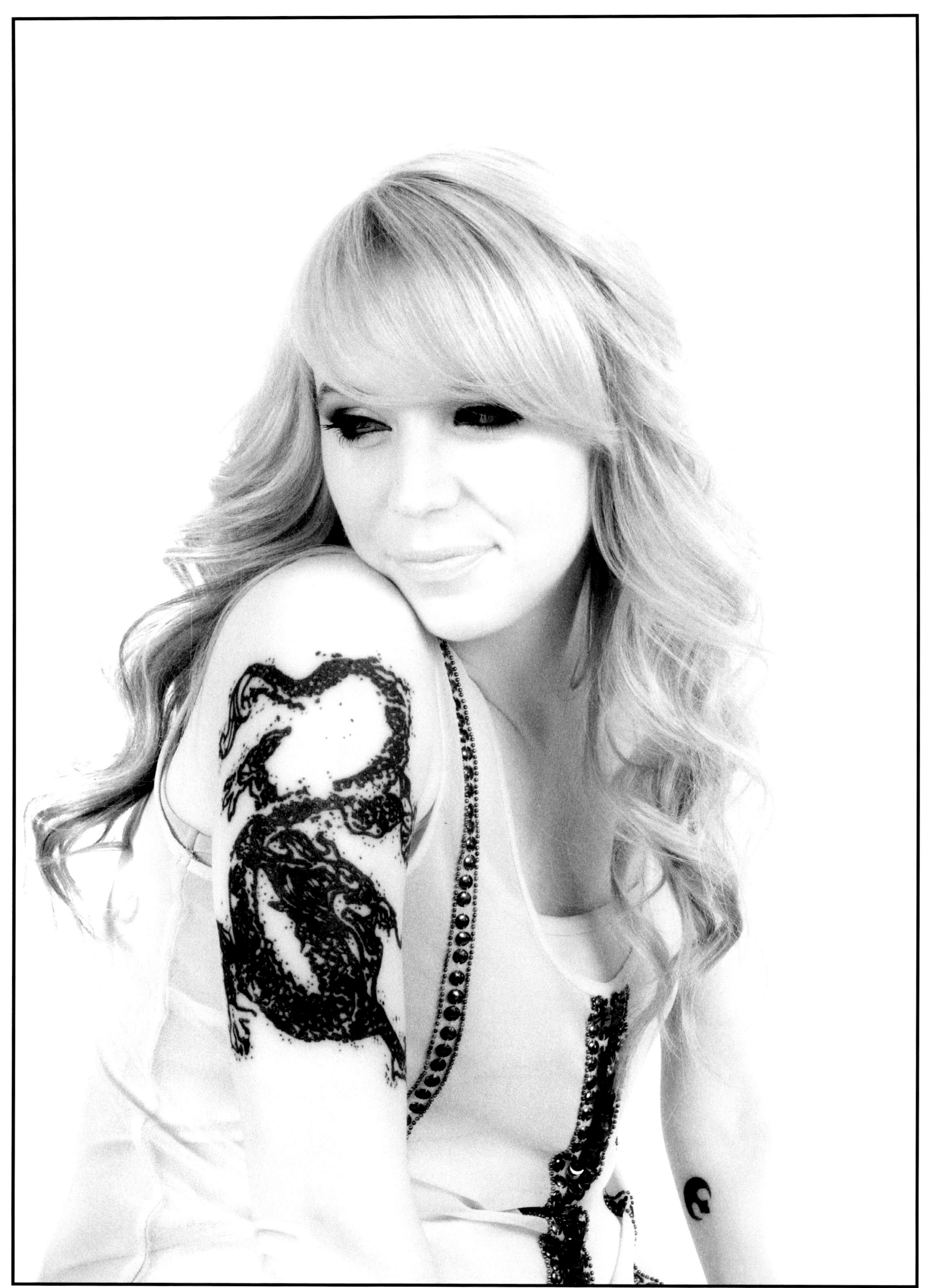

This tattoo was a long time in coming. There was a woman who was designing an album cover and she included this in my first album cover and I loved it because it's not a cartoon; I'm not particularly fond of cartoon-like tattoos. I loved that it was abstract. I was born in the year of the dragon, so I definitely wanted a dragon tattoo. When I came across it, it had all of these little dots in it and I had the tattoo artist copy it perfectly. I was on tour with Pink for a couple of months and we were in Las Vegas. Her husband owns Hart & Huntington Tattoo and we were all getting tattoos until five o'clock in the morning. I knew I wanted to get this one but I didn't have it, so I was going through a book of designs and thought, "Well, I'm here and everyone else is doing it so I'm going to get one." It's fate; the world wanted me to get this one not the one I found in Vegas because the guy who was supposed to tattoo me said, "Alright Suzie, you're next," and just then Pink walked in and said, "I need a tattoo…" and he did her tattoo instead of mine. I was so tired and we had to get up early the next day, so I left and didn't get it done. About half a year later I ended up getting it done in Toronto on Queen Street. Some people love it, but some people really don't like it. When I brought it in even the tattoo parlor where I had it done said they didn't like it, but I said, "I'm doing it!" The girl with the dragon tattoo…!

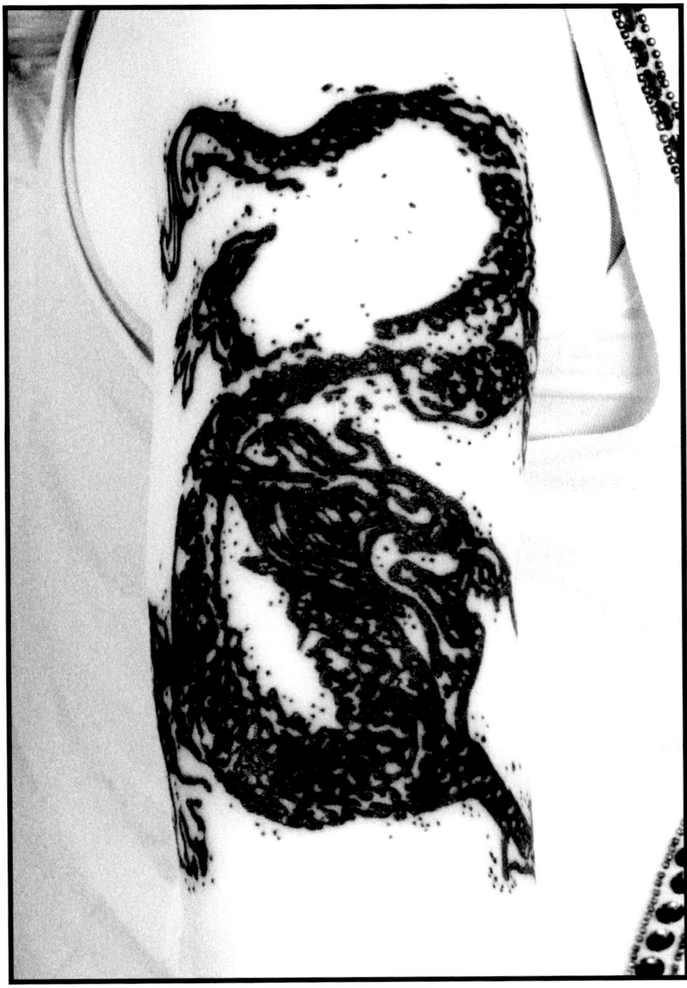

–Suzie McNeil

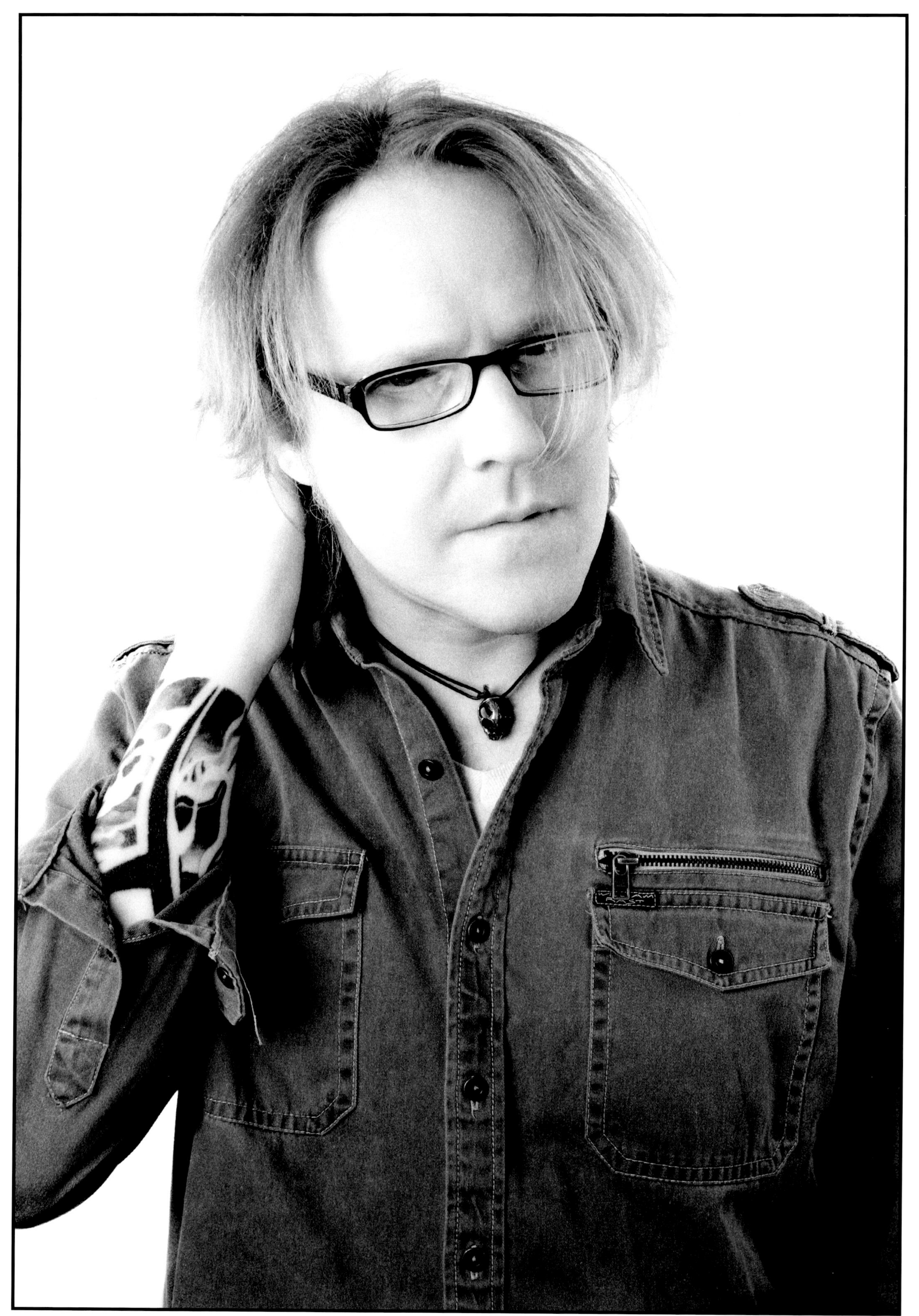

I choose these tattoos to talk about because that was the first big project on my body by my friend Kore Flatmo, a fantastic artist. I met Kore the same time Fear Factory started and he was starting as a tattoo artist. Then he started working at this place in LA at the time called Purple Panther, right across the street from Guitar Center, I think it was near that area, Sunset Blvd. I went to Kore first to get one piece done and it was the Universal Life Church crucifix on my arm that I got from The Cure's 93 album cover. I was looking for a guy to do it, so a friend of mine said, "Oh, you should go to Kore, he's rad." So, I went to Purple Panther, talked to him, looked at my design and he's like, "sure, I'll do it." I sat and talked with him and he's a really cool dude and we became good friends. I just loved his atmosphere, loved his vibe, and so we started working, I started becoming a project for him in some way. He always came up with ideas. He said, "I wanna do this, I wanna add this to your cross like this Rosicrucian kind of cloud on top of it". He did this entire arm and we just expanded, you know. Since I've known him, since '92, maybe '91, he came to me early on and we had been working, and he goes "Man, I got this great idea I want to put on you." It was like a gift he was giving me. So he had these tribals designed and said, "I just pictured them on your forearms" because when I was on stage—he came to an early Fear Factory show—"I can see you on stage just holding the microphone and have these things like you're a warrior going into battle and this is your shield and this is your weapon," so it was like a total gift of a concept and an artistic friendship that we created between us. I consider Kore Flatmo a close friend to this day, even though I rarely see him and I haven't been tattooed by him in a few years. I'm dying to get another one, more work; it was a gift from a close friend.

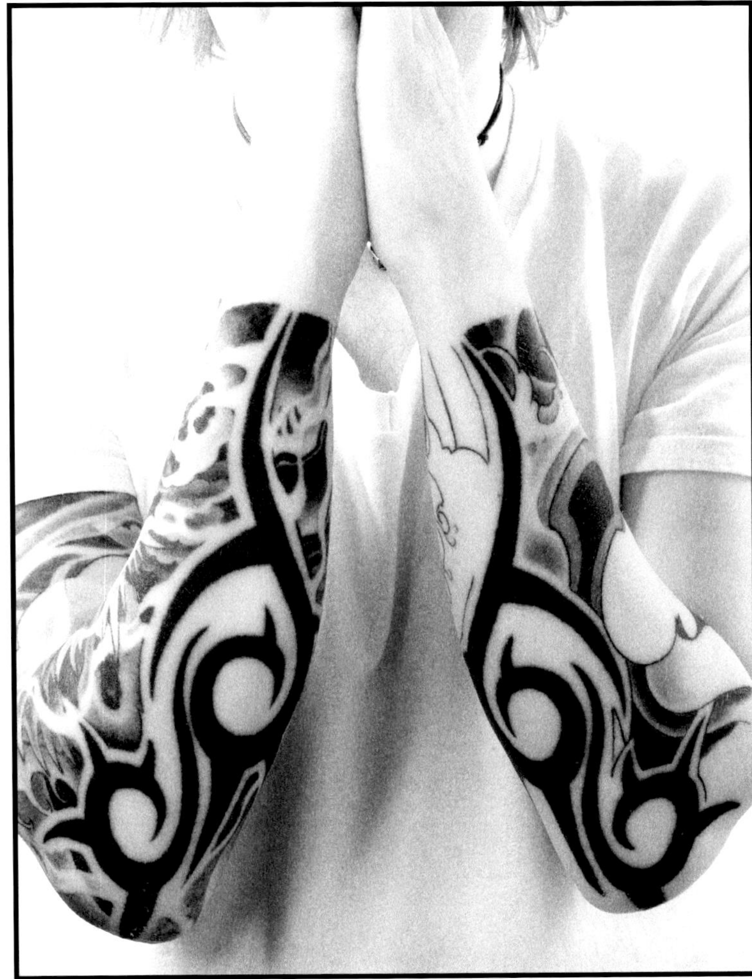

–Burton C. Bell

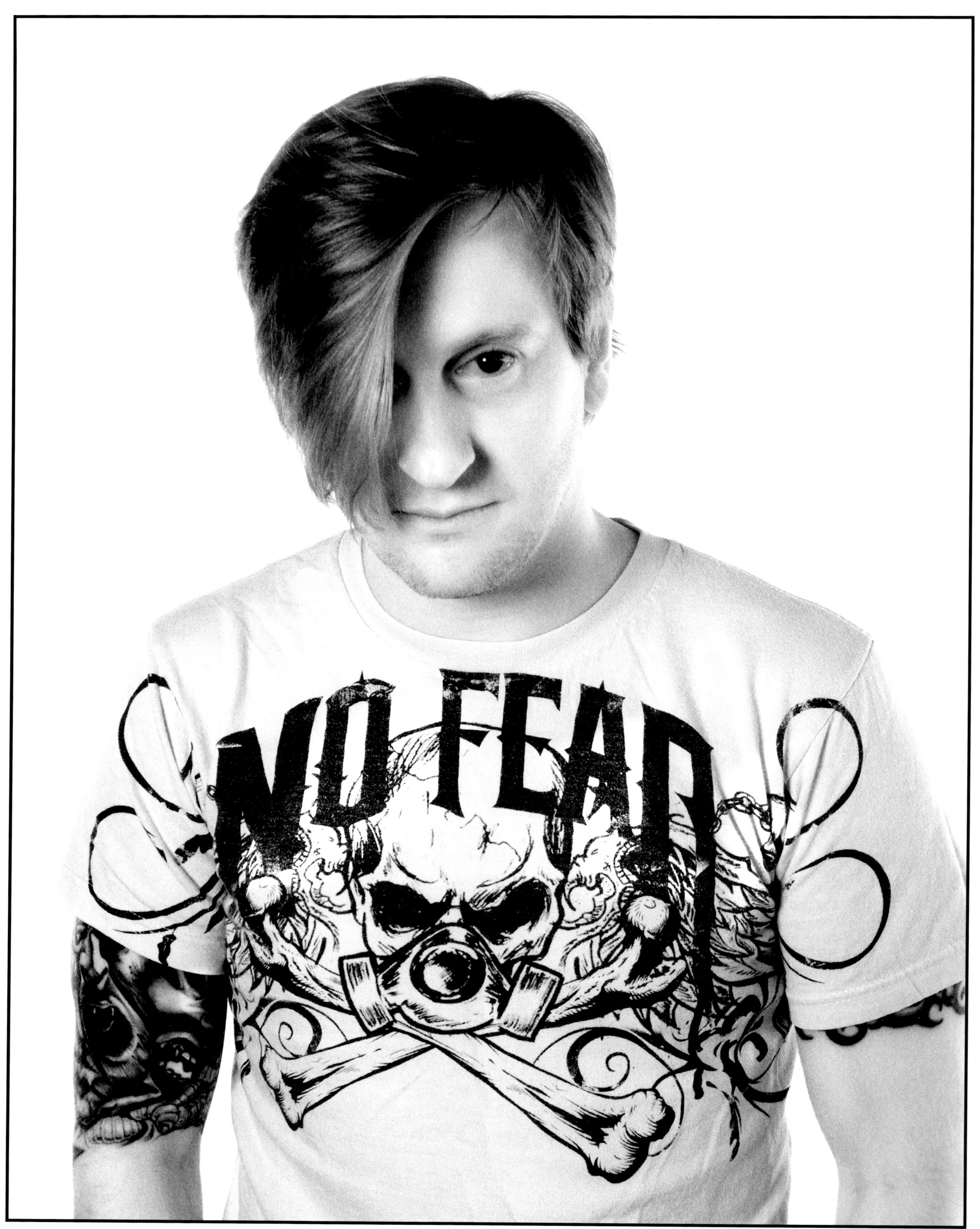
NO FEAR

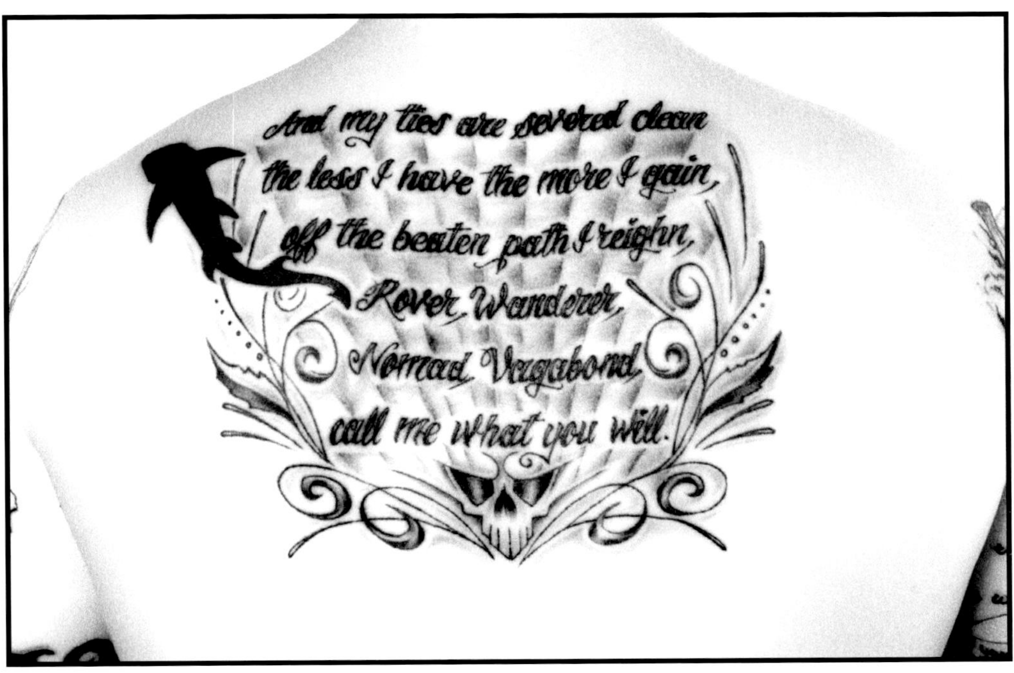

As probably a lot of people know, I'm a massive Metallica fan and it's the Metallica lyrics from the song "Wherever I May Roam" from their *Black* album. I was excited to get this piece because one, I'm a massive Metallica fan and two, I have two children back home, that are young. My wife, you know, a nice girl...I found out when I was away on tour, that she was cheating on me with God knows how many other people, so I got home and it's my, how should I say, my way of cutting my ties with her except for my children.

–Michael "Moose" Thomas

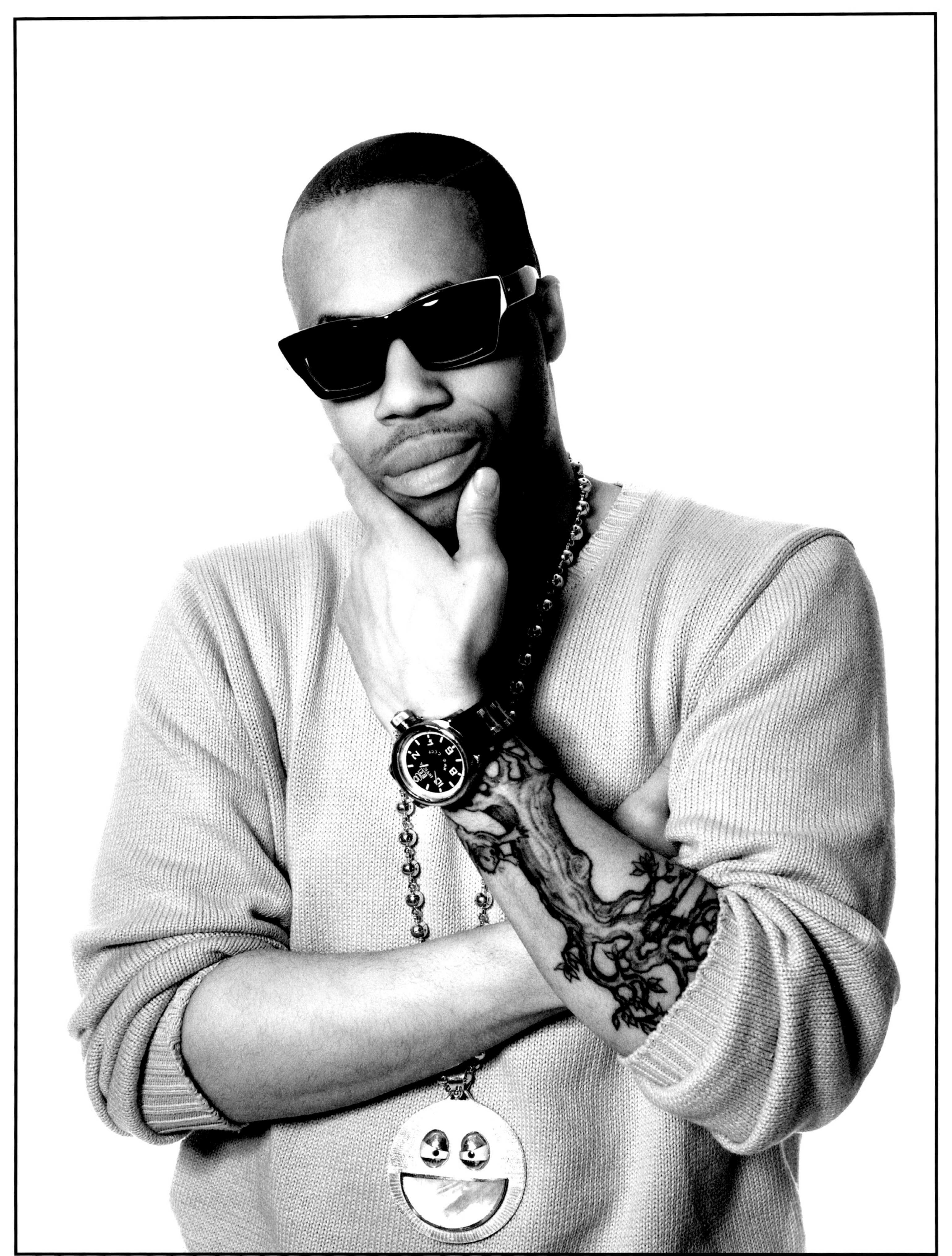

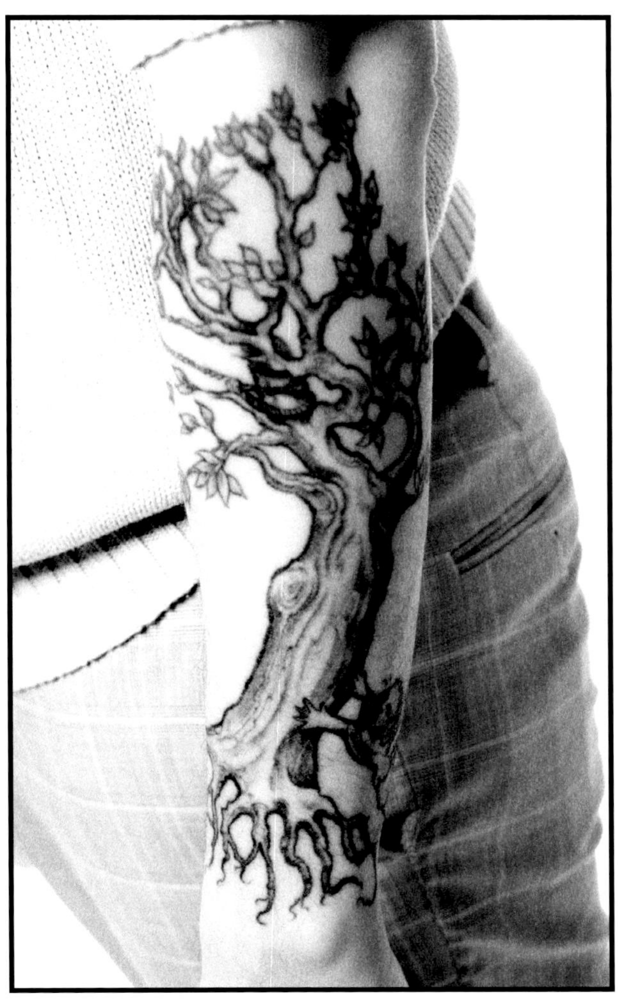

It started off me wanting to get a forearm tattoo, just because I thought a tattoo on the forearm would be kind of dope. I wanted to get something that represented my family: I wanted to get a family tree. So in this family tree, if you look closer to my wrist, the roots actually spell out "family," which is really dope because it's not something that's overt, so you're not just going to look and see "family." If I tell you that it spells out "family," then you'd be like, "oh, that's crazy." So the roots spell out family and the family tree is actually kind of uprooted a little bit so it's not actually all the way in the ground. There's a cherub that's holding it up from the bottom and then there's another cherub, that tied a rope to the tree that's holding it up and that has to do with what I believe in in terms of my family and faith. The family tree is one of the most important things to me, if not *the* most important, but even when the family is uprooted or there's issues or problems, we rely on our faith to hold us up. And never let that tree fall over, that's where the cherubs come into play.

–Kardinal Offishall

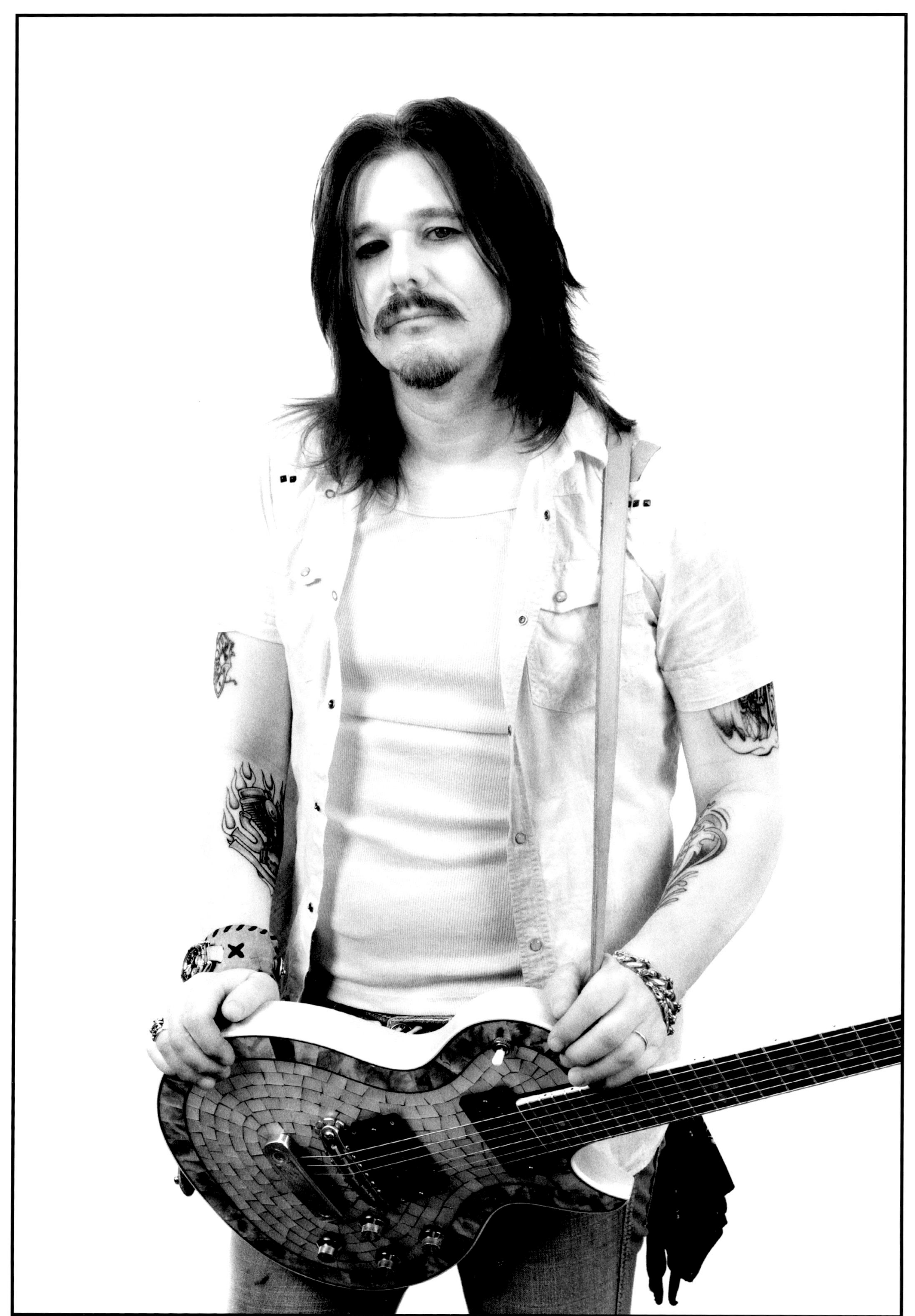

This tattoo is my 1965 Harley Davidson motor. I bought the bike from my friend Del James and my buddy Jack Ferraris built the bike and Jesse James built the motor. I've had it for a long time and I've ridden it all over the country. Last January I was in an accident. Some dumbass made a left hand turn in front of me and knocked me down; I broke both of my legs, one of them very badly with a plate and a rod in there now. In my recovery, one of the things I really wanted to do was rebuild the bike—the frame, front end, wheel, tank, just about everything except the motor, tranny, and back wheel were gone. I had to replace everything and this time I built it all myself. What's important to me about putting this on may arm is, as I said, this bike means a lot to me and it's what I do outside of music. I love to work on bikes, I love to ride bikes; I'm definitely more a rider. It keeps me sane. Those long days of riding when you just like to clear your mind, or you are deep in thought. Having this is more than a hobby to me and I immortalized it on my arm. My good buddy Mariano from Buenos Aries did it for me. Argentina is one of my favorite places in the world and the last time we were down there, even though I had a show every day, we inked up the arm. All of us musicians do that; put a little ink on and then have to play a couple of shows. It's all part of it. So there you go…me and my 1965 Harley Davidson.

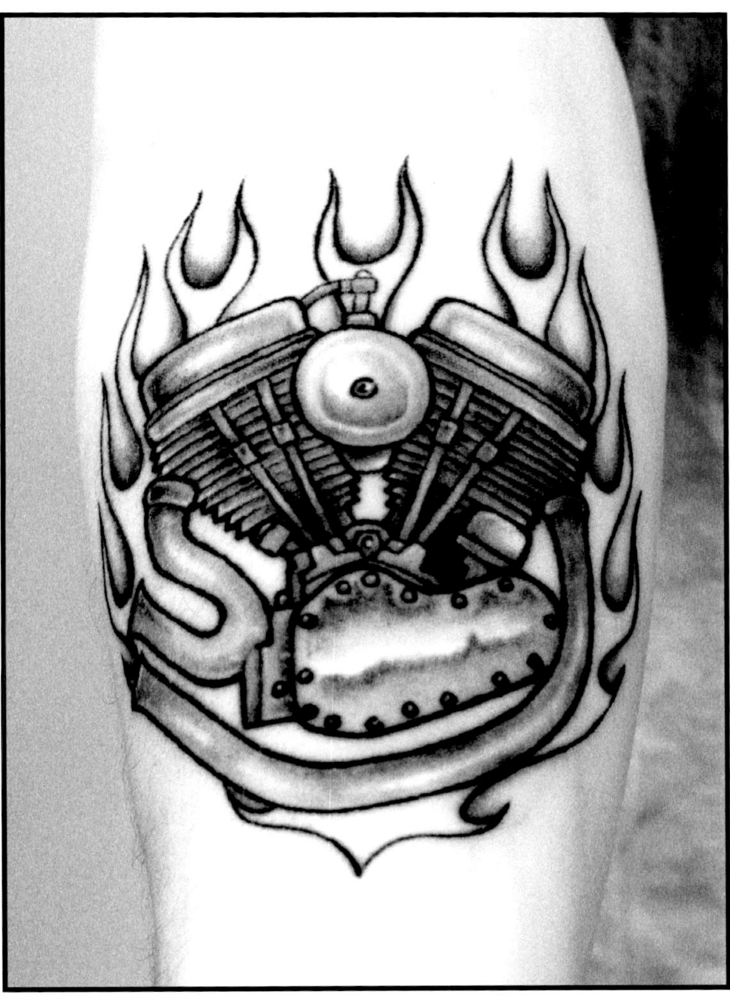

–Gilby Clarke

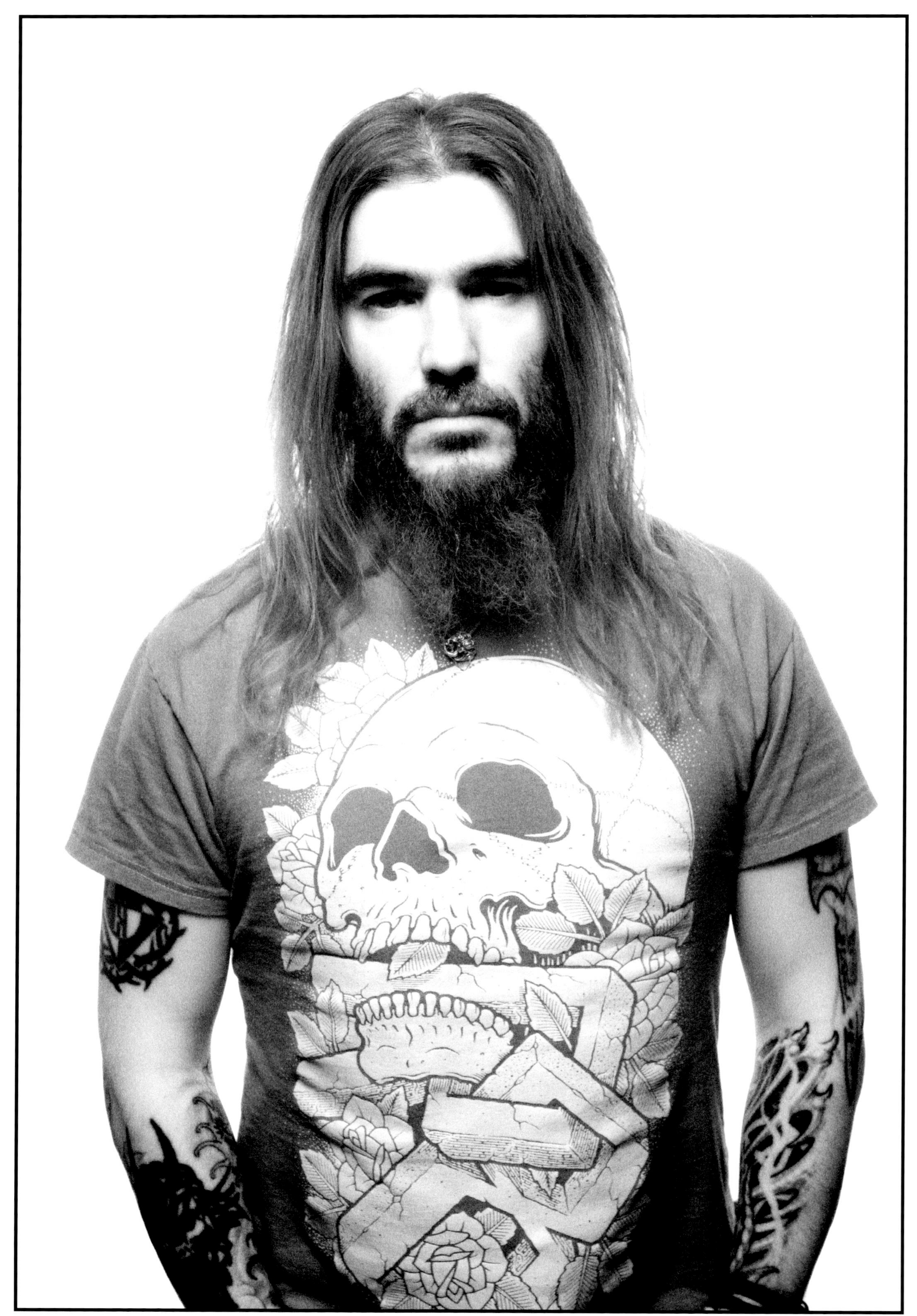

So, my cluster of horrible tattoos. Really bad tattoos. My first tattoo, originally people used to make fun of me, saying it was the Overkill logo. Now that Overkill isn't around anymore, it looks like the Avenged Sevenfold logo. My girlfriend at the time bought it for me. It's flash off the wall, it's a skull with some wings and some crossbones underneath it. I've had a lot of people who were on crank tattoo me and they were very affordable, which is the reason that I did it, but they've made some really bad tattoos along the way. To me, there's kind of a charm about keeping bad tattoos. I know it's very popular to cover up a tattoo but I think in some ways there's a coolness about keeping, it's kind of a reminder, about how you do stupid shit, you make mistakes. So this kind of looked like a Machine Head symbol, I think maybe on the first day, but it has since turned into a black splotch that is just a black scar really. At some point, I was with another cranked out guy on the road and I said, "Hey, I want to get a sword right here and the sword is going to go down." So he sat down and he tattooed me for however long he tattooed me and at the end, I sat there, I look at it and kind of bent my arm and I was like, "Oh man, a bendable sword! Fuck!" So, another bad tattoo. I've somehow tied it all together with a good tattoo. I got my wife's name in a classic sailor ribbon and that kind of makes the whole thing tie together, but yes, this is my cluster of really bad tattoos. I'm not going to get them covered up because I'm proud of them and I like to sit there and suffer once in a while. Yeah, you can do stupid shit.

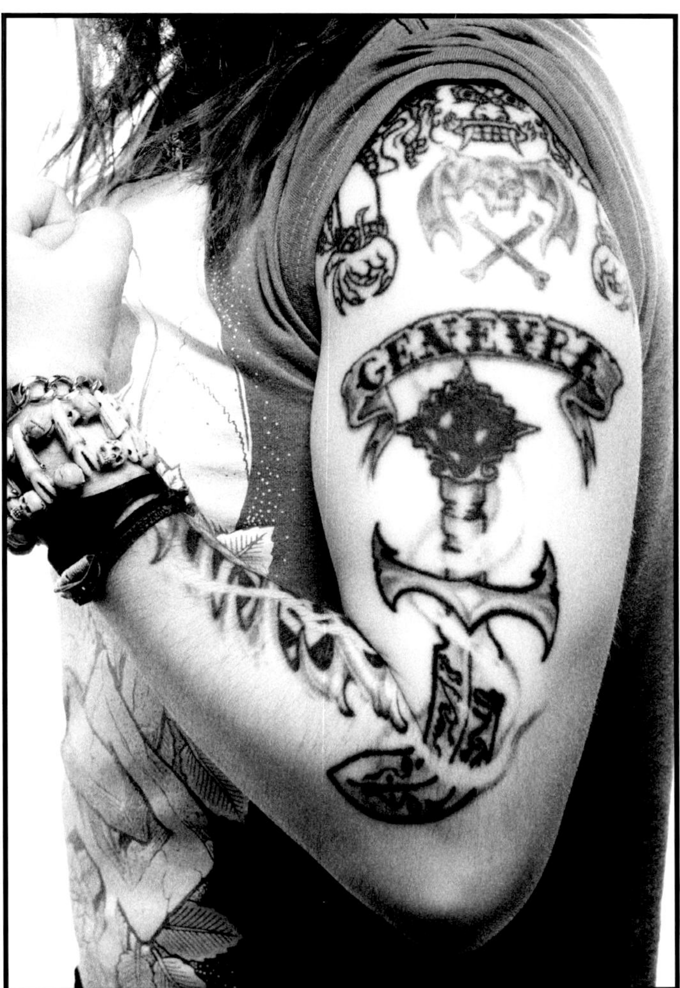

–Robb Flynn

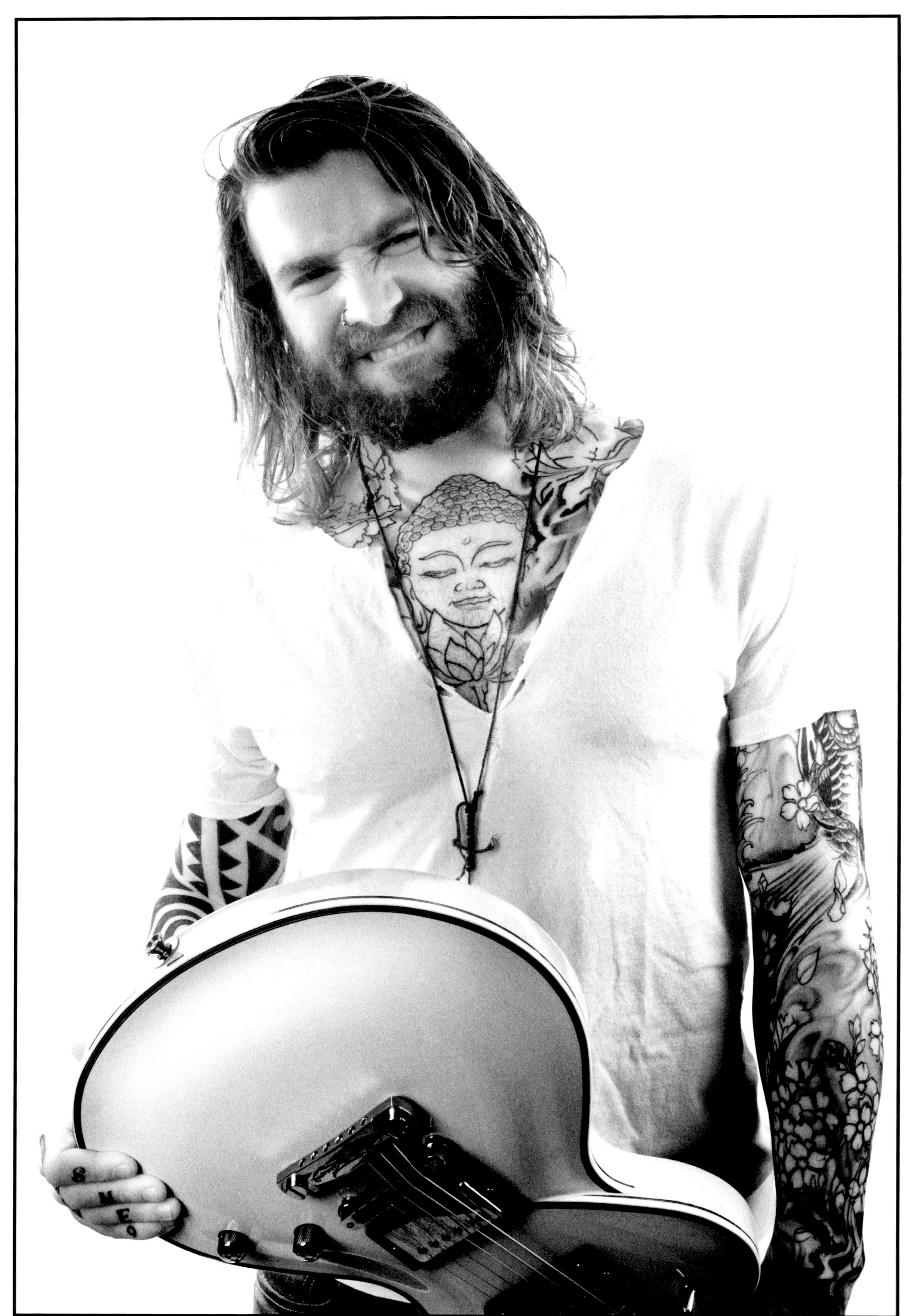

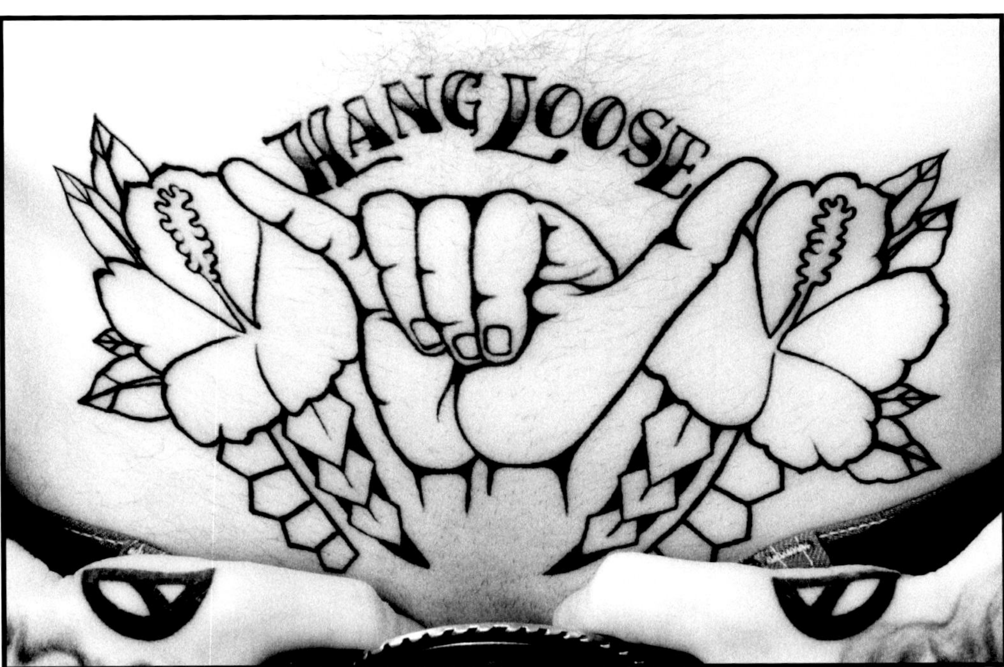

We were in Costa Rica with a bunch of buddies and we were surfing the whole trip. We came back and we all decided to get a big group tattoo, that "hang loose" symbol and I thought it would be a good idea to get it right above my dick because it's got double meaning and it's hilarious. So I went and got it done and I came back and nobody else got it done, so I'm the only one with the hang loose tattoo.

–Dan Steinke

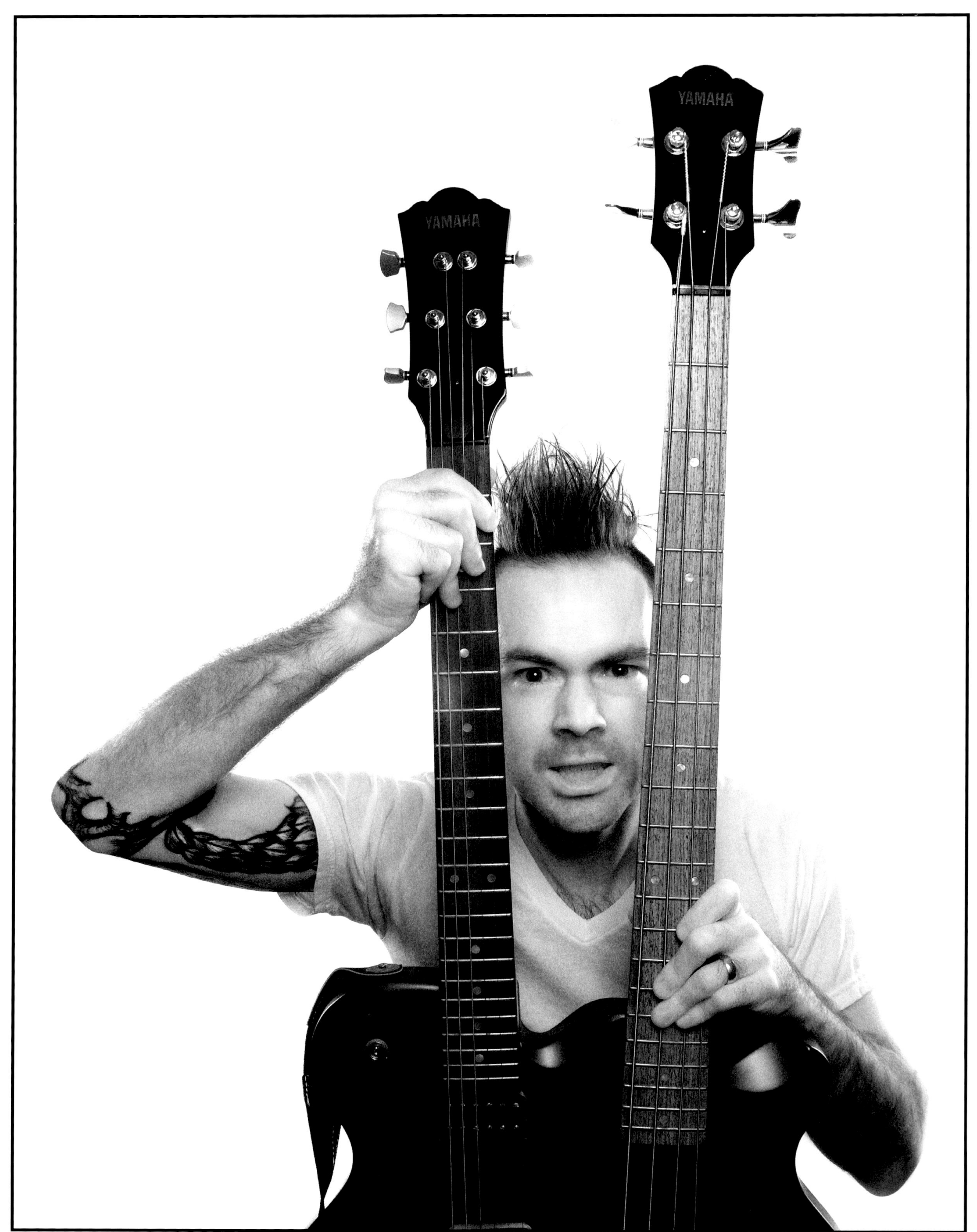
YAMAHA
YAMAHA

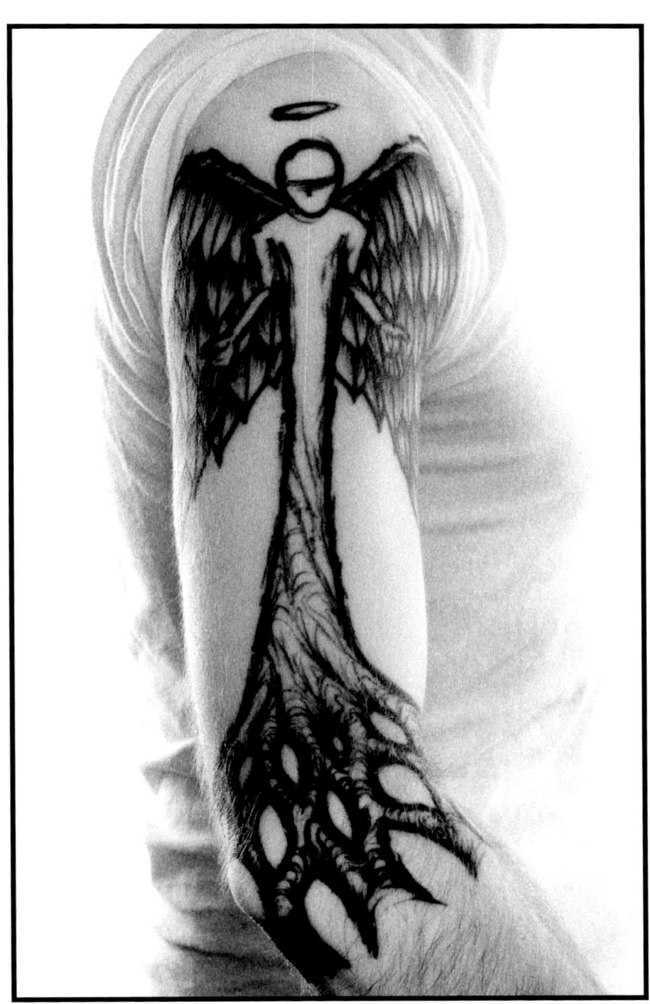

I really only have one tattoo story, because I only have one tattoo. I don't remember how many years ago, but I flew out to Vancouver for an artist named Steve Moore to do the work and because there was a limited amount of time on my trip, we did it all in one 5½-hour sitting. I want to say that I was cool and I was a tough guy, but I was in excruciating pain. He started at the bottom, so there was no turning back. The intention behind it? You can see it's the angel on the shoulder. It's pretty much as simple as that age old idea of just having a good conscience, as a reminder to do the right thing. It seemed like being on tour and being out there on the road, there is definitely enough little devils on your shoulder and all around you and even on your skin, but just around you in general. So when deciding to get something, I was like, really the only thing I needed, was a reminder to make good choices, because there's plenty of reminders to make bad ones out there on the road. The intention was that this good conscience would be rooted and grafted to my forearm and my being and if, on occasion, it decides to take the high road, then it eventually is going to pull me up with it and if I decide to take the...ah... darker path, then I'm going to pull it down with me.

–James Black

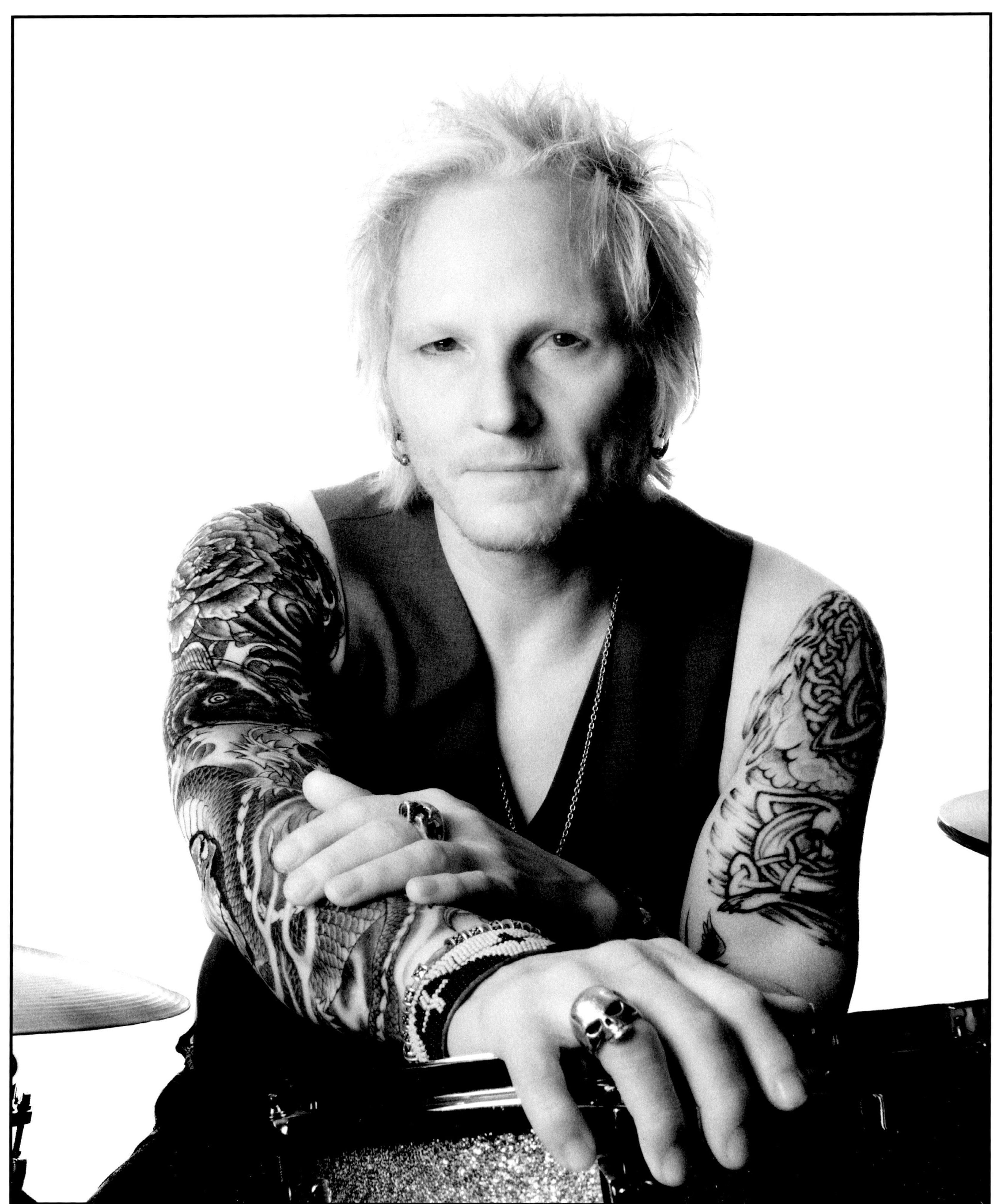

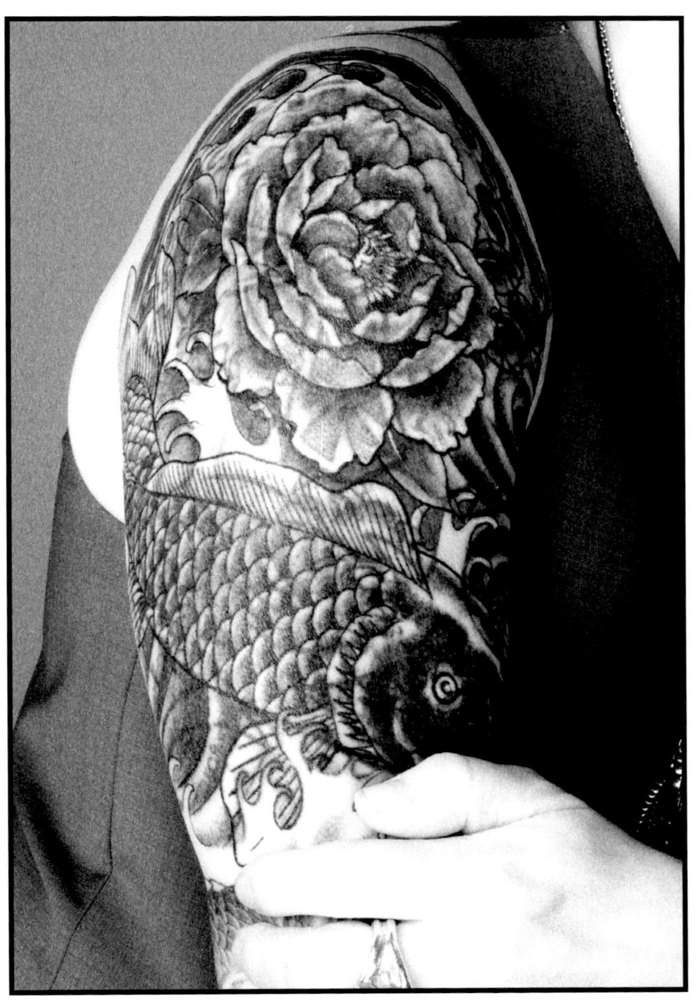

I didn't have any tattoos when I joined Guns N' Roses. I had none, and the band basically said, go to the tattoo shop and get a couple of tattoos immediately. I went down to Kevin Quinn's shop and my first tattoo was some Celtic knot work. I'm half Norwegian, so I thought, "Oh, I'll go Norwegian," so I got the Celtic stuff and then after that, Kevin Quinn came on the road with Guns N' Roses and did some stuff over on this arm, which I just had covered up by Mark Mahoney. This is a project that I was waiting to reveal at this photo shoot. It's fairly new. I just finished it about a month ago and I'm very happy with it. The big piece is a dragon. I actually, went into the shop to get a small dragon, just on my forearm and this is what I came out with. Mark just started to draw this free hand and then said, "Hey, we need to cover this up, too" so he, we went all Japanese, which really isn't his style, he's most famous for black and grey, but I was with him and I like him and he's a friend, so we did the momo flower, koi fish, the Japanese dragon, and then we added this Japanese skull on my elbow. He had this sticker that we put on there and I was like, "Wow, go for it." So that's really the story of this arm. I went in for a little dragon and Mark said, "No, you can't do a little dragon, it just wouldn't be right".

–Matt Sorum

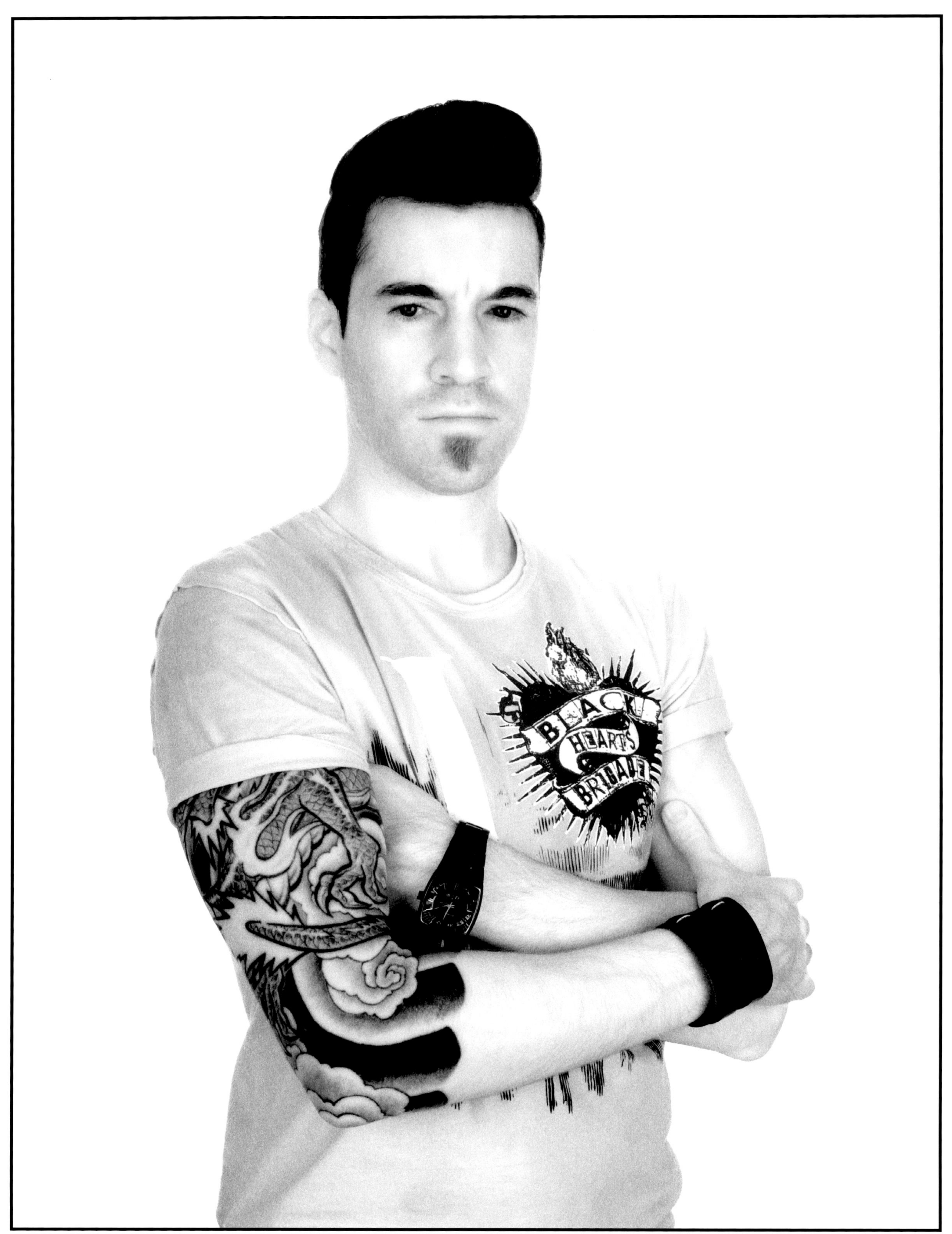
BLACK
HEARTS

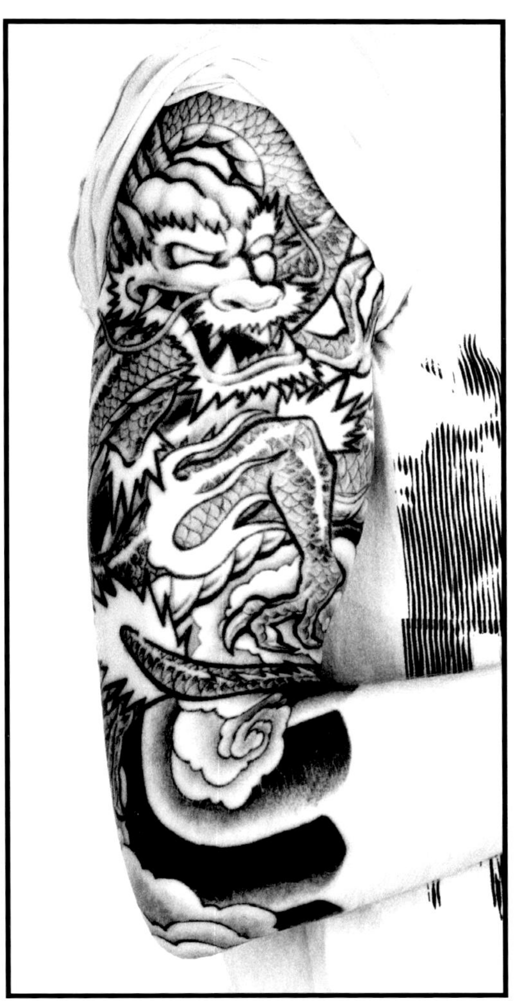

I got my right sleeve around 2000, I think just before Theory of a Deadman was signed. It was my second tattoo and it took 20 hours to do. I got it done by Donavan at Lady Luck Tattoos in Langley, British Columbia, about 20 minutes outside of Vancouver. I've since gone back and gotten two more from Donavan. I had always wanted a dragon and loved that style of artwork. After one of the sittings, which was 4 or 5 hours long, I went directly to a friend's rock show at The Commodore downtown. After a couple of drinks I started to feel totally fucked up—I must have had low blood sugar or something. Security grabbed me and said, "You gotta go. You're wasted," and I had to leave the club. It had a huge flight of stairs and when I got to the top I blacked out and fell all the way down smashed my head at the bottom and got a concussion. The security dragged me out thinking I was wasted but I wasn't and pleaded with them to let me back in so I could get my friend and go home. I had a headache for two weeks. Some tattoos hurt a little, some hurt a lot I guess.

–Tyler Connolly

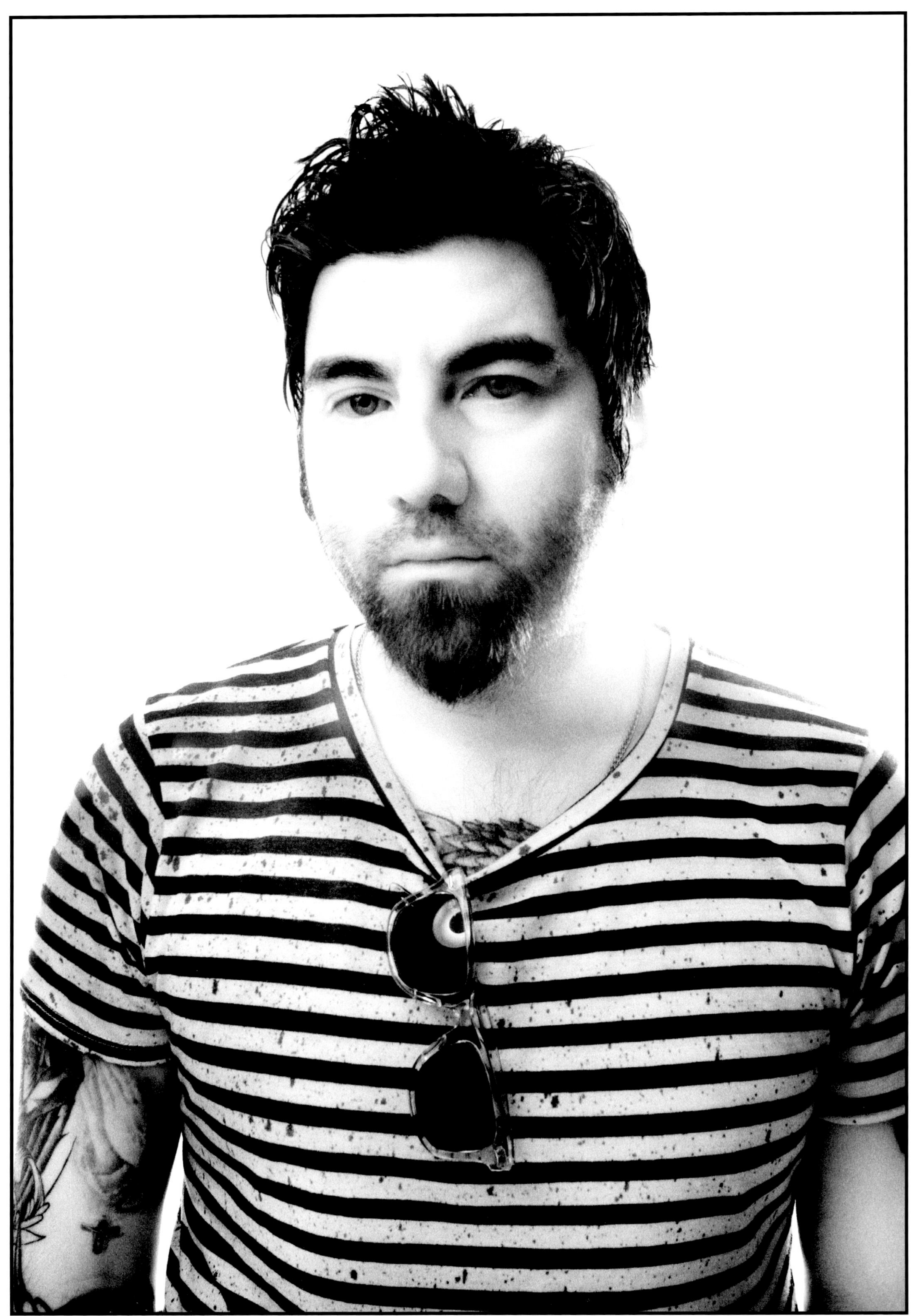

I'm not a fan of hardly any of my tattoos. I've always just gotten tattoos on a whim and it started as soon as I turned 18, when I was able to get tattooed. I just started getting them and not thinking too much about them. This tattoo actually is something I've wanted for a while, it's a Baphomet. I'm really into a lot of religious art, be it Catholicism or Satanism or anything. Stuff like that is usually always attractive to me art-wise, so now I think as I move forward, any tattoos will stick with that theme. This one I got in Brussels, probably about 1½ years ago. This is the last tattoo I've gotten and it's kind of funny because it's right next to my praying hands, which is one of my first tattoos which is really faded. There's no deep meaning behind it other than I just really like the artistic look of religious art or anything similar to that. A cool thing about this is I thought about getting a Baphomet, and I was in Brussels at the airport. I was picking up my wife, she was flying in to meet me, and this guy recognized me and started talking with me. He's a tattoo artist and on a whim, he said, "Hey, I'm coming to the show tomorrow. Do you want any tattoos?" I've seen a lot of his art and he's a really good artist, so I told him I want a Baphomet. So the next day he showed up at the show. He had drawn it out and it was awesome. I mean it was pretty much the same as you see here. He elaborated a little bit and it's not a typical Baphomet, but it's his own art and so I really dig the fact that it's original. He came to the show and did most of it before the show. I bandaged it up, sang the show, got off stage and he finished it up, the shading and stuff. This the last one I got and it's one of my favorites.

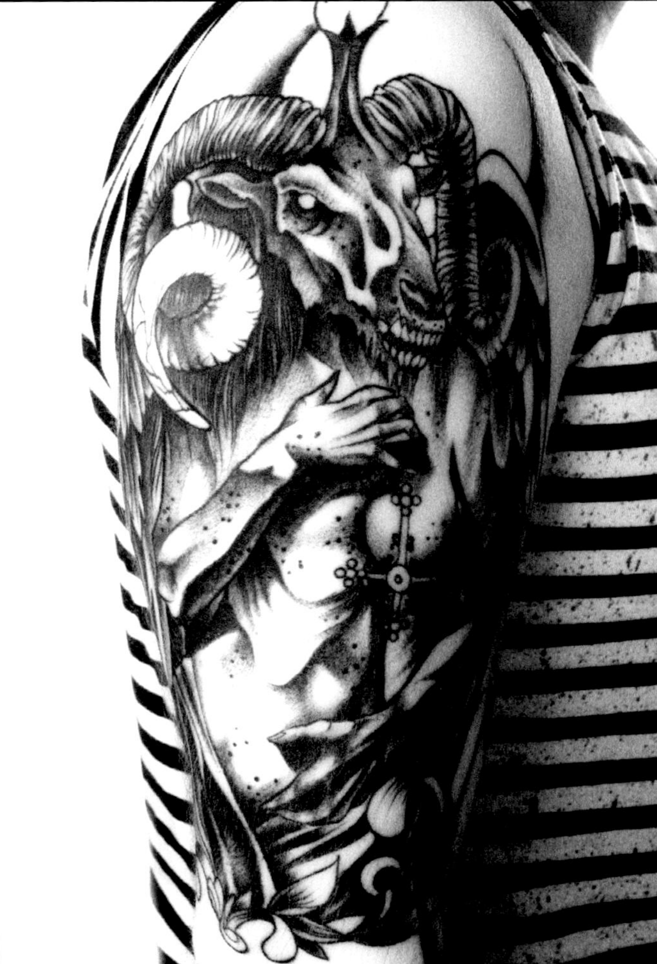

–Chino Moreno

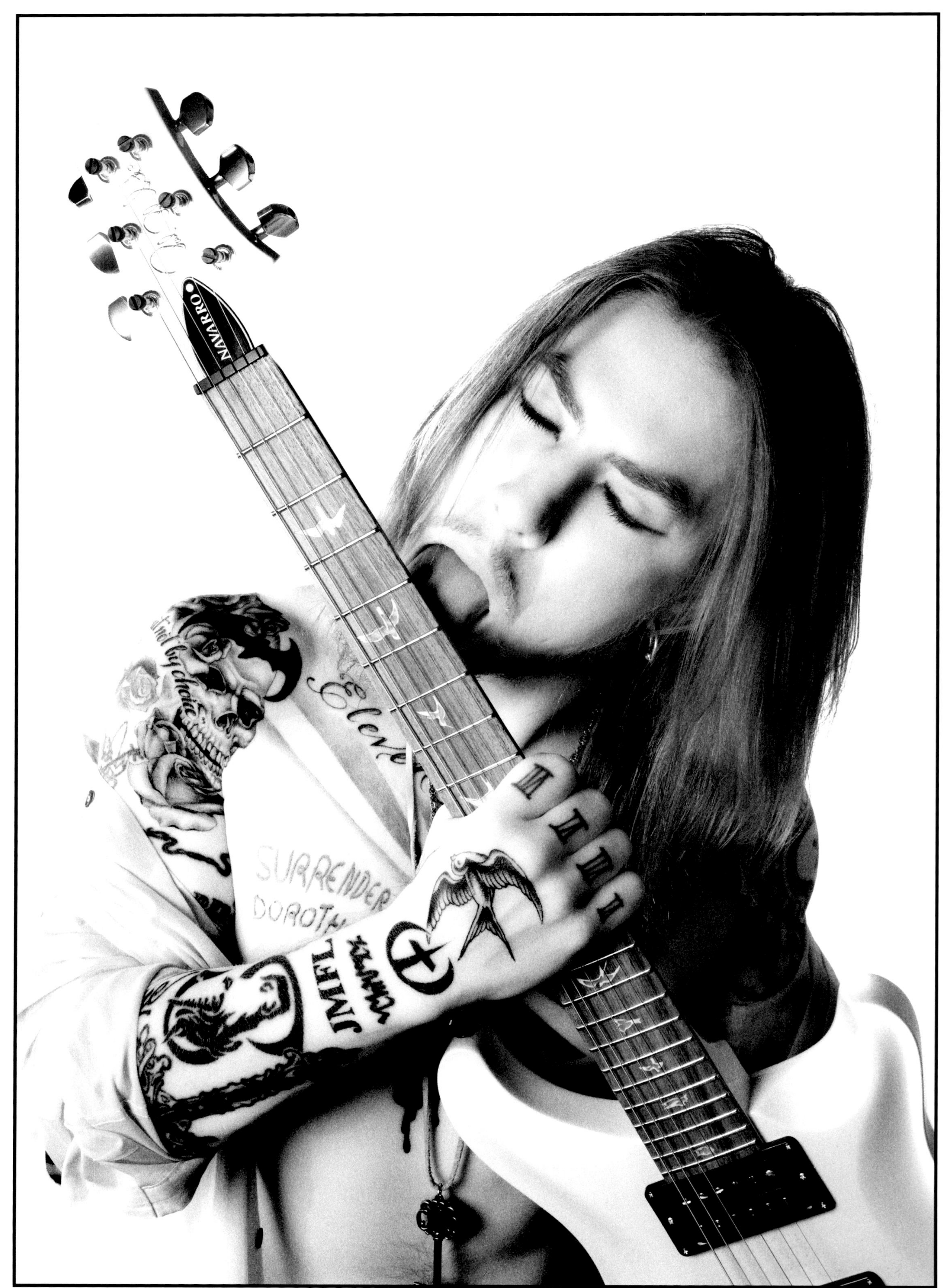
NAVARRO
SURRENDER
JMFL

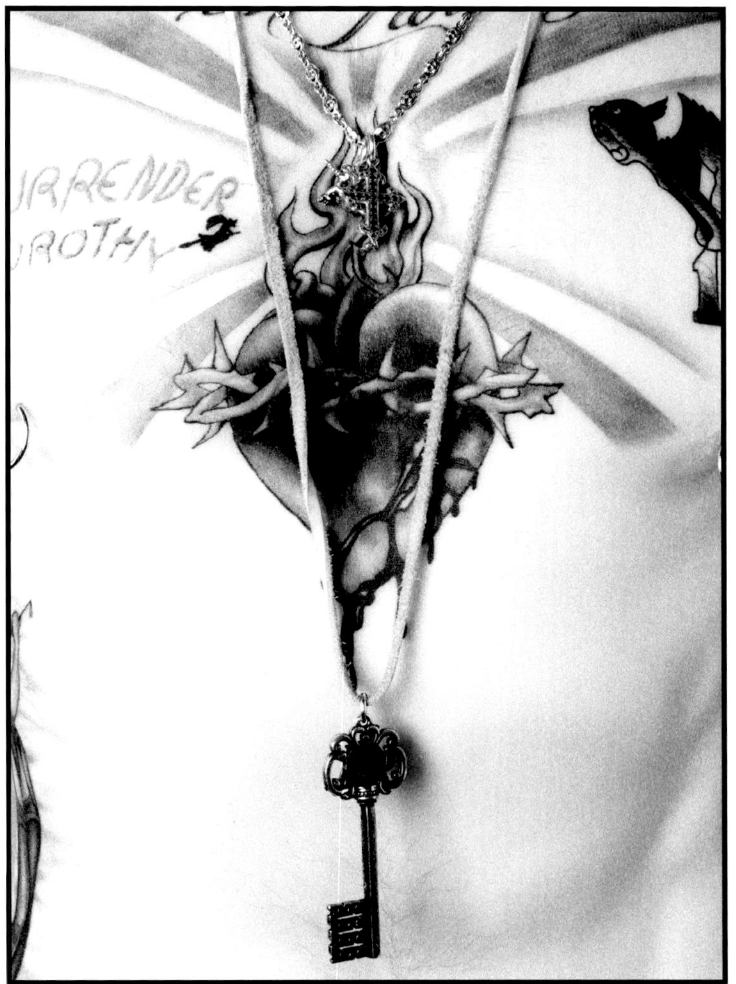

This is a sacred heart done by Freddy Negretty, one of the pioneers of the black and grey style. He works out of Shamrock Social Club in Hollywood, California, on the Sunset Strip, and this particular sacred heart is a cover up. I'm not one for cover ups generally speaking, but I initially had my ex-wife's initials on my chest and I would've kept them because it was a time in my life, except that the initials were done poorly on a lazy heroin-filled night back in the day, I think probably by a heroin-filled artist as well, so I wanted to kill two birds with one stone, get the cover up done and get a better piece of work done. I went and saw Freddy and we came up with the sacred heart design, which is something I've always wanted, and he really brought out a three dimensional vibe to it, which was certainly something I was lacking in that area, so I'm super happy with it.

–Dave Navarro

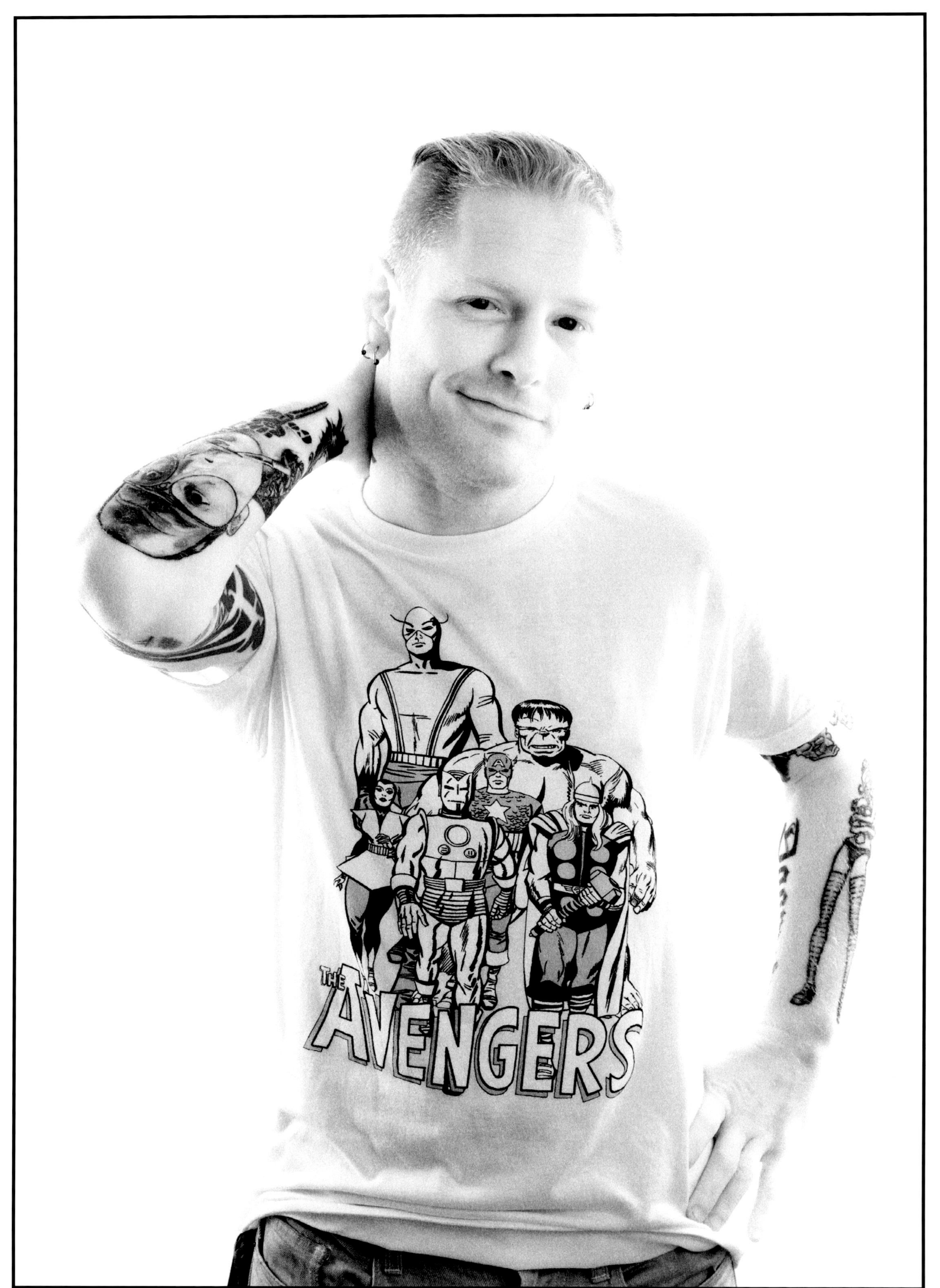
THE
AVENGERS

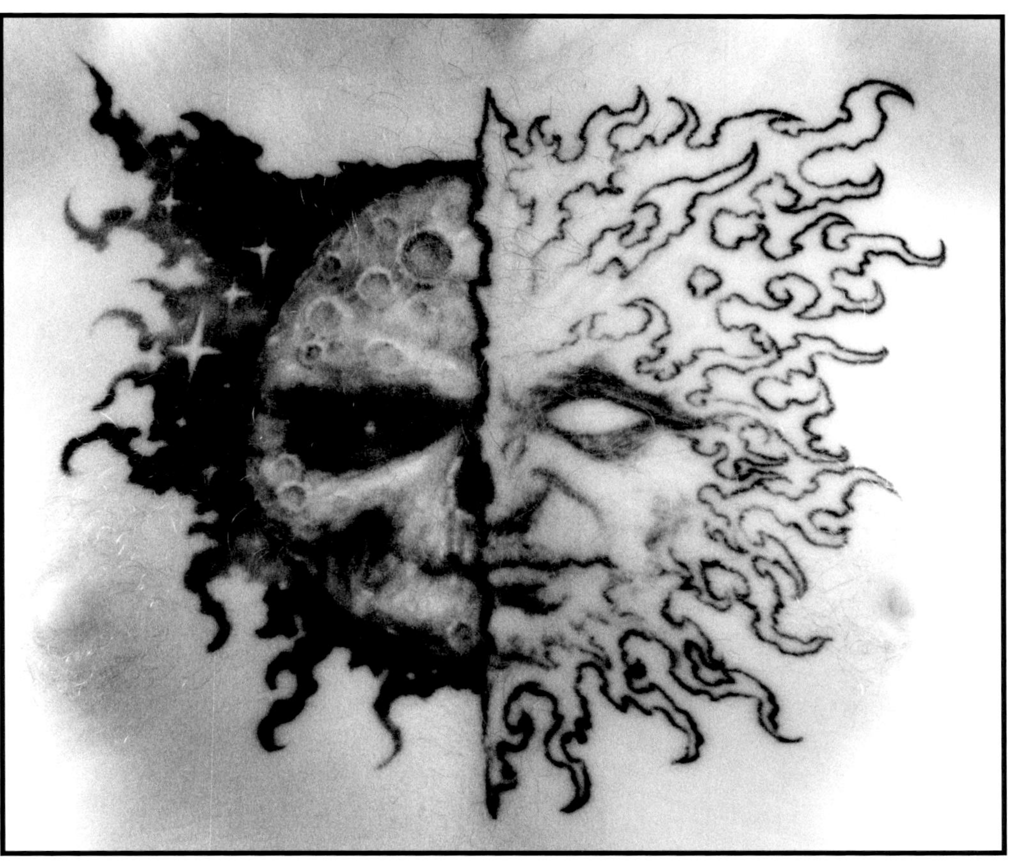

I'd have to say the piece that means the most to me, or is the most important is probably the one I've got on my chest— the Paul Booth piece. It's not that it's anything dramatic or anything like that but it's kind of the key to all of my pieces. Everything that I try to get is all about balance. It's about Yin and Yang, it's about the duality of everything; how there's light and there's dark in all of us and that to me represents everything that I'm trying to do, not only in music, but also in my life; the way I am towards other people, my family, my friends, the band. It's just about finding that perfect balance. Sometimes it's a little on one side and sometimes it's a little on the other, but one thing I've realized is you can't have the light without the dark. You can't have the madness without the sanity. It's taken a while to see that there's a certain grasp that you have to have on it, but it's definitely made me a better person. It's made me figure out that if I go too far one way, I'm not who I want to be. If my tattoos were a map, this would be the legend and that's really what it's all about. It's not the first one I got, but I think it's the one that tells the story the most right out of the gate, and it's working out pretty good so far.

–Corey Taylor

BIOS

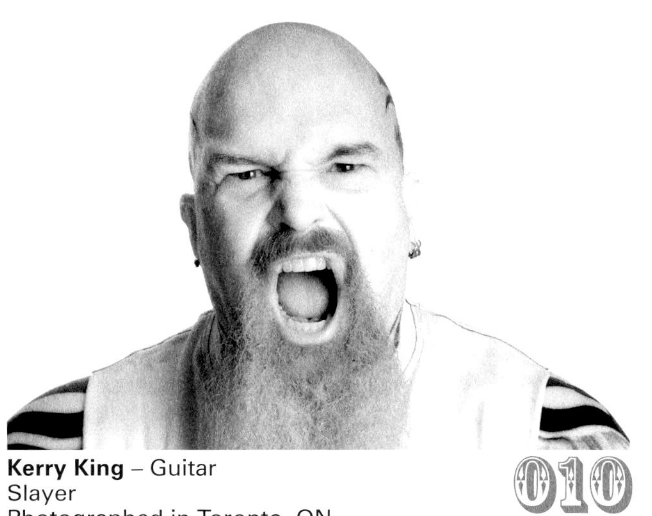

Kerry King – Guitar
Slayer
Photographed in Toronto, ON
July 29, 2010

010

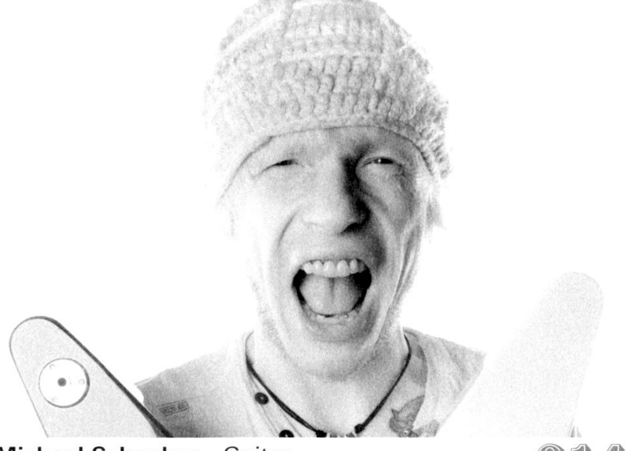

Michael Schenker – Guitar
Michael Schenker Group, Scorpions
Photographed in Toronto, ON
March 4, 2012

014

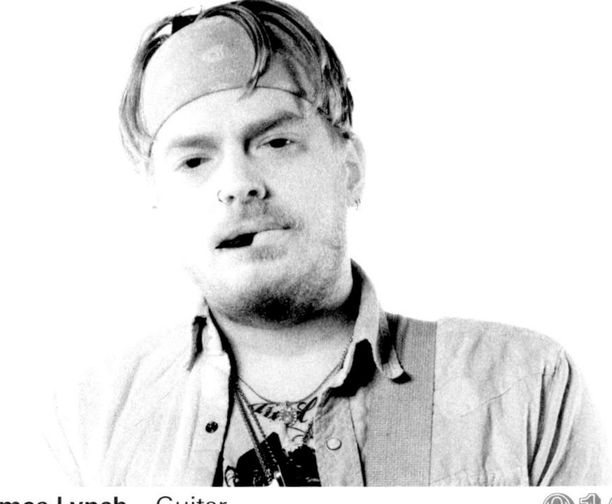

James Lynch – Guitar
Dropkick Murphys
Photographed in Toronto, ON
February 22, 2012

018

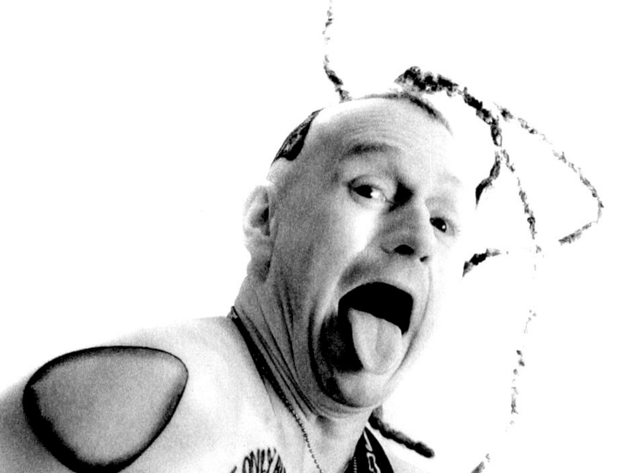

Rev Jones – Bass
Mountain, Michael Schenker Group, Steelheart
Photographed in Anaheim, CA
January 18, 2010

012

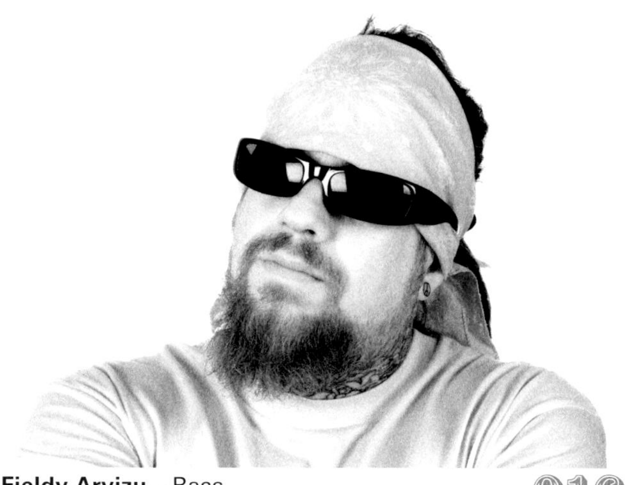

Fieldy Arvizu – Bass
Korn
Photographed in Toronto, ON
March 31, 2011

016

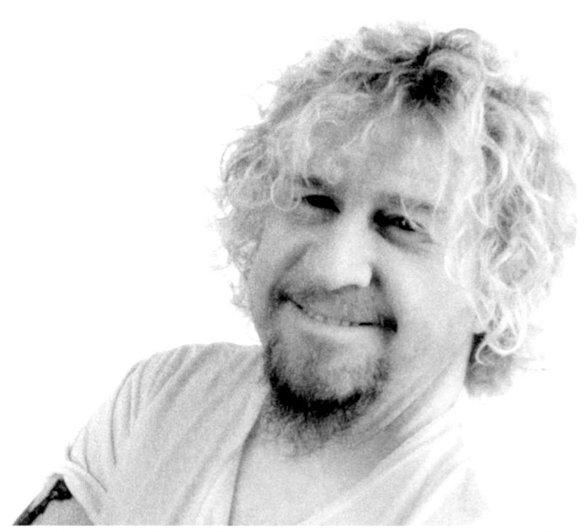

Sammy Hagar – Vocals, guitar
Montrose, Van Halen, Chickenfoot
Photographed in Toronto, ON
May 24, 2009

020

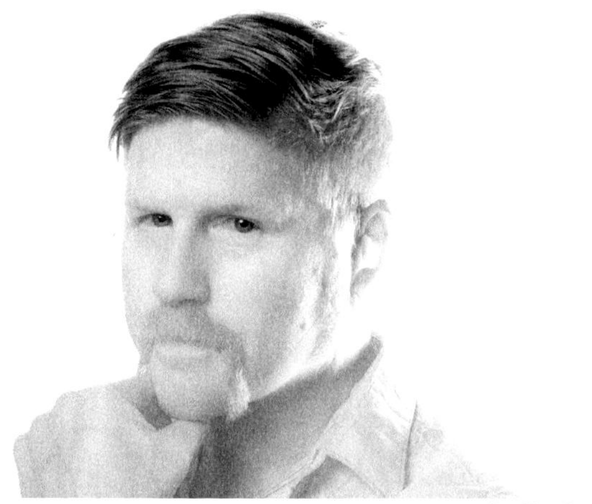

Bill Kelliher – Guitar, vocals 022
Mastodon
Photographed in Toronto, ON
November 25, 2011

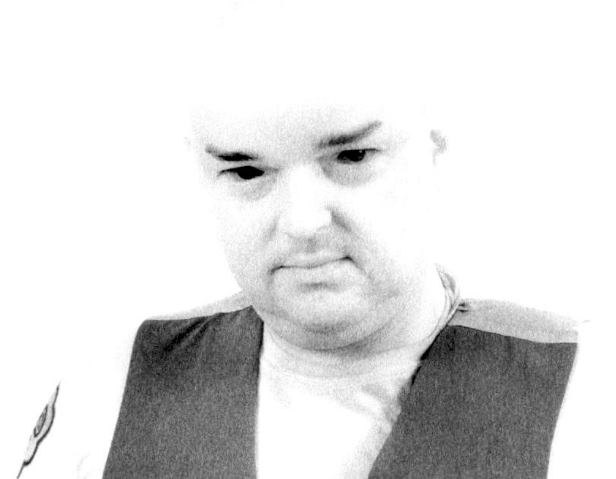

Alain Johannes – Guitar 024
Eleven, Them Crooked Vultures
Photographed in Toronto, ON
May 14, 2010

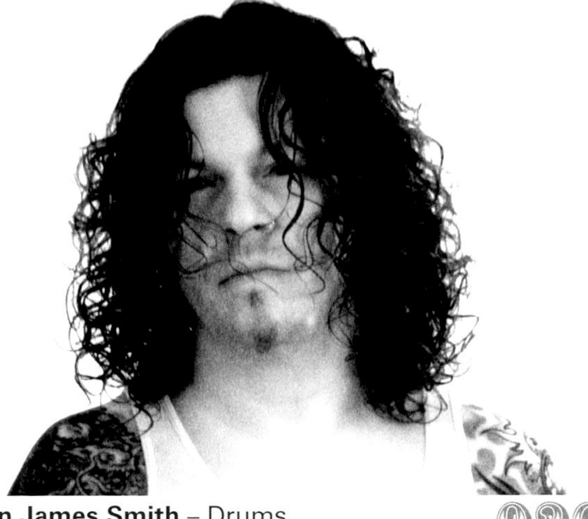

Darren James Smith – Drums 026
Harem Scarem
Photographed in Whitby, ON
February 27, 2010

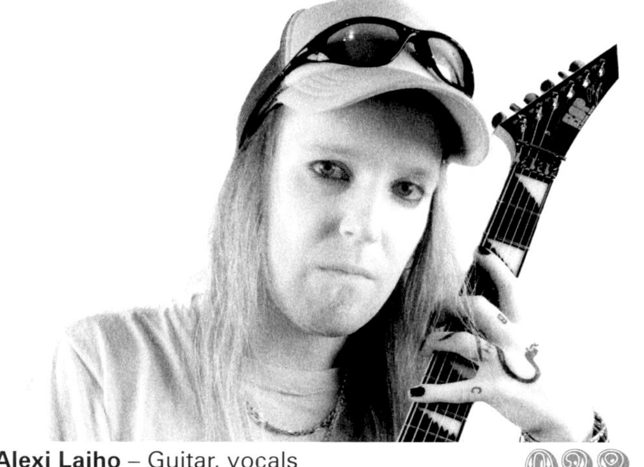

Alexi Laiho – Guitar, vocals 028
Children of Bodom
Photographed in Toronto, ON
July 23, 2011

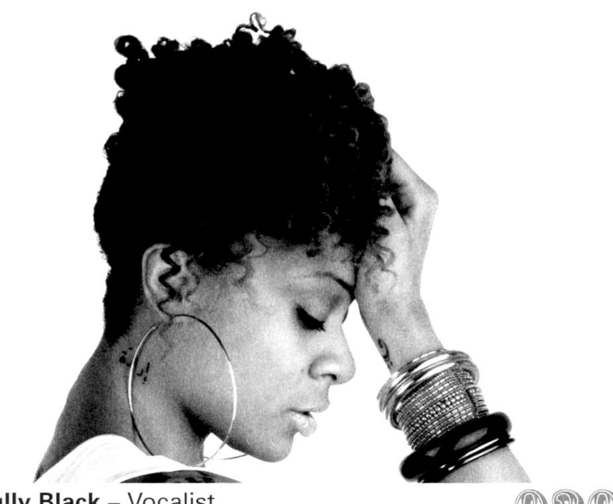

Jully Black – Vocalist 030
Photographed in Toronto, ON
August 27, 2009

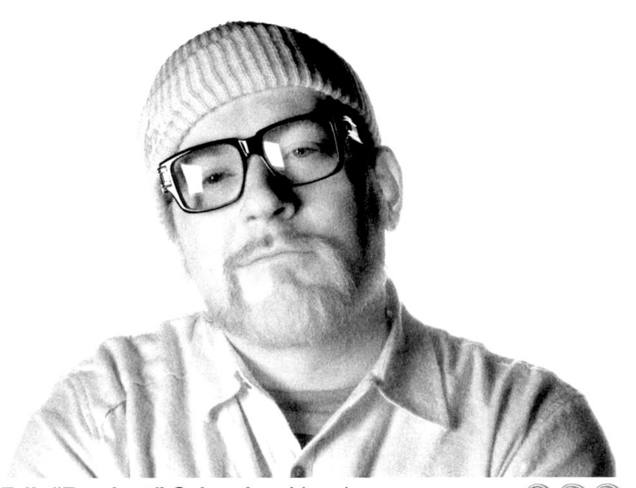

Erik "Everlast" Schrody – Vocals 032
House of Pain, Everlast
Photographed in Toronto, ON
April 9, 2011

James Rota – Guitar, vocals 034
Fireball Ministry
Photographed in Hollywood, CA
April 25, 2011

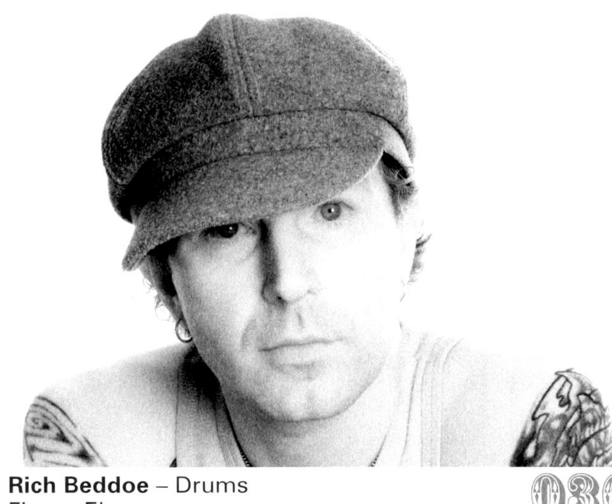

Rich Beddoe – Drums 036
Finger Eleven
Photographed in Hamilton, ON
February 26, 2012

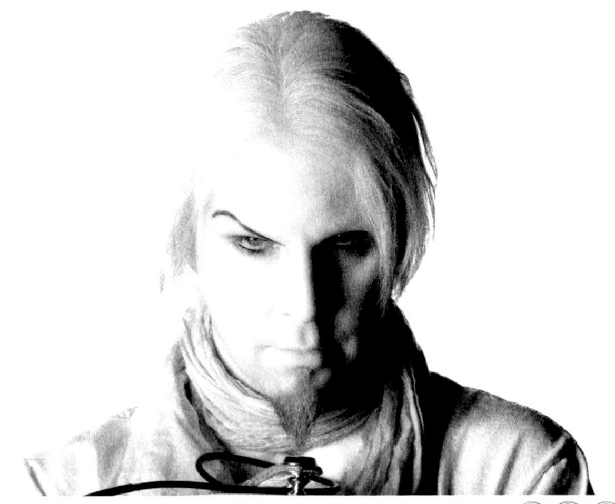

John 5 – Guitar 038
Rob Zombie, Marilyn Manson
Photographed in Toronto, ON
November 28, 2009

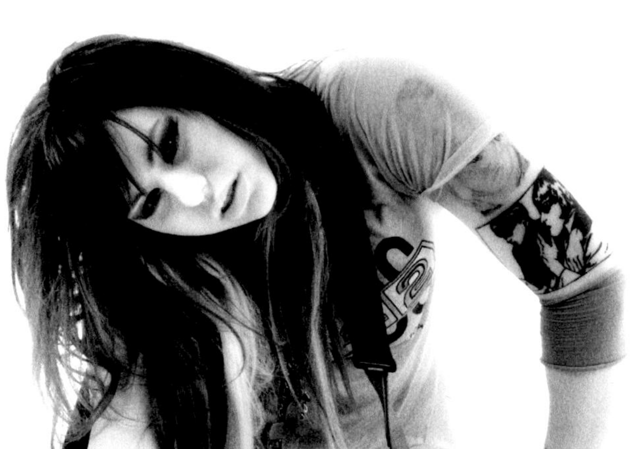

Care Failure – Guitar, vocals 040
Die Mannequin
Photographed in Toronto, ON
February 6, 2010

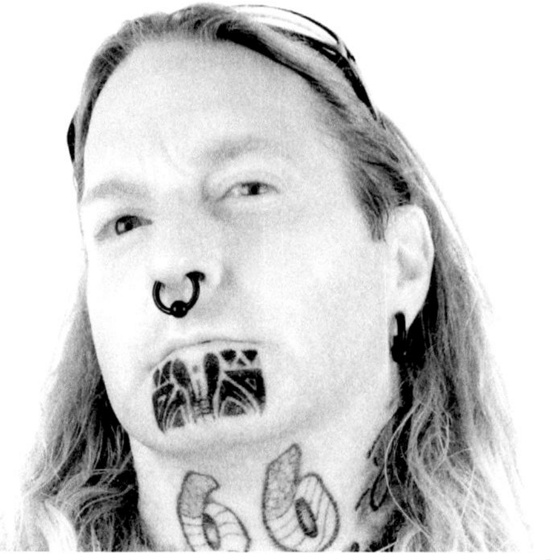

Dez FaFara – Vocals 042
Devil Driver
Photographed in Toronto, ON
July 23, 2011

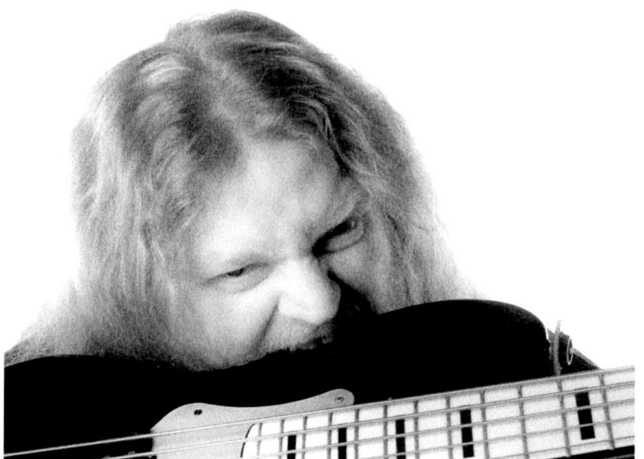

Byron Stroud – Bass 044
Fear Factory, 3 Inches of Blood, City of Fire
Photographed in Toronto, ON
March 24, 2012

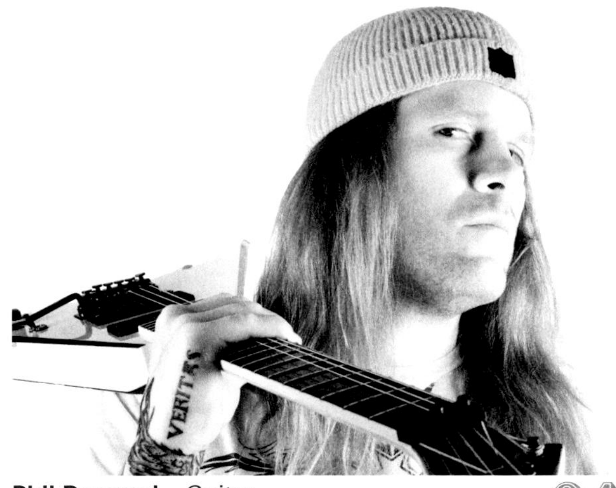

Phil Demmel – Guitar 046
Machine Head
Photographed in Dublin, CA
April 21, 2011

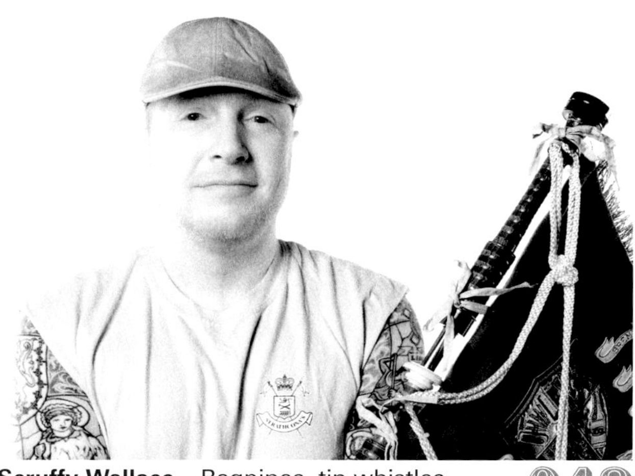

Scruffy Wallace – Bagpipes, tin whistles 048
Dropkick Murphys
Photographed in Toronto, ON
February 22, 2012

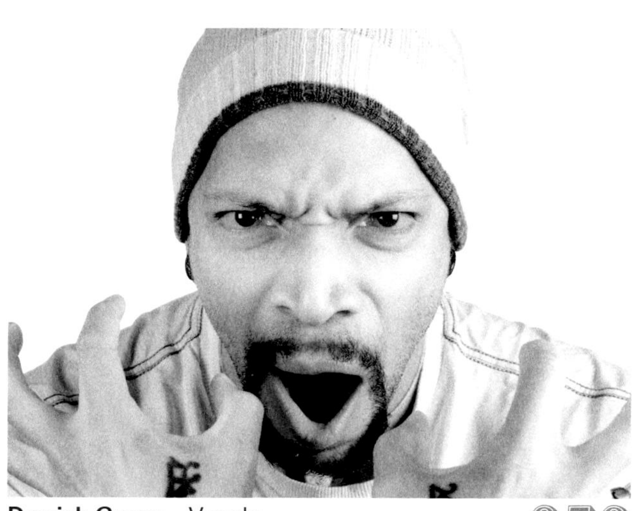

Derrick Green – Vocals 050
Sepultura
Photographed in Toronto, ON
April 18, 2011

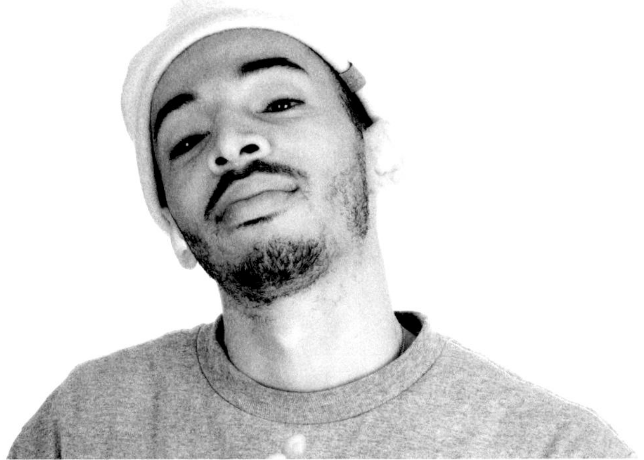

Chris McAdoo – Rapper 052
Hollyweird
Photographed in Atlanta, GA
January 25, 2011

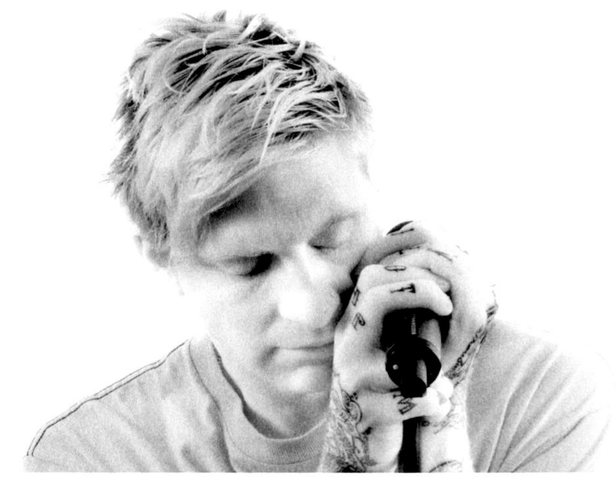

Brian Byrne – Vocals 054
I Mother Earth
Photographed in Toronto, ON
April 25, 2010

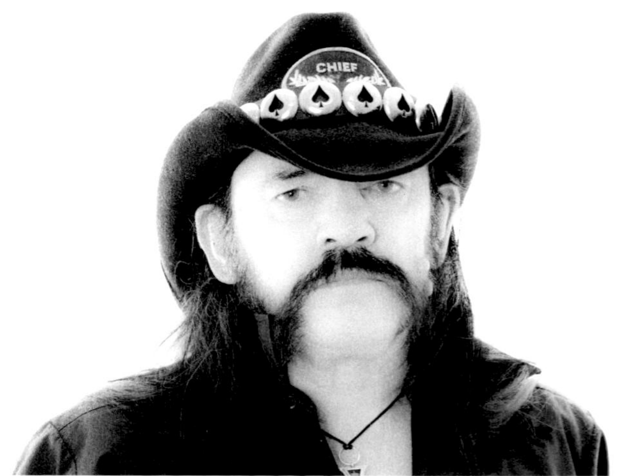

Lemmy Kilmister – Bass, vocals 056
Motorhead
Photographed in Oshawa, ON
February 7, 2012

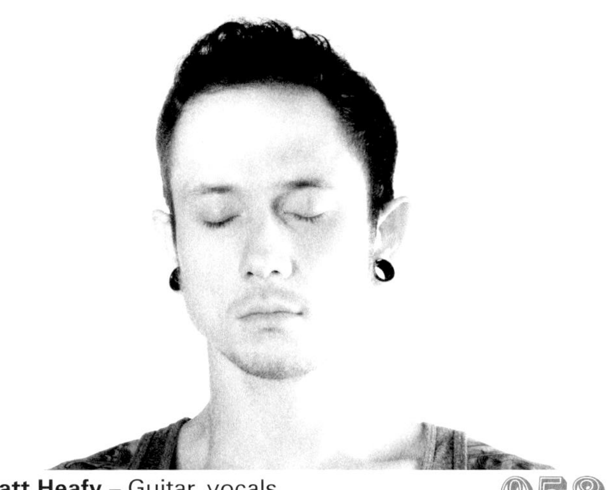

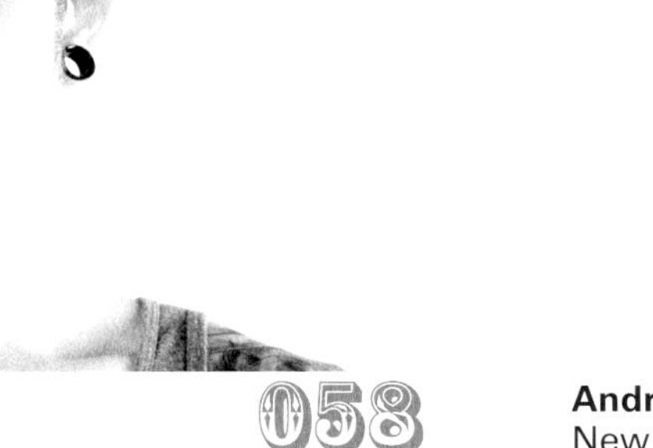

Matt Heafy – Guitar, vocals
Trivium
Photographed in Toronto, ON
February 14, 2012

058

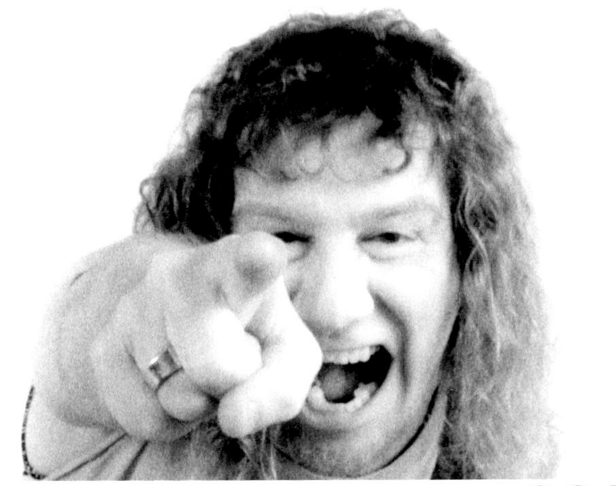

Steve "Lips" Kudlow – Vocals, guitar
Anvil
Photographed in Toronto, ON
May 19, 2010

060

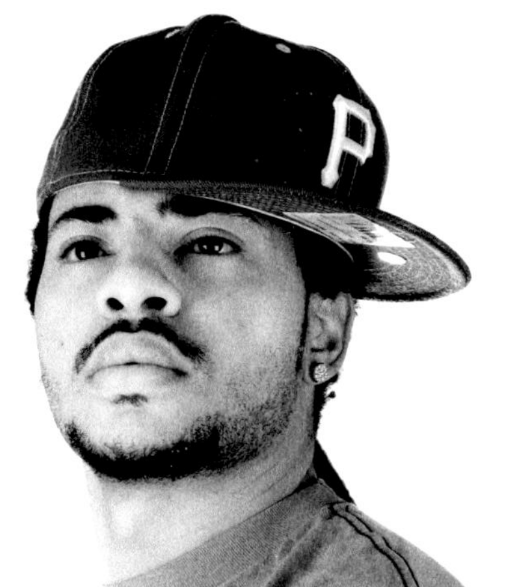

Pill – Rapper
Photographed in Atlanta, GA
January 25, 2011

062

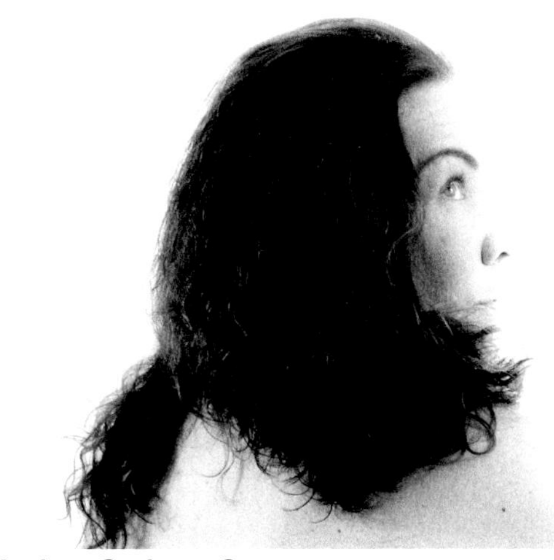

Andrea Gruber – Soprano
New York Metropolitan Opera
Photographed in New York, NY
August 4, 2009

064

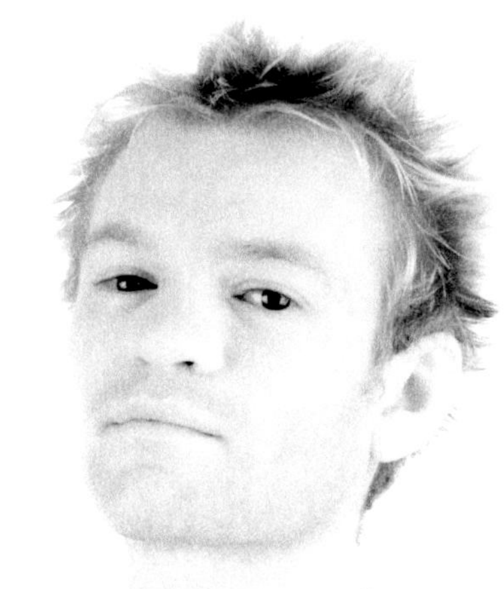

Deryck Whibley – Vocals, guitar
SUM 41
Photographed in Bel Air, CA
June 12, 2009

066

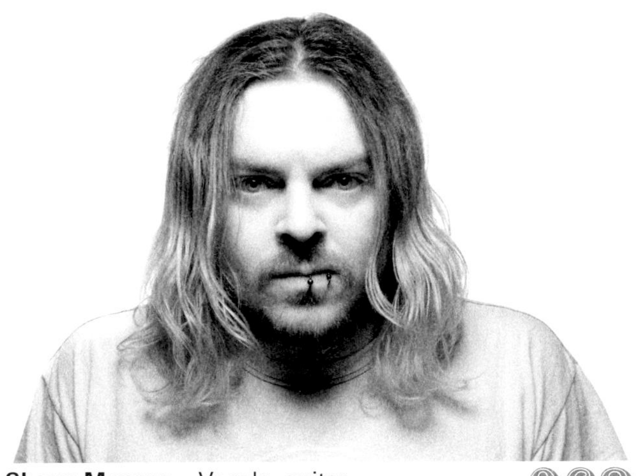

Shaun Morgan – Vocals, guitar
Seether
Photographed in Toronto, ON
May 26, 2011

068

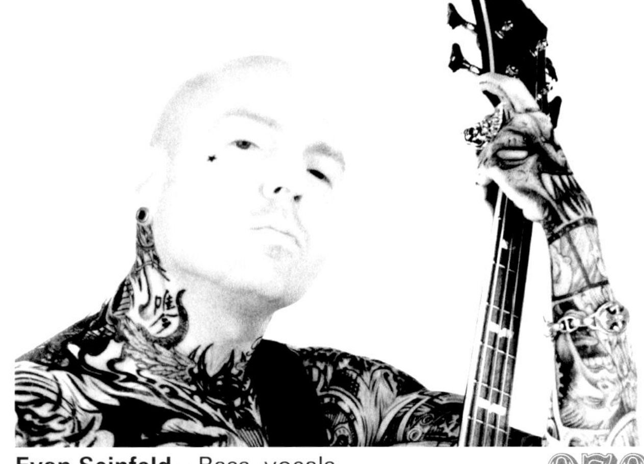

Evan Seinfeld – Bass, vocals
Biohazard, The Spyderz
Photographed in Van Nuys, CA
June 9, 2009

070

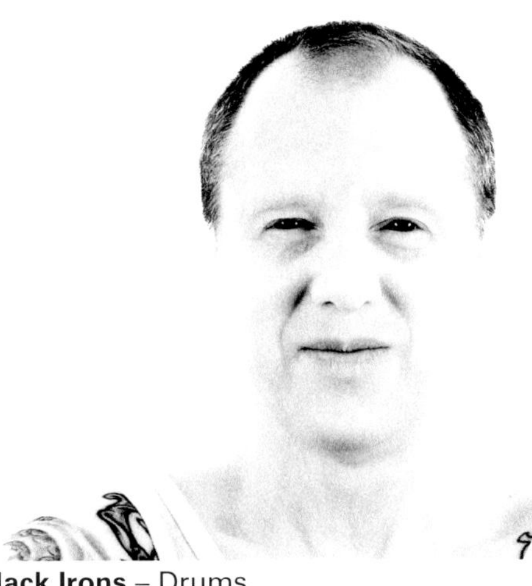

Jack Irons – Drums
Eleven, Red Hot Chili Peppers, Pearl Jam
Photographed in Los Angeles, CA
January 20, 2010

072

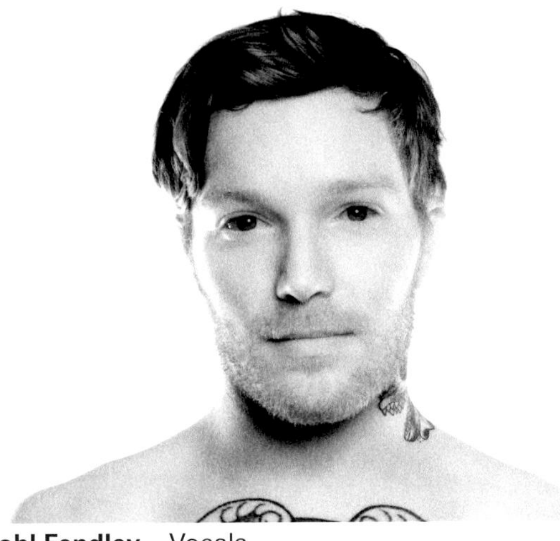

Johl Fendley – Vocals
Baptized in Blood
Photographed in Toronto, ON
October 17, 2011

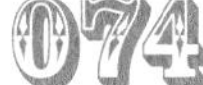

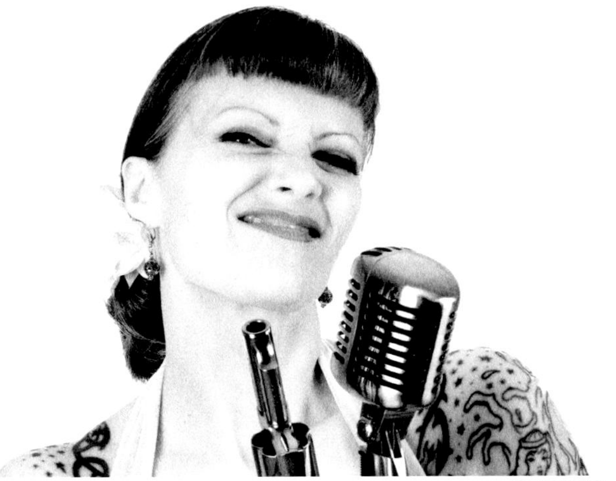

Bernadette Seacrest – Vocalist 076
Bernadette Seacrest and her Provocateurs,
Bernadette Seacrest and her Kris Dales
Photographed in Atlanta, GA
January 26, 2011

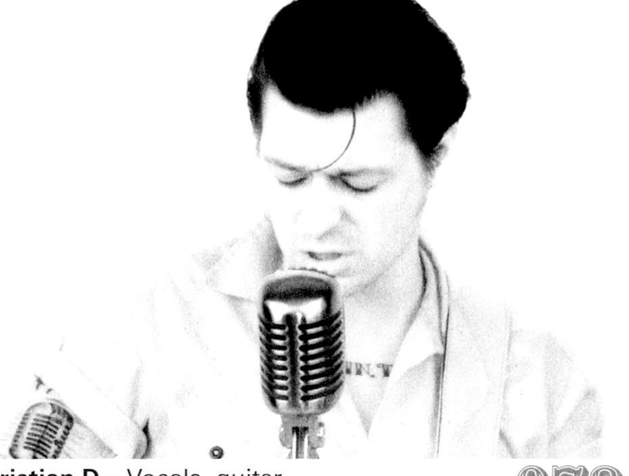

Christian D – Vocals, guitar 078
Christian D and the Hangovers
Photographed in Toronto, ON
December 7, 2008

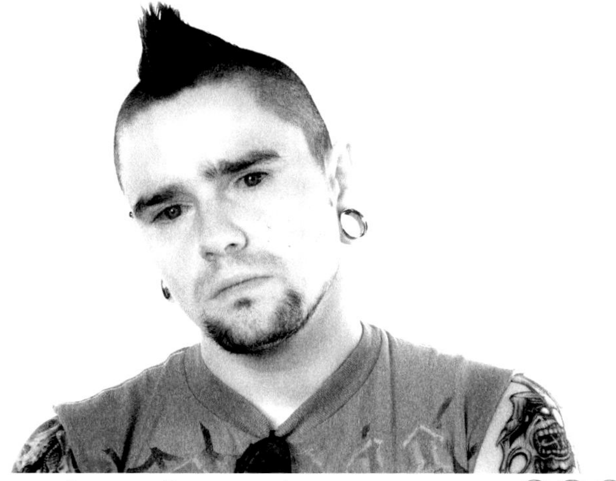

Jason James – Bass, vocals 080
Bullet for My Valentine
Photographed in Toronto, ON
September 14, 2011

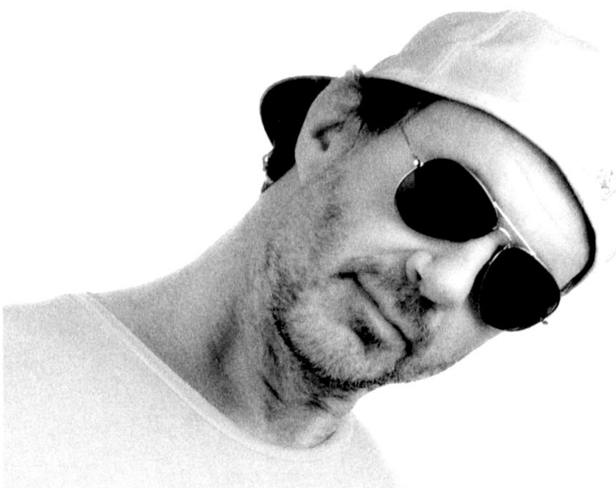

Chad Smith – Drums 082
Red Hot Chilli Peppers, Chickenfoot
Photographed in Toronto, ON
May 24, 2009

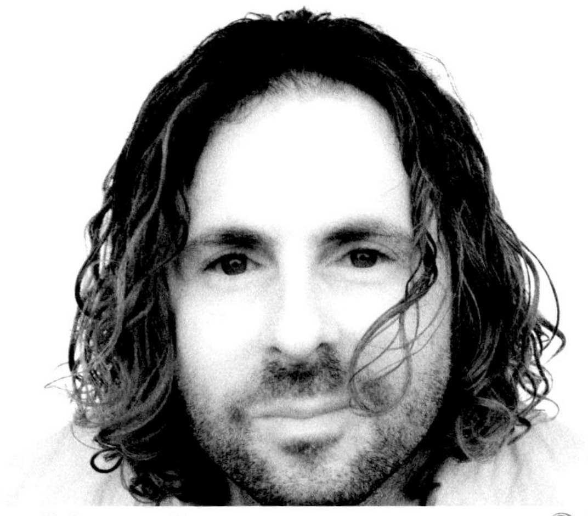

Tony Polermo – Drums 084
Papa Roach
Photographed in Rochester, NY
September 16, 2011

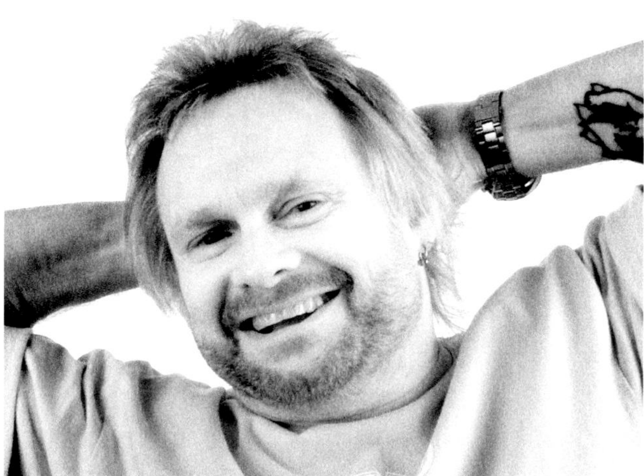

Michael Anthony – Bass 086
Van Halen, Chickenfoot
Photographed in Toronto, ON
May 24, 2009

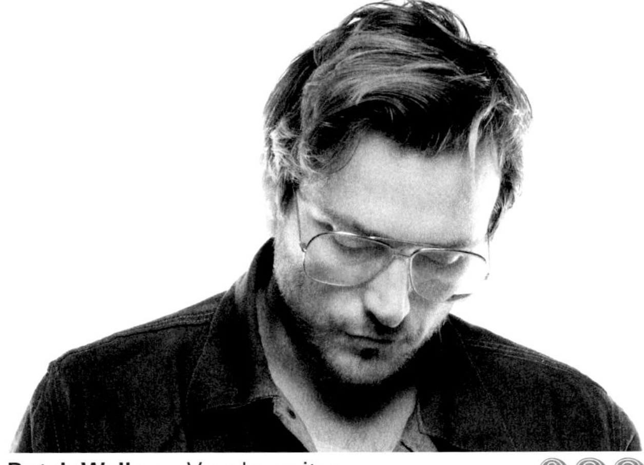

Butch Walker – Vocals, guitar 088
Butch Walker,
Butch Walker and the Black Widows
Photographed in Toronto, ON
October 19, 2011

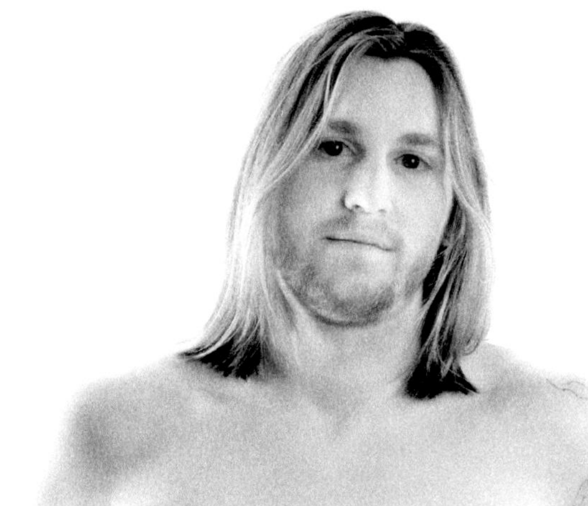

Dustin Steinke – Drums 090
Bleeker Ridge
Photographed in Orillia, ON
May 2, 2012

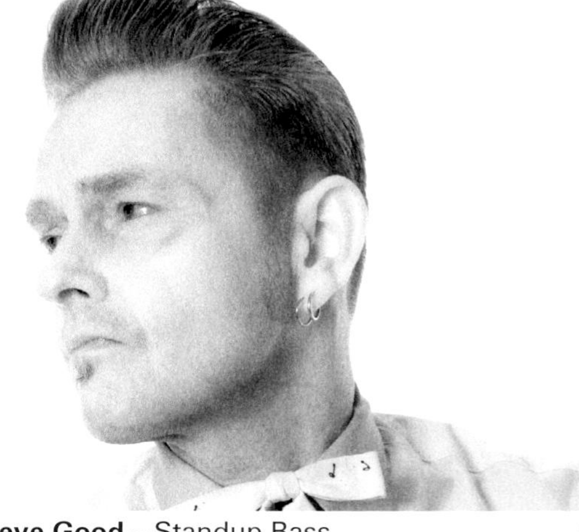

Steve Good – Standup Bass 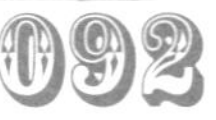 092
Tennessee Voodoo Coupe
Photographed in Toronto, ON
February 15, 2012

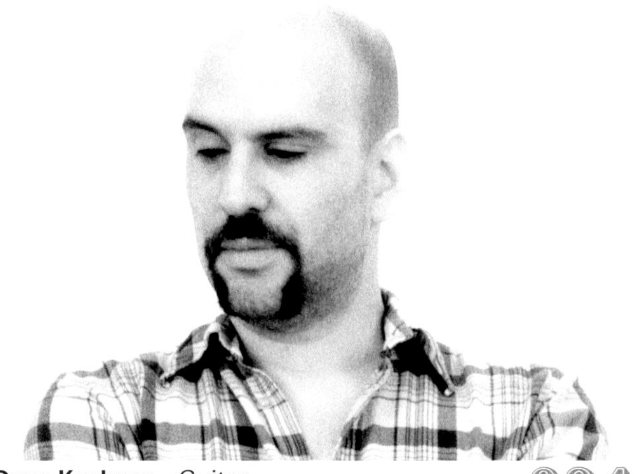

Dave Kushner – Guitar
Velvet Revolver
Photographed in Hollywood, CA
October 15, 2010 094

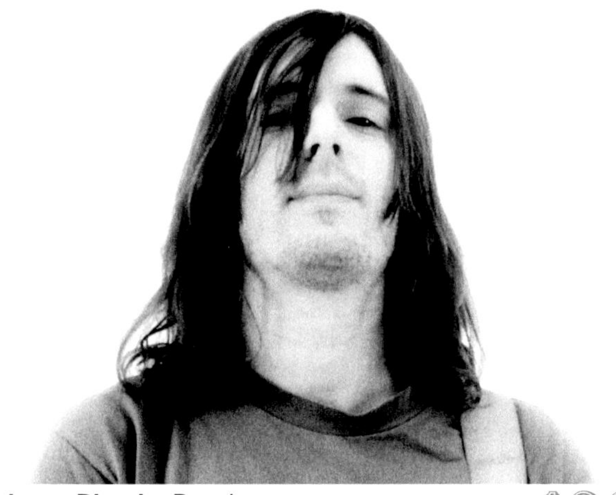

Anthony Bleed – Bassist
Die Mannequin
Photographed in Toronto, ON
February 6, 2010 100

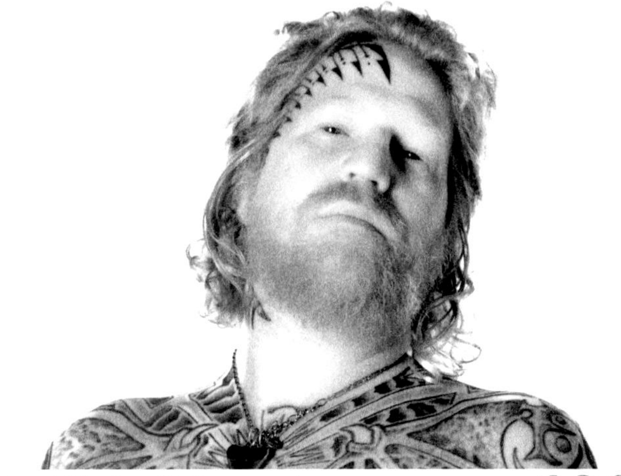

Brent Hinds – Guitar, vocals
Mastodon
Photographed in Toronto, ON
September 18, 2010 106

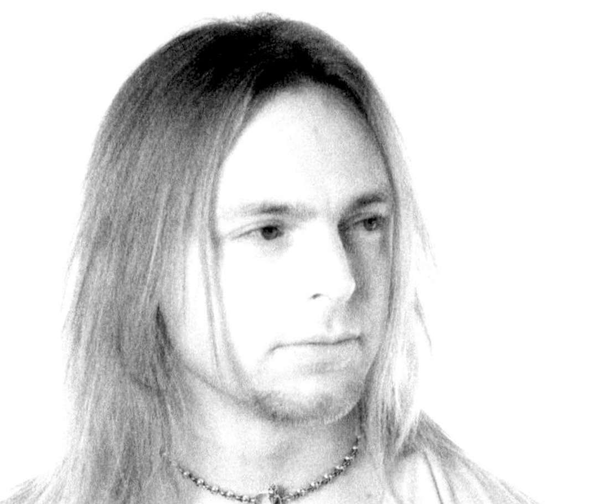

Matt Tuck – Guitar
Bullet for My Valentine
Photographed in Toronto, ON
September 14, 2011 096

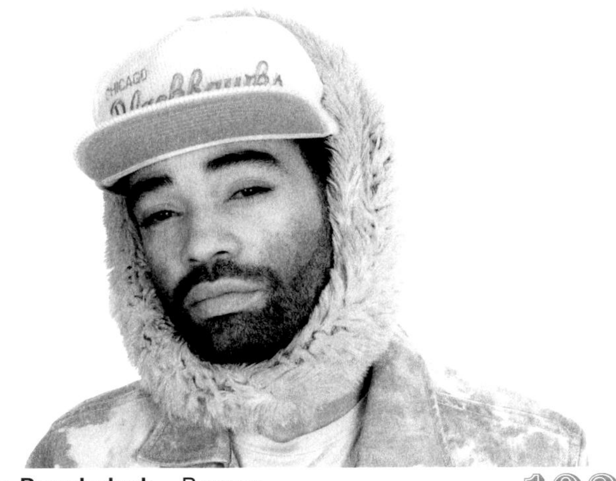

Mr. Bangladesh – Rapper
Photographed in Atlanta, GA
January 25, 2011 102

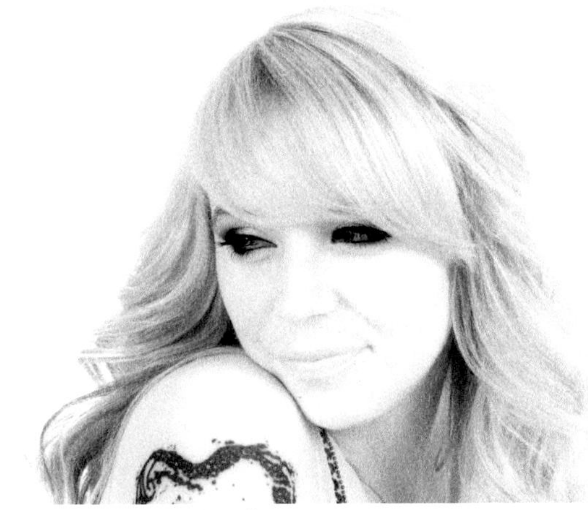

Suzie McNeil – Vocalist
Photographed in Toronto, ON
April 24, 2010 108

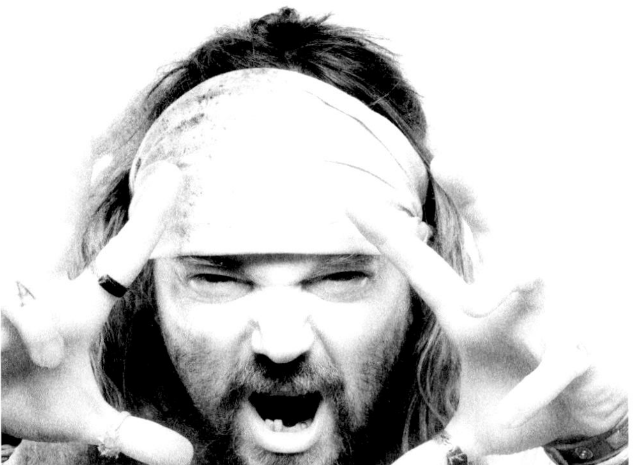

Max Cavalera – Guitar, vocals
Sepultura, Soulfly, The Cavalera Conspiracy
Photographed in Toronto, ON
October 17, 2011 098

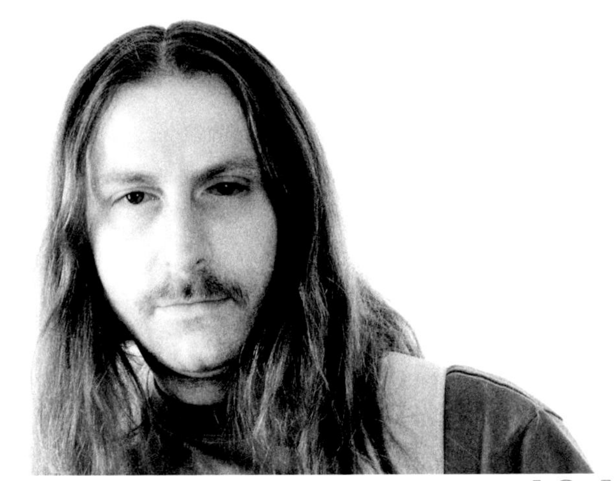

Martin Mendez – Bass
Opeth
Photographed in Toronto, ON
April 7, 2012 104

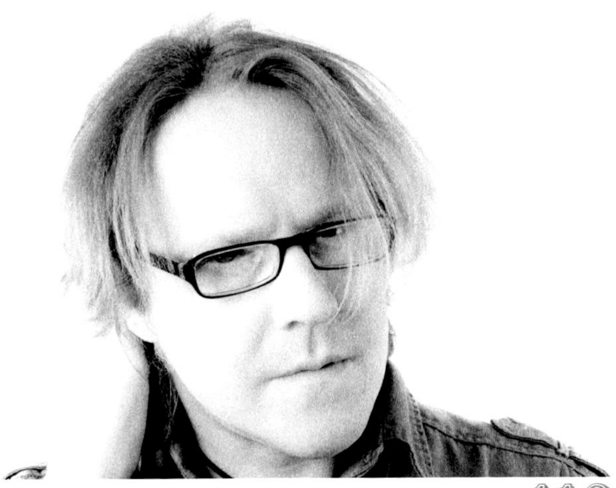

Burton C. Bell – Vocals
Fear Factory
Photographed in Guelph, ON
September 20, 2011 110

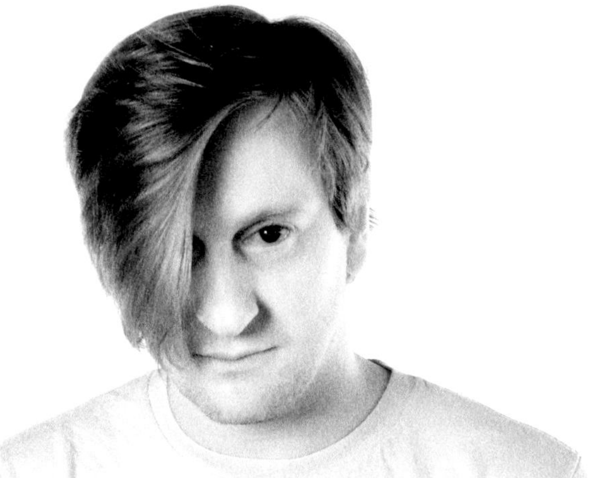

Michael "Moose" Thomas – Drums 112
Bullet For My Valentine
Photographed in Toronto, ON
September 14, 2011

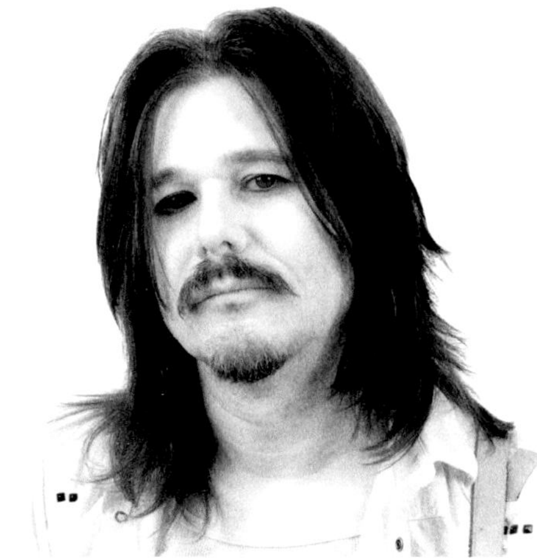

Gilby Clarke – Guitar 116
Guns N' Roses
Photographed in Sherman Oaks, CA
October 11, 2010

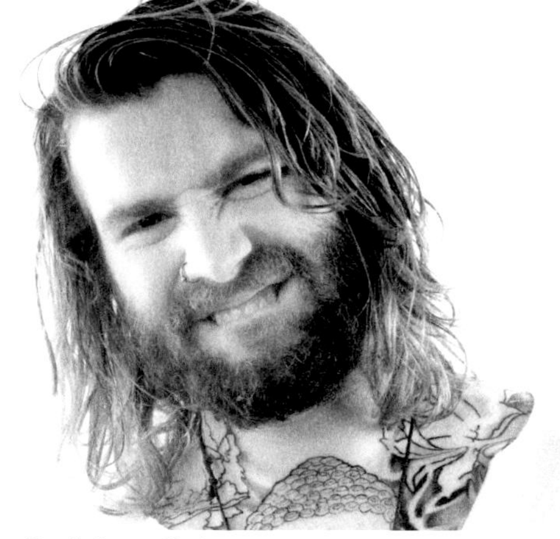

Dan Steinke – Guitar 120
Bleeker Ridge
Photographed in Orillia, ON
May 2, 2012

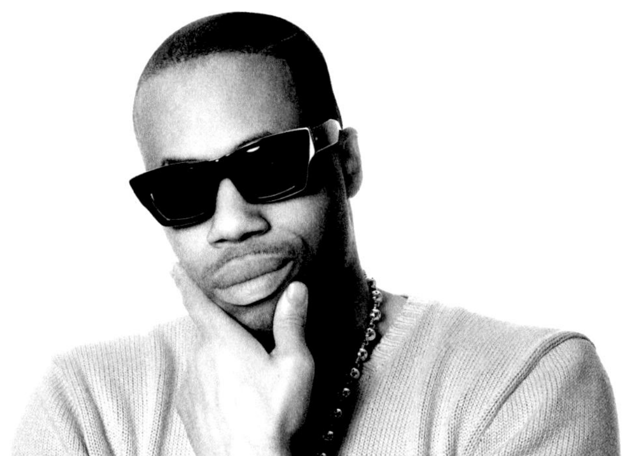

Kardinal Offishall – Vocalist 114
Photographed in Toronto, ON
November 10, 2010

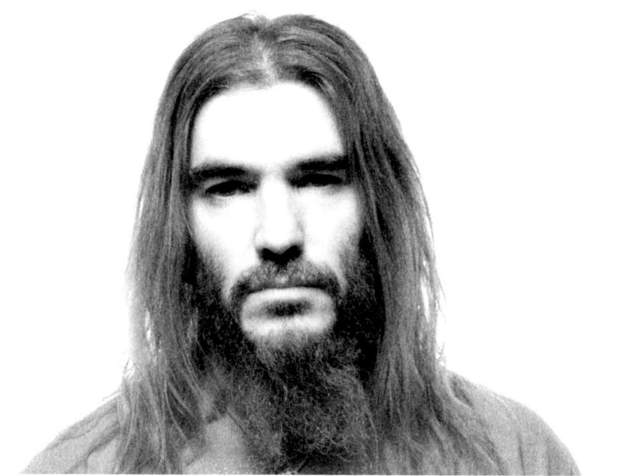

Robb Flynn – Guitar, vocals 118
Machine Head
Photographed in Toronto, ON
January 28, 2012

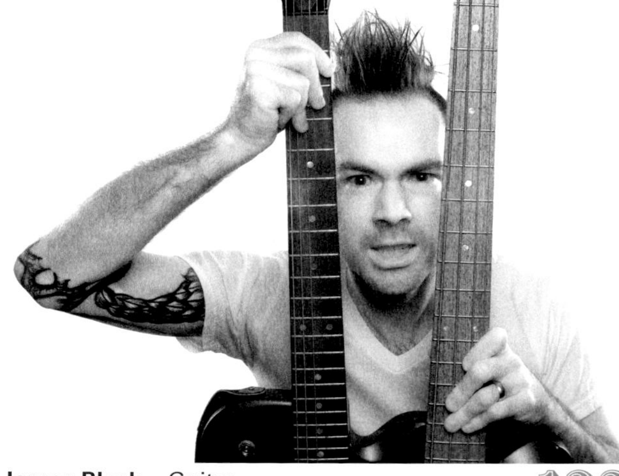

James Black – Guitar 122
Finger Eleven
Photographed in Toronto, ON
October 26, 2011

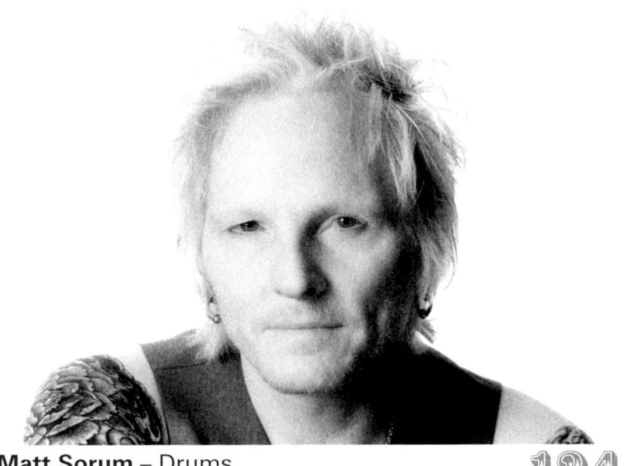

Matt Sorum – Drums 124
The Cult, Guns N' Roses, Velvet Revolver
Photographed in Hollywood, CA
April 25, 2011

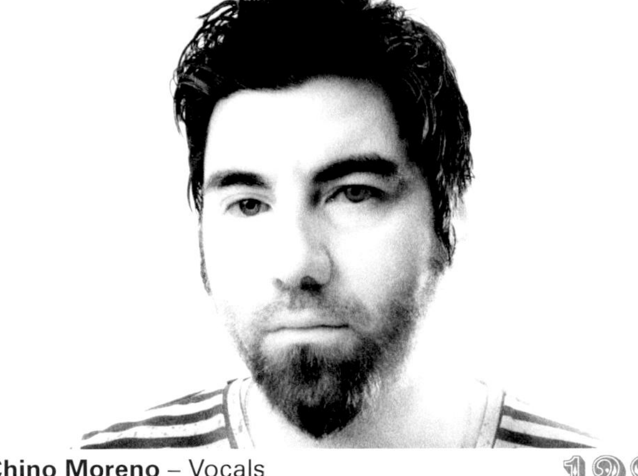

Chino Moreno – Vocals 128
Deftones
Photographed in Burbank, CA
January 22, 2012

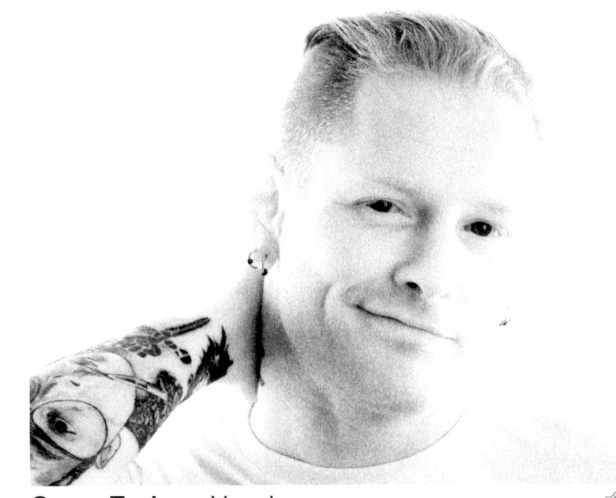

Corey Taylor – Vocals 132
SlipKnot, Stone Sour
Photographed in Toronto, ON
August 11, 2012

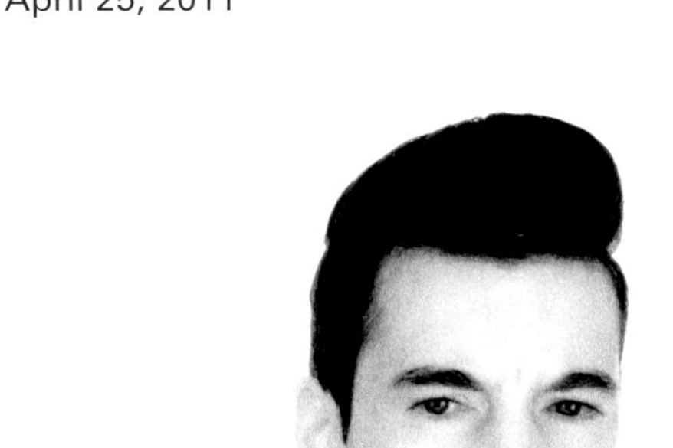

Tyler Connolly – Vocals, guitar 126
Theory of a Deadman
Photographed in Toronto, ON
June 28, 2009

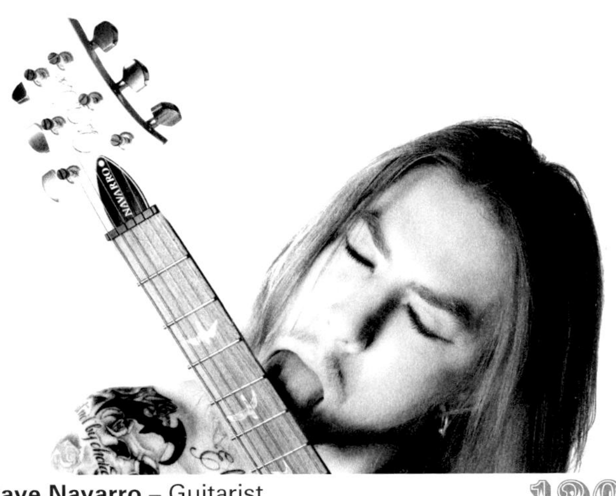

Dave Navarro – Guitarist 130
Jane's Addiction
Photographed in Toronto, ON
February 27, 2012

ABOUT INFRARED

Infrared (IR) photography is created using special equipment to capture the infrared spectrum of light. For the portraits in this book, I used a converted Nikon D2X camera that "sees" this invisible light.

When many people think of infrared, they think heat. Far infrared is used in thermal imaging. Near infrared is used in IR photography. The near IR spectrum ranges from 700 nm to 900 nm. The far IR spectrum ranges from 9,000 nm to 14,000 nm. The visible light spectrum ranges from 400 nm to 700 nm.

At first glance, a black-and-white image that you see in this book may look like any other monochromatic image until you start looking a little more closely; objects which appear dark in visible light, may appear lighter in IR. For example, many fabrics that appear black are IR-reflective and will appear white in the final image.

Generally, IR light interacts differently than visible light with skin and tattoo ink. IR wavelengths do not penetrate skin very deeply and give it a milky, ethereal appearance, while tattoo ink absorbs the IR wavelengths, rendering a much higher contrast between the skin and the ink. It's this effect that makes these portraits unique and allows you to see these artists in a whole new light.

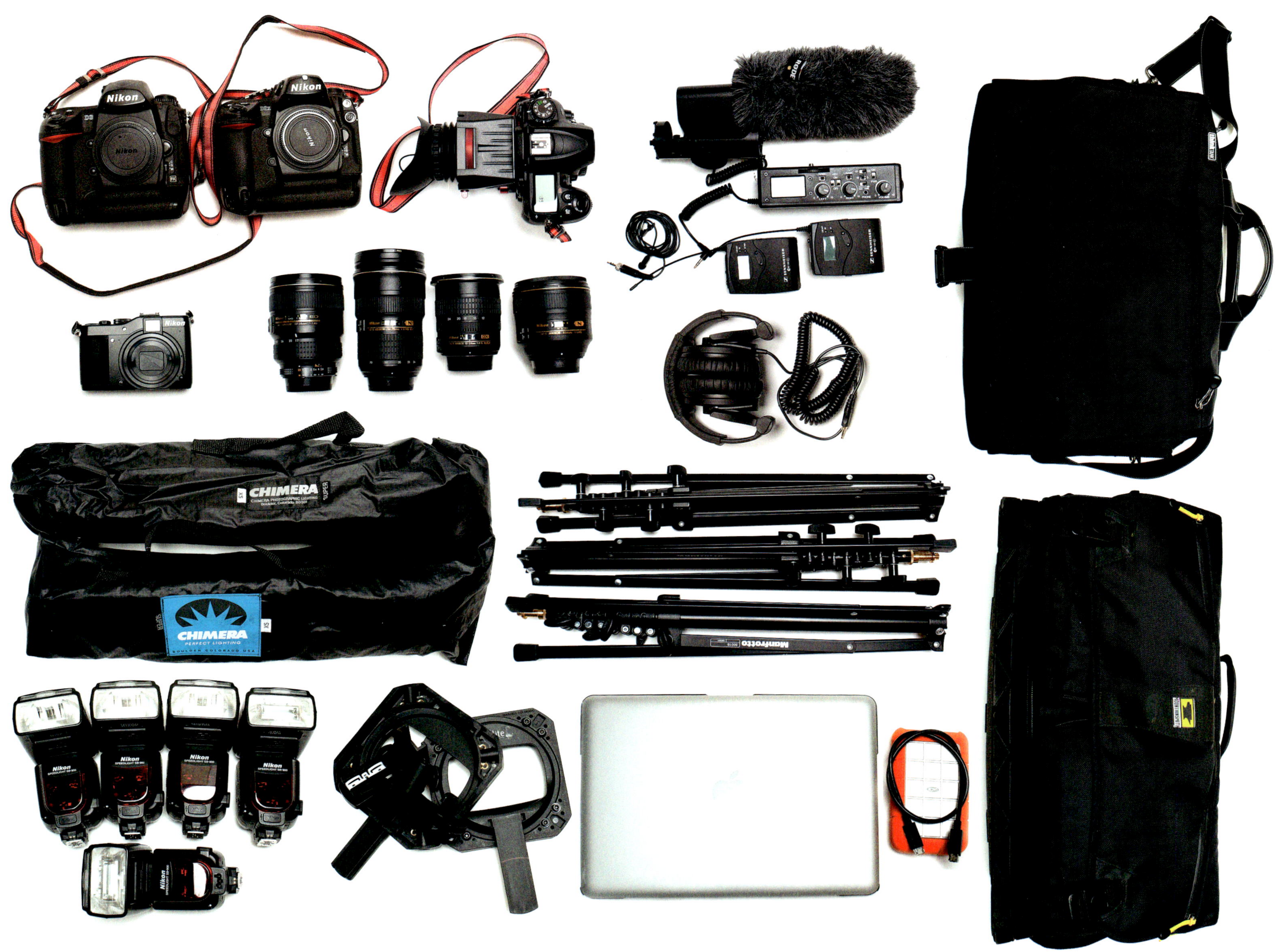
Nikon
Nikon
CHIMERA
CHIMERA
PERFECT LIGHTING
Manfrotto

MUSICAL
INK